P9-DOG-712

James Newton Poling

DELIVER US FROM
EVIL

*Resisting
Racial and Gender
Oppression*

FORTRESS PRESS ◆ MINNEAPOLIS

DELIVER US FROM EVIL
Resisting Racial and Gender Oppression

Interior design: David Lott
Cover design: Brad Norr Design

Library of Congress Cataloging-in-Publication Data

Poling, James N. (James Newton), 1942–
    Deliver us from evil : resisting racial and gender oppression / by
James Newton Poling.
        p.   cm.
    Includes bibliographical references and index.
    ISBN 0-8006-2904-3 (alk. paper)
    1. Christianity and justice.   2. Good and evil.   3. Racism—
Religious aspects—Christianity.   4. Racism—United States.
5. Afro-Americans—Crimes against—United States.   6. Sexism—
Religious aspects—Christianity.   7. Women—Crimes against—United
States.   8. Sexism—United States.   9. United States—Race
relations.   10. United States—Moral conditions.   I. Title.
BR115.J8P65   1996
261.8'34—dc20   95-45088
                                                                                CIP

The paper used in this publication meets the minimum requirements of American National Standard for Information Sciences—Permanence of Paper for Printed Library Materials, ANSI Z329.48–1984.

Manufactured in the U.S.A.   AF 1-2904

00   99   98   97   96   1   2   3   4   5   6   7   8   9   10

DELIVER US FROM
EVIL

Dedicated to
Toinette M. Eugene
Friend, Companero, Mentor
Courageous Womanist Theologian

CONTENTS

ACKNOWLEDGMENTS

I wish to acknowledge my indebtedness during the research and writing that led to this book:

To Nancy Werking Poling, editor, writer, my life-partner, and courageous woman.

To former and present students, who have taught me much about theology and experience.

To clients who taught me by engaging in their own healing process.

To colleagues who read and critiqued my manuscript: Brenda Consuelo Ruiz, Toinette Eugene, Emilie Townes, Donald Matthews, Gilbert Bond, Marie Fortune, Evelyn Kirkley.

My thanks to The Divinity School, Rochester, New York, for sabbatical study leave, June to December, 1994.

PREFACE

S ome years ago several students, clients, and colleagues challenged me to take evil in the world more seriously, and with their help I began to see with new eyes.

I remember the story of a White woman whose father had beaten her, imprisoned her in closets, and controlled every aspect of her life until she got married. All the while he functioned as a local church leader and deacon. When, as an adult, she shared her story with pastors and other church leaders, she was stigmatized as a neurotic who needed special care and discipline rather than treated as a person suffering from injustice.

For much of the time I knew her, I offered her pastoral care and counseling according to textbook advice on how to help a person who was unstable and needy. I missed seeing that her behavior was a form of resistance to evil. In spite of childhood abuse and professional incompetence by pastors like me, she refused to be consoled and continued to seek help and solace from leaders of the church. Seen from another perspective, she insisted that pastors and teachers ordained by the church live up to our responsibilities. She insisted that we understand her pain and provide the resources she needed for healing and for the expression of her spirit.

As I began to see her behavior as resistance rather than neurosis, I had to face the limitations of my own ministry, and I became concerned about the silence of the church. Why did I see her resistance as a problem rather than a resource, and how could I help my community see her courage in the midst of evil?

A few years later I listened to the story of an African American man, a victim of his father's terror and tyranny. Because he had been an active leader at school and church, teachers and church leaders had known about his family's problems. But no one intervened to protect this young child, whose physical and psychic survival was a daily challenge. I learned from this man how racism created the family isolation that allowed the violence to continue.

I was again disturbed that in his search for healing, the young man, labeled a "difficult" person, was often marginalized by the church. People criticized him for being overly sensitive to criticism and unable to participate in the accepted styles of friendship and support. However, over the course of many conversations, he gradually taught me to question the norms by which care and nurture are dispensed by the church. Labeling him a difficult person actually served to protect the rest of us from dealing with the pain in his life, and from facing the racist limitations on the church's definitions of community. His resistance to the labels taught me how the church's racism contributes to family violence and marginalization.

Again, I was forced to encounter my limitations as a minister. How could I overcome my inclination to see his resistance to racism as a problem, and how could I help my community recognize his resilience and strength in the midst of evil?

These relationships led me to the conviction that something was wrong in my ministry and in the community where I practiced my Christian life. These two persons were abused by their families as children, and when they came to the church, they were violated again. This book is an attempt to understand the roots of evil in persons, families, churches, and society, so that we can recognize resistance to evil as a force for good.

INTRODUCTION

DELIVER US FROM EVIL

As Christians, we pray, "Deliver us from evil." Sometimes we mean "Deliver us from the Evil One," the one who is destroying our spirits and our bodies. In this prayer we ask God to protect us from violence, and we join with all victims of violence who cry for protection from evil persons and systems.

Sometimes we mean "Deliver us from doing evil," from being someone who does evil deeds that hurt others. In this prayer we confess our sins to God, repent of our ways, and commit ourselves to a new life of love and justice in our relationships with others.

Deliver us from evil is a prayer of resistance. In this prayer, we resist the evil from without that threatens us with harm, and we resist the evil from within that threatens to violate others. Whether we are victims of violence or perpetrators of violence, Jesus' prayer is a promise that we will receive strength to resist evil.

RESISTANCE TO EVIL

This is a book about resistance to evil. I am interested in the stories of individuals and groups who have lived courageous lives by resisting evil forces, and who have revealed for us all the resilient love of God. Even when God's love and creativity seem to have been destroyed and distorted, acts of resistance have proven God's love again. What enables some people to resist and survive the power of evil?

The thesis of this book is that a liberated and critical consciousness that has been tested and proven over many generations of struggle enables some individuals and groups to resist and survive the power of evil. There are historical communities of resistance whose destruction has been

planned and implemented by evil forces. Yet the resistance of these communities has continued. The following definition of resistance to evil will
guide the historical exploration of chapters 1 to 5.

> Resistance to evil is a form of liberated and critical consciousness that
> enables persons or groups to stand against evil in silence, language, and
> action.[1]

Of the many communities of resistance—for example, the Jews during
the Holocaust and the indigenous Indians during the European conquest
and domination—this book focuses especially on two groups: African
American women and men during slavery and racism in the United States,
and European American women during centuries of patriarchal exploitation and violence. While I have much to learn from the continuing
struggles of other groups, my reason for choosing these two is because of
their personal influence in my own life and their historical importance in
the history of the United States.

In the last five hundred years persons from the African diaspora have
experienced capture, murder, enslavement, torture, rape, lynching, massive poverty, forced labor, and other forms of oppression. Like other
groups who have been systematically oppressed for centuries, African
Americans have experienced intolerable levels of sustained violence
against their bodies and spirits. The memories of loss and tragedy are profound. African American communities in the United States continue
to experience levels of poverty, violence, and oppression in striking contradiction to a society where others have affluence and power. Out
of these centuries of suffering, rich and powerful witnesses of God's love
and power have been forged to form the basis of Black and womanist
theology. The contrast of suffering and hope in this movement inspires
my work.

The resistance movements of European American women have rejected
the subordinate status of women in church and society in the United
States. The physical and sexual violence that so many women have experienced as children and adults dramatize the terror that is at the root of
their oppression. For thousands of years, women have been exchanged
and violated by men vying with one another for power. Their exclusion
from leadership in church and society, which functioned as extensions of
a system of male dominance, defines their place in the social order. As the
oppression of women has been thematized and illustrated, new forms of
resilient hope have been brought forth. "The emergence of feminist consciousness"[2] reveals a long history of resistance to oppression and male
dominance. This alternative vision represents new hope for the future.

THE NATURE OF EVIL

This book explores the nature of evil from the perspective of the communities of resistance. Because evil thrives best in situations of deception and mystification, it is difficult and crucial to define it carefully, which I will do more completely in chapter 6. For now, I will define evil as follows:

> Evil is the abuse of power in personal, social, and religious forms that destroys bodies and spirits. Evil is an abuse of power because the power of life comes from God, and all power should be used for good. Whenever power is used to destroy the bodies and spirits of God's creation, there is evil.[3]

Evil has a personal dimension. In situations of interpersonal violence, for example, someone decides to cause physical harm to another, and someone is injured. Even in situations usually understood as impersonal evil, someone's life and health is always at stake. Chapters 1 and 2 will explore resistance and evil in personal and interpersonal situations.

Evil has a social dimension. By social dimension I mean the economic, institutional, and ideological forces that create the likelihood that various forms of evil will occur. Violent parents are able to injure their children because societies grant parental authority. All power is socially constructed and its use and abuse is a social event. Chapters 3 and 4 will explore resistance and evil in social situations.

Evil has a religious dimension. Every personal and social event is embedded in religious horizons of meaning and value. In fact, the very concepts of good and evil make religious value judgments about ultimate reality. When they struggle against evil, resistance communities appeal to a religious worldview. Religious evil occurs whenever the theology and/or practices of religious groups are used to destroy bodies and spirits. Religious evil is the most dangerous kind of evil, because it obscures the possibility of a transcendent reality to which communities of resistance can appeal. Resistance to religious evil will be an underlying theme in many chapters of this book.

DEBATE AND BETRAYAL

A study of United States history will demonstrate that evil maintains itself through a process of debate and betrayal by those in power. In certain historical periods, communities of resistance have more successfully brought their moral claims to the public arena for debate. These times have increased hope that power could be more fairly distributed and that all people in a society would have access to the resources necessary for life and creativity. In my research, I discovered such times just before and after the Revolutionary and Civil Wars. Prior to the wars, religious and political leaders debated the issues of freedom and full citizenship for African American women and men and for White women. These debates brought hope for just power arrangements. However, after both wars, debate was stifled, with structures of injustice and oppression firmly reestablished. African American women and men and White women found themselves in desperate conditions, without the protection they had hoped would come. The communities of resistance experienced this as a betrayal, especially by those who had supported their claims in the past.

I have come to the conviction that such debate and betrayal is one of the ways evil maintains itself. Public debate not only creates opportunities for new moral claims to be asserted, but also enables those who have power to reconceive their interests in more effective ways. During times of transition, debate, which offers oppressed groups the hope of social change, in fact often betrays their trust, as those with power close ranks against the groups they had promised to support. In my discussion, I will be examining debate and betrayal so that we may recognize its insidiousness.

AN EXERCISE IN PRACTICAL THEOLOGY

Practical theology is a subdiscipline of theology that generates theological reflection on the doctrines and practices of religious communities out of sustained attention to the suffering and hope of persons toward the goal of transforming the society.[4]

The suffering and hope of African American women and men and of European American women provide the focus for this project in practical theology. I draw on my experience as a pastor, teacher, and pastoral counselor to dozens of survivors of family violence. I pray that my work will help to stop the violence against those who are most vulnerable in church and society. Furthermore, I hope pastors and church leaders will come to see that those people we sometimes view as "neurotic" or "difficult" may in fact be resisting evil and may help us all identify its presence.

In traditional theology, evil is the systematic distortion and violation of God's creation. The life, death, and resurrection of Jesus Christ is God's transformation of the possibilities of human life in the midst of evil. This study is committed to exposing false theologies that have been used for evil purposes, and to searching for theologies that can resist evil and transform human life for the good. I hope this project will result in courageous and healing practices in the church that bring liberation and healing for all members of society.

Practical theology requires interdisciplinary research. I bring to it my training in theology, pastoral counseling, and psychology. However, I have been encouraged by several colleagues to take the discipline of history more seriously, because ideologies of race and gender in the United States have been constructed over several centuries.[5] A number of historians have carefully studied slavery, racism, and sexism with special attention to debates among prominent men. I am indebted to scholars who have worked with primary sources and provided us with the results of their efforts. I am of the conviction, which is based on my study of these secondary sources, that race and gender have been constructed within the crucible of debate about practical problems, such as whether baptism would undermine or sanction slavery as an institution. This debate took place over many decades, and the idea that baptism and freedom can be separated continues to subtly influence White Christians. Therefore, it is necessary to remember the history of the ideas and practices through which race and gender have gained their power.

Theology, especially Christology, is another major discipline addressed in this project. Jesus' name was on the lips of many African American women and men who resisted slavery, and Christ has been proclaimed by many White women who have resisted patriarchy. Jesus Christ was also invoked to promote White supremacy and male dominance. This means that Christology is central to understanding both resistance and evil. I will turn to womanist and feminist theologians for insight into how the Christ-symbol can be deconstructed and reconstructed for the sake of justice and love.

The reader will notice appeals to Black womanist, Black male, and feminist theologians throughout this book. Black womanists, sometimes called Black feminists, are Black women intellectuals who are writing about their experiences in United States society, which discriminates on the basis of race, gender, and class. The creativity and courage of this group has inspired me to try to understand racial and gender evil. I pray that my work fairly represents the moral claims of womanist scholars and that my analysis will challenge the White community to strengthen our resistance to the evils of racism and sexism on behalf of God's new commonwealth of freedom and justice. I also am indebted to Black male theologians, who have been especially creative since the Black Power movement of the 1960s and whose insights provide crucial understandings throughout my study. Feminist theologians have produced an important body of analysis, especially about gender power arrangements, and many have also been among the most creative White writers willing to look at race and class oppression.

MY ACCOUNTABILITY

Part of my motive for this work is my own cry—*deliver me from evil*. As I have understood more about the role of religion in promoting evil, I have been more convicted of my own complicity as a white man. For many years, my guilt immobilized me into passivity, but now I refuse to accept my ongoing ignorance and evil. I can act in solidarity with the victims of violence. I can criticize the social ideologies and institutions that perpetuate this evil. I can deconstruct my inherited theology and its flaws. I can explore my own motives for participating in the evils of racism and sexism. I do my work because of a moral and theological commitment as a follower of Jesus Christ.

However, I am faced with the limitations of my own ignorance and hidden self-interests. I can work on the internal distortions I see, but I cannot work on the distortions that are unconscious and systemic. How do I examine the evil that is hidden? By being accountable to the communities of resistance. In this work I have maintained accountability in four ways. First, as part of an network of scholars and colleagues who are working on similar issues and perspectives. I especially acknowledge my connections with the Society for Pastoral Theology, with informal groups of womanist and Black male theologians, and with feminist theologians. These groups have given me significant critical responses to my work over many years. Second, I have submitted this manuscript by contract with several scholars and practitioners who have given me detailed challenges.[6] Third, I work as a pastoral counselor in solidarity with the movement of survivors of physical and sexual violence who are striving to bring their insights and critical feedback to church and society. Fourth, I have discussed my ideas on four trips to Nicaragua, and have submitted my manuscripts to colleagues there in order to test the implications for the suffering and hope of Christians in the Two-Thirds World.[7]

SUMMARY OF CHAPTERS

The five chapters in Part I focus on the history of the resistance to racial and gender oppression. In chapter 1, I review Harriet Jacobs's story of resistance in the everyday life of an African American woman in the nineteenth century. Her resistance discloses the existence of evil persons and systems that tried to destroy her spirit. In one of his most famous case studies, Sigmund Freud introduces us to Dora, a young woman who came to him for help but who resisted his interpretation of her life. Our review of this case in chapter 2 helps us understand how the resistance of women is often defeated by psychological assumptions that ensure that gender oppression will be maintained.

The United States (American) Revolution released a worldwide hope for freedom. Yet in the midst of that burst of freedom, African Americans were enslaved, and White women were oppressed within a cult of domesticity. In chapter 3, I ask how seemingly well-intentioned leaders betrayed the hope of the revolution. The Civil War led to the Emancipation Proclamation and to the hope for Reconstruction. African American women and men and White women won temporary gains through committed and dedicated political action. Yet, by 1877, Reconstruction had failed, and an organized backlash enforced by terrorism and lynching had recreated apartheid, disfranchisement, and Jim Crow segregation in both North and South. Women's suffrage was delayed until 1920. In chapter 4, I ask how evil maintains its dominance in the face of the commitment and dedication of resistance movements.

Resistance communities organized themselves throughout the first half of the twentieth century through labor unions, education, and court cases. Resistance to apartheid laws and racial discrimination created civil rights organizations and an energetic feminist movement. Backlash and betrayal seem to characterize the end of the century. In a brief review in chapter 5, I will test my historical thesis about resistance and betrayal.

Part II focuses on resistance to evil in the name of Jesus. Understanding resistance is the key to defining evil. In chapter 6, I will examine the dynamics of resistance to evil by seeing how specific communities of resistance understand themselves. Evil is the abuse of power that is destructive to persons and communities. Chapter 7 develops a practical, working definition of evil and provides an analysis that supports resistance.

Survivors of racial and sexual violence raise questions about Christian doctrines such as obedience, servanthood, and veneration of the crucified, male Jesus. Chapter 8 examines the spirited debate about Christology among womanist and feminist theologians. In chapter 9, I suggest that White men consider some tentative proposals on Christology. What can we learn about faith in Jesus Christ from the witness of communities of resistance?

The conclusion will focus on the praxis of a faith based on prophetic acts of solidarity. New practices of goodness can begin to forge partnerships that cross the chasms of privilege and power and create new possibilities for healing, community, and justice for all people.

PART ONE

RESISTING
RACIAL AND GENDER
OPPRESSION

RACE, GENDER, AND WHITE SUPREMACY

The Case of Harriet Jacobs

In her autobiography, Harriet Jacobs reveals the trauma that faced many young African American women during slavery.

> [When] I entered on my fifteenth year . . . my master began to whisper foul words in my ear. Young as I was, I could not remain ignorant of their import. I tried to treat them with indifference or contempt. The master's age, my extreme youth, and the fear that his conduct would be reported to my grandmother, made me bear this treatment for many months. . . . He tried his utmost to corrupt the pure principles my grandmother had instilled. He peopled my young mind with unclean images, such as only a vile monster could think of. I turned from him with disgust and hatred. But he was my master.[1]

At first, the master Dr. Flint's concern for his reputation and his young wife's jealousy prevented him from raping Harriet Jacobs. A physician and respected leader in the community, he wanted to preserve his image as a moral and upright man. Unlike the plantation, where anything could happen with impunity, and the large cities, where anonymity prevented many evil deeds from being discovered, the small town offered Harriet Jacobs some protection. Mrs. Flint discovered her husband's interest, and while she had no sympathy for Harriet Jacobs, she was determined to prevent a sexual relationship from taking place. However, she was no match for her crafty husband.

> I pitied Mrs. Flint. She was a second wife, many years the junior of her husband; and the [wicked] miscreant was enough to try the patience of a wiser and better woman. She was completely foiled, and knew not how to proceed. She would gladly have had me flogged for my supposed false

oath; but, as I have already stated, the doctor never allowed any one to whip me [except himself].[2]

This stalemate continued for some time, with Harriet Jacobs able to avoid being raped but not able to stop the escalating sexual harassment.

Dr. Flint had raped at least eleven women, and was determined to rape Harriet Jacobs. As a serial rapist, he should have received the most severe punishment, yet he was protected by law and custom from any consequences of his evil deeds.

> My master was, to my knowledge, the father of eleven slaves. But did the mothers dare to tell who was the father of their children? Did the other slaves dare to allude to it, except in whispers among themselves? No, indeed! They knew too well the terrible consequences.[3]

Harriet Jacobs fell in love with a "young colored carpenter, a free born man."[4] She asked for permission to marry, but it was rejected and she was verbally abused in the process. Dr. Flint threatened her: "Do you know that I have a right to do as I like with you,—that I can kill you, if I please?" She answered: "You have tried to kill me, and I wish you had; but you have no right to do as you like with me."[5]

When Harriet Jacobs is courted by "a White unmarried gentleman,"[6] a lawyer named Mr. Sands, she is flattered, and her resistance takes another direction. Three motives converge: first, she hopes to be sold to Mr. Sands and eventually win freedom for her children;[7] second, she wishes to exercise her own choice of sexual partner ("It seems less degrading to give one's self, than to submit to compulsion. There is something akin to freedom in having a lover who has no control over you, except that which he gains by kindness and attachment"[8]); and third, she wants to spite her master ("I knew nothing would enrage Dr. Flint so much as to know that I favored another; and it was something to triumph over my tyrant even in that small way."[9]) This decision introduces the spiritual conflict of the narrative. Slavery created the kind of oppression that meant Jacobs's resistance against rape, abuse, and harassment required her to violate conventional moral standards.[10]

> O virtuous reader? You never knew what it is to be a slave; to be entirely unprotected by law or custom; to have the laws reduce you to the condition of chattel, entirely subject to the will of another. You never exhausted your ingenuity in avoiding the snares, and eluding the power of a hated tyrant; you never shuddered at the sound of his footsteps, and trembled within hearing of his voice. I know I did wrong. No one can feel it more sensibly

than I do. The painful and humiliating memory will haunt me to my dying day. Still, in looking back, calmly, on the events of my life, I feel that the slave woman ought not to be judged by the same standard as others.[11]

The pain of her choice is most poignant when she reveals that she is pregnant by Mr. Sands to her grandmother, who responds by sending her away and saying she never wants to see her again. The grandmother's worst fears have come true for another generation of women, and temporarily her resistance crumbles and she blames Harriet Jacobs for her decision. This is the fearful moment every mother wants to avoid. "The mother of slaves is very watchful. She knows there is no security for her children. After they have entered their teens she lives in daily expectation of trouble." In a few days, they were reconciled, and her grandmother "laid her old hand gently on my head, and murmured, 'Poor child! Poor child!'[12]

Having two children with Mr. Sands provides short-term relief during pregnancy and caring for the babies, but Dr. Flint is a stubborn man, and his abuse gets worse. "When I was told that Dr. Flint had joined the Episcopal church, I was much surprised. I supposed that religion had a purifying effect on the character of men; but the worst persecutions I endured from him were after he was a communicant."[13] When she confronted him with his hypocrisy, "His voice became hoarse with rage. 'How dare you preach to me about your infernal Bible!' he exclaimed. 'What right have you, who are my negro, to talk to me about what you would like and what you wouldn't like? I am your master, and you shall obey me.' "[14] Then Harriet Jacobs added: "No wonder the slaves sing,—'Ole Satan's church is here below; Up to God's free church I hope to go."[15]

In the climax of this part of the story, Harriet Jacobs is sent to the plantation, where she is isolated as part of the plan to break her spirit. There she accidently hears that her children are also to be brought to the plantation for the purpose of "breaking them in." She flees, spends time in the swamp, and then hides for seven years in the crawl space of her grandmother's attic, just several dozen yards from Dr. Flint's house.

HARRIET JACOBS'S RESISTANCE

What forms of liberated and critical consciousness enable individuals to stand against evil in silence, language, and action? What does this resistance tell us about racial and gender evil?

I am indebted to several contemporary scholars for insights about Harriet Jacobs's narrative, and about how similar structures of racial and sexual oppression continue to control the lives of many people today. My premise is that important parts of the foundation of modern capitalistic society were constructed in the nineteenth century, and that its ideologies continue to define the nature of power in our time. Neither Harriet Jacobs nor the millions of slaves created the slave society. The slave economy was a creation of the White male religious imagination. In analyzing this story, we will explore how this religious imagination was formed and maintained in the face of its obvious injustice and evil.

Dr. Flint used his power to rape, physically assault, abuse, and control the lives of his slaves; yet he was a respected citizen, a successful doctor and businessperson, and a Christian. We need to understand Dr. Flint as an individual created by the systems of racism and patriarchy of that time.

As a victim of physical assault, sexual harassment and abuse, Harriet Jacobs exercised minimal control over her labors and loves. Certainly her resistance was justified. To accept this assumption is to give hermeneutical privilege to the least powerful person, namely Harriet Jacobs, in order to ask how the abuse of power was organized at that time.

Such an evil situation could exist only if individual, social, and religious imagination had created the possibility for it to do so. Although we do not have access to Dr. Flint's mind—what he was thinking, and how he justified his own behavior—we can explore the writings his contemporaries, which reveal the internal and external situations of men like Dr. Flint, and demonstrate the manner in which they rationalized their treatment of slaves. In this section, we first review the story from Harriet Jacobs's perspective, and then ask about the rationale of White slaveholders.

The narrative by Harriet Jacobs, who wrote under the pen name of Linda Brent, has become important for several reasons. Even though scholars for many years discredited her story as a fabrication written by Abolitionists for a political and ideological agenda, it has recently been authenticated by Jean Fagan Yellin[16] and is now accepted as one of most accurate of the slave narratives. It is also one of the few slave narratives to overcome the sensibilities of nineteenth-century Victorian society and speak openly about sexual abuse of Black women by slaveholders.[17] Furthermore, Harriet Jacobs's story is a remarkable literary achievement by an author of any century, because it discloses both her extraordinary resistance to violent and dehumanizing oppression and at the same time reveals the author's internal struggle with her feelings that she betrayed her own principles.[18] Harriet Jacobs's story illustrates how the United States slavocracy organized race and gender as forms of social control.

Harriet Jacobs reported that when she was young the protection of her mother and grandmother shaped her consciousness. Later, her identification with her grandmother and the memory of her own life before the onset of emotional, physical, and sexual violence sustained her.

Much of her resistance occurred in silence. When her father died, she was not allowed to grieve or even see his body until a day later because her mistress wanted her to pick fresh flowers for a party. Even though she served at the table of the master's family, she could not ask for food, and was often denied any, surviving on that given to her when she passed her grandmother's house. During one painful exchange with Dr. Flint, she said, "I felt too feeble to dispute with him, and listened to his remarks in silence."[19] In fact, most of the time, Harriet Jacobs was forced to endure abuse and deprivation in silence, because she was a slave who had no right to "feel that [we] were human beings."[20]

Sometimes, however, she resisted by speaking out, using what Shawn Copeland calls "sass":

Linda Brent, [and] her grandmother, Mary Prince . . . use language to defend themselves from sexual and physical assault and to gain psychological space and strength. *Language* was a crucial form of resistance. In these narratives, women model audacious behavior: wit, cunning, verbal warfare, and moral courage. These Black women *sass!* *The Random House Dictionary of the English Language* defines sass as impudent or disrespectful back talk. Enslaved Black women use sass to guard, regain, and secure self-esteem; to obtain and hold psychological distance; to speak truth; to challenge "the atmosphere of moral ambiguity that surrounds them," and, sometimes, to protect against sexual assault.[21]

In one argument, Harriet Jacobs defended her right to love and marry whom she wanted.

"I have half a mind to kill you on the spot. . . . So you want to be married, do you?" said he, "and to a free nigger."

"Yes, sir."

"Well, I'll soon convince you whether I am your master, or the nigger fellow you honor so highly. If you *must* have a husband, you may take up with one of my slaves." . . .

I replied, "Don't you suppose, sir, that a slave can have some preference about marrying? Do you suppose that all men are alike to her?"

"So you love this nigger?" said he, abruptly.

"Yes, sir."

"How dare you tell me so!" he exclaimed, in great wrath. After a slight pause, he added, "I supposed you thought more of yourself; that you felt above the insults of such puppies."

I replied, "If he is a puppy I am a puppy, for we are both of the negro race. It is right and honorable for us to love each other. The man you call a puppy never insulted me, sir; and he would not love me if he did not believe me to be a virtuous woman."

He sprang upon me like a tiger, and gave me a stunning blow. It was the first time he had ever struck me; and fear did not enable me to control my anger. When I had recovered a little from the effects, I exclaimed, "You have struck me for answering you honestly. How I despise you!"[22]

Harriet Jacobs's most effective resistance came in the form of actions that exposed the contradictions of Dr. Flint's racism.[23] She asked for permission to marry a free Black man who loved her and thus showed that her desire was her own. To win her freedom, she formed a liaison with Mr. Sands, a White man, with whom she had two children. Finally, she ran away from Dr. Flint and hid in her grandmother's attic space for seven years so that he would not abuse her children further. In these actions, she showed a critical and liberated consciousness that supported her resistance to the domination of racial and gender oppression.

THE NATURE OF WHITE SUPREMACY

Harriet Jacobs's resistance discloses the evil of slavery. The following definition is adapted from The Cornwall Collective and Patricia Collins's thought:

> [T]he "matrix of domination" is a "system of attitudes, behaviors and assumptions that objectifies human persons on the basis of [socially constructed categories such as race, gender, class, etc.], and that has the power to deny autonomy, access to resources and self-determination to those persons, while maintaining the values of the dominant society as the norm by which all else will be measured."[24]

At least three parts of this definition merit discussion.

1. *Domination is a "system of attitudes, behaviors and assumptions that objectifies human persons on the basis of [socially constructed categories such as race, gender, class, etc.]."*

Dr. Flint expressed his attitude toward his many slaves through his question, "Do you know that I have a right to do as I like with you,—that I can kill you, if I please?"[25] Because his status as a White male slaveholder gave him power to use human beings as he wanted, he used control, abuse, violence, and rape to effectively dehumanize the persons in his power. Although damaging to any person with less power or status, his attitude was especially destructive for those toward whom his sexual and aggressive impulses were directed. In psychological terms, his social attitudes, behaviors, and assumptions toward African Americans, especially African American women, became even more dangerous when his power was fueled by his sexual desires. In psychoanalytic terms, Dr. Flint formed an narcissistic attachment to Harriet Jacobs that endangered her freedom and her life. He acted to possess her through harassment and attempted rape, and it was only through extraordinary courage, inner strength, and luck that Harriet Jacobs was able to resist and finally escape his clutches. For years after she arrived in the North, she lived in constant fear that he would capture and imprison her again. The story of Dr. Flint illustrates the importance of understanding psychological motives and dynamics in studying racial oppression.

2. Domination *"has the power to deny autonomy, access to resources and self-determination to those persons."*

In addition to his own attitudes, behaviors, assumptions, and psychological desires, Dr. Flint also had the economic and social power to control Harriet Jacobs and other human beings. He controlled their labor by deciding how, when, and where they would work, and he kept the profit from their work. He controlled their time by keeping them busy every day at exhausting tasks, telling them where to sleep and what to eat, and by requiring them to ask permission for anything they wanted to do on their own. He controlled their bodies because the society protected him when he physically beat, put in jail, or murdered them. Dr. Flint had tyrannical power that he exercised without fear of sanctions from church or society.

Far from being punished for his abusive power, Dr. Flint was rewarded with economic gain and social status. He was a physician, wealthy and highly respected, and a high achiever according to the norms of his society. Apparently, he joined the Episcopal church because it was expected of someone of his status. Of it, he said, "It was proper for me to do so. I am getting on in years, and my position in society requires it."[26]

Dr. Flint's power did not come because of his narcissism and personal evil, but because of his accommodation to the values of church and society. His power to deny resources, autonomy, and self-determination to other human beings came as a result of meeting social expectations, not by revolting against them. In order to understand this kind of evil, we must look beyond the individual to the way society establishes and enforces economic power and social norms.

3. Domination *"maintains the values of the dominant society as the norm by which all else will be measured."*

Harriet Jacobs's resistance also helps us see how the values of the dominant society functioned as norms that could be used against others. For example, Dr. Flint's wife chose to accept her husband's sexual abuse of Black women as the price she was willing to pay to profit from his economic and social status. Even though she was upset about his feelings for Harriet Jacobs, she was not sympathetic to his victim. The decision of most White southern women to join White men in their racist attitudes and behaviors is considered by many Black womanist scholars to be a choice for class privilege in spite of gender oppression.

Harriet Jacobs said, "The young wife soon learns that the husband in whose hands she has placed her happiness pays no regard to his marriage vows. Children of every shade of complexion play with her own fair babies, and too well she knows that they are born unto him of his own household. Jealousy and hatred enter the flowery home, and it is ravaged of its loveliness."[27] This observation points to the existence of interlocking, although distinct, forms of oppression. As the normative power in the family, Dr. Flint imposed a life of hard work, violence, rape, and death upon those who had no protection or human rights. Slavery also meant a life of contradictions and inner conflict for White women and children who chose to adapt to the tyranny of the patriarchal institution.

Mr. Sands, the White lawyer who fathered Harriet Jacobs's children, is often overlooked or interpreted as a benevolent White person in the narrative. He does treat her with more respect, does not physically abuse her, and provides some measure of protection against Dr. Flint's rage. However, Mr. Sands, as far as we know, took little personal risk to support Harriet Jacobs and his children. Engaging in a sexual liaison with a Black women in slavery was part of the accepted pattern in Southern society, and his social status protected him from any of the consequences that Harriet Jacobs faced. When Harriet Jacobs hid in the attic and, later, when she feared for her safety in the North, Mr. Sands did little to help. Even though he was more benevolent than Dr. Flint, he stayed within the expectations of his racial, gender, and class status and risked little of himself to combat slavery. In this way, he bore complicity for the slave system as well.

DEBATE AND BETRAYAL

While Dr. Flint was becoming a prominent and wealthy citizen in North Carolina, political and religious leaders in the nation were engaged in vigorous debates about race and gender. Benjamin Rush was a leader of the antislavery movement in the North, and Thomas Jefferson was a southern moderate who believed that slavery was a stain upon the new United States. In spite of these men's doubts, actions, and writings, slavery continued to prosper as an institution throughout the nineteenth century. Yet both Rush and Jefferson betrayed the antislavery cause in fundamental ways, and thus illustrate our theme of betrayal of the communities of resistance.

Dr. Flint's real name was James Norcom (1778–1850),[28] whose lifespan overlapped that of Thomas Jefferson (1743–1826) and Benjamin Rush (1745–1813). Important similarities characterize their lives. All three were slaveholders: Norcom had 50 slaves, and Jefferson had 200 slaves in 1780 and 267 slaves in 1822. Rush was a slaveholder until 1794. Respected citizens and community leaders, the three men were educated, religious, wealthy White men who benefited greatly from the organization of society.

Differences among them also existed. Jefferson was a nationally prominent politician, an author of the Declaration of Independence, and the third president of the United States (1801–1809). Rush was a nationally prominent political leader, a signer of the Declaration of Independence, a physician, and the founder of the field of American psychiatry. Although we have no written witness from Dr. Norcom related to his beliefs about life and slavery, Jefferson and Rush left us volumes.

Because Jefferson and Rush were prolific writers who participated in the contemporary debates about slavery, historical research has gained insight into their personal and public ideas. Studying Jefferson offers insight into a man similar in many ways to Dr. Norcom, and reading Rush's works offers insight into the mind of a northern Abolitionist. Together, Jefferson and Rush provide access to the White male imagination of the late eighteenth and early nineteenth centuries.

Thomas Jefferson

In the history of the slave debates at the end of the eighteenth and beginning of the nineteenth century, Thomas Jefferson has come to assume a prominent place for several reasons, but primarily because he expressed views typical of many southern slaveholders and even many abolitionists of the time. He was troubled by slavery and believed that it was a major problem for the integrity of the new nation. He feared the moral compromises White people made because of racism, and he feared the rage and violent revolt of African Americans. He believed that the result of slavery might well be a race war that could destroy the United States.

Yet Jefferson also opposed assimilation of "Negroes," believing that "intermixture of blood" would destroy the country. He believed that only a homogeneous European "lovely white"[29] could create the republic he envisioned. In all these values and attitudes, Jefferson typified moderate southerners, northerners, and even Abolitionists.

However, the economic and political forces of the time had already made his dream irrelevant. By the middle of the eighteenth century, the southern colonies were already committed to a slave economy, and the coming of "King Cotton" by 1793 had strengthened the motive for promoting the slave system. In 1792, the nation raised 6,000 bales of cotton; by 1810, 178,000 bales.[30] Cotton, tobacco, rice, indigo, and other crops raised all over the South with slave labor created wealth for both North and South. There was corresponding growth in the Black population, which went from 757,181 in 1790 to 1,377,808 in 1810, forming approximately 19% of the total population.[31]

Jefferson was in a bind because of conflicting internal values and attitudes, and because of an external reality that did not correspond to his own desires. Part of Jefferson's struggle occurred because of his sincere commitment to equalitarian natural rights for all "men," most clearly seen in the Declaration of Independence, which he helped to author. Winthrop Jordan summarizes Jefferson's beliefs:

> Rights belong to men as biological beings, inhering in them . . . because "all men are created equal and independent" and because "from that equal creation they derive rights inherent and inalienable." The central fact was creation: the Creator, whose primary attribute was tidiness, would scarcely have been so careless as to create a single species equipped with more than one set of rights.[32]

Granted his religious and moral position, Jefferson believed that Negroes were human beings who deserved and desired freedom just as much as Europeans. Therefore, slavery was wrong as an economic and political system. In this sense, Jefferson was sympathetic with some of the arguments of the Abolitionists of the North. In one of his classic statements, he emphasized the injustice and evil of slavery.

> Indeed I tremble for my country . . . when I reflect that God is just: that his justice cannot sleep forever: that considering numbers, nature and natural means only, a revolution of the wheel of fortune, an exchange of situation, is among possible events: that it may become probable by supernatural in-

terference! The Almighty has no attribute which can take side with us in such a context. . . . Nothing is more certainly written in the book of fate than that these people are to be free.[33]

In this statement, Jefferson also discloses his fear of slave revolts, which he believed could create the conditions for a race war leading to extermination of White or Black people, which was horrifying to him. He feared that the system of slavery permitted "one half the citizens thus to trample on the rights of the other, transforms those into despots, and these into enemies, destroys the morals of one part, and the *amor patriae* of the other."[34] As we shall see, Jefferson had two conflicting values—one "for freedom and his larger equalitarian faith,"[35] but also one against assimilation and interracial community.

Jefferson was also a slaveholder, with all of the attitudes and values of his economic and social location. Even though he mentioned several times that he might free his slaves, he freed only a few, and, in a letter to a friend, he confesses his own violence toward the slaves. Ronald Takaki summarizes the correspondence:

As a slavemaster, Jefferson personally experienced what he described as the "perpetual exercise of the most boisterous passions." He was capable of punishing his slaves with great cruelty. He had James Hubbard, a runaway slave who had been apprehended and returned in irons to the plantation, whipped and used as an example to the other slaves. "I had him severely flogged in the presence of his old companions," Jefferson reported. On another occasion, Jefferson punished a slave to make an example of him in "terrorem" to the others, and ordered him to be sold to one of the slave traders from Georgia. "If none such offers," he added, "if he could be sold in any other quarter so distant as never more to be heard among us, it would to the others be as if he were put out of the way by death." Clearly, Jefferson was no "prodigy," able to retain his manners and morals undepraved by the brutalizing circumstances of slavery.[36]

Jefferson was troubled by his own violence but he tended to blame the institution of slavery for corrupting him rather than take responsibility for his own behavior. He channeled his mixed feelings into intellectual analysis of the problem of slavery. For example, he agonized over whether Africans were equal to Europeans in intelligence.

Comparing them by their faculties of memory, reason, and imagination, it appears to me that in memory they are equal to the whites; in reason much inferior, as I think one could scarcely be found capable of tracing and comprehending the investigations of Euclid; and that in imagination they are dull, tasteless and anomalous. . . . [N]ever yet could I find that a black had uttered a thought above the level of plain narration; never see even an elementary trait of painting or sculpture.[37]

He was strongly influenced by the theory of environmentalism, which blamed any deficits in the African Americans on the brutality of slavery itself. But he went beyond this theory to a belief in the natural inferiority of "the Negroes." "I advance it therefore as a suspicion only, that the blacks, whether originally a distinct race, or made distinct by time and circumstances, are inferior to the whites in the endowments both of body and mind. . . . It is not their condition then, but nature, which has produced the distinction."[38]

Under the guise of ending slavery and preventing a future race war, Jefferson endorsed colonization, a idea that persisted into the twentieth century. As president, Jefferson conducted official conversations with countries in Africa and Latin America about accepting large numbers of "Negroes," although no realistic plan for financing or logistics ever materialized. In his support of colonization, Jefferson demonstrates his wish for the Negro problem to just go away and for the United States to be homogeneously white and European.

Sexuality presented Jefferson with another difficulty. His belief in the superiority of Europeans and the purity of races left him concerned about "mixture of blood." In the following meditation, he speculates about White beauty and Black sexuality in a way that reveals his underlying racial prejudice.

Are not the fine mixtures of red and white, the expressions of every passion by greater or less suffusions of colour in the one, preferable to that eternal monotony, which reigns in the countenances, that immoveable veil of black which covers all the emotions of the other race? Add to these, flowing hair, a more elegant symmetry of form, and their own judgment in favour of the whites, declared by their preference of them, as uniformly as is the preference of the Oran-ootan [orangutan] for the black woman over those of his own species. The circumstances of superior beauty, is thought worthy attention in the propagation of our horses, dogs, and other domestic animals; why not in that of man?[39]

In this paragraph, Jefferson, clearly expressing his preference for the English and Nordic traits of beauty and contrasting them sharply with that of the Africans, assumes a hierarchical relationship between Englishmen, Africans, and apes in a way that emphasizes the animal aspects of what he thought of as lower types. As Winthrop Jordan interprets it, Jefferson reveals the common perception of Europeans and European Americans about the inferiority of Black persons and their "perverted" sexuality.

> Red and white were the ingredients of beauty, and Negroes were pronouncedly less beautiful than whites; Negroes desired sexual relations especially with whites; black women had relations with orang-outangs. On a deeper level the pattern of his remarks was more revealing of Jefferson himself. Embedded in his thoughts on beauty was the feeling that whites were subtler and more delicate in their passions and that Negroes, conversely, were more crude. He felt Negroes to be sexually more animal—hence the gratuitous intrusion of the man-like ape. His libidinal desires, unacceptable and inadmissible to his society and to his higher self, were effectively transferred to others and thereby drained of their intolerable immediacy. . . . Yet Jefferson was never completely at rest. His picture of Negroes as crudely sensual beings, which was at once an offprint of popular belief and a functional displacement of his own emotional drives, kept popping up whenever Negroes came to mind.[40]

Given Jefferson's racial prejudice and fears expressed in his *Notes on Virginia* (1784), charges made against Jefferson one year after he became president were ironic. In 1802, James T. Callendar accused him of fathering five children with Sally Hemings, a Black woman who was a slave on his plantation—a charge of miscegenation and fornication. This scandal swirled around him for the rest of his political career. (He was president from 1801 until 1809 and died in 1826.) In spite of diligent historical research, "Jefferson's paternity can be neither refuted nor proved from the known circumstances or from the extant testimony. . . ."[41] Jefferson himself never responded to the charges.[42] An important question that goes beyond the facts of the matter is why the charges became a scandal, especially when sexual abuse of Black women by White men was quite usual at the time. Takaki suggests:

> Everywhere in the controversy, there was irony. Both Jefferson's critics and his defenders were demanding what Jefferson himself had also demanded: White men must vigilantly guard themselves against their own "strongest passions" and must not "stain" the blood of the white republic. The code of white racial purity required that violators be severely punished. . . . Yet there was nothing Jefferson could have done to wipe away the "stain" upon the nation: He had become the receptacle of the nation's guilt as white men imputed to him the passions they could not contain and the sins they could not confess. In the process, they were reaffirming in their own minds the principles of republicanism, determined to expel the "enemy"—interracial sex and impurity—from the "bowels" of the new nation.[43]

The scandal represented exactly the dilemma of White men of that time. The doctrine of White supremacy paradoxically required White dominance over all persons of color (including dominance in the bed), and also required a myth of racial purity that prevented intermarriage and sexual liaisons. In Jefferson's scandal, the truth about the sexual abuse of Black women was disclosed, but in a way that reinforced White supremacy. By castigating Jefferson, the president, for miscegenation, the public was pretending to be horrified at something that happened all too frequently, namely, the rape and abuse of Black women by White slaveholders.

Benjamin Rush

Benjamin Rush, an Abolitionist, nevertheless shared some of the same assumptions as Thomas Jefferson about "the Negroes." As a physician, Dr. Rush was primarily interested in medicine as a solution to social problems. He believed that certain people, namely those who were mentally and physically ill, could be cured through intensive treatment in asylums.

> Rush viewed illness in strikingly republican terms: Sickness was the consequence of vices such as idleness, intemperance, and the loss of self-control over the appetites of the instinctual life, especially sexuality. "This appetite, which was implanted in our natures for the purposes of propagating our species, when excessive, becomes a disease of both the body and mind," the doctor noted. The results of sexual excess, Rush warned, were horrible. Promiscuous intercourse or masturbation produced "seminal weakness, impotence, dysury, tabes dorsalis, pulmonary consumption, hypochrondriasis, loss of memory, manalgia, fatuity, and death."[44]

Rush believed that marriage, diet, temperance, hard work, and study could cure these illnesses. That is, instinctual excesses were the problem, and repression and sublimation of these drives into work was the cure. For stubborn cases, he prescribed a regimen of purging (artificial diarrhea) and bloodletting (twenty to forty ounces of blood at a time). He also prescribed that patients be isolated in rooms without human company, and sit in special chairs with straps and a head vice to prevent movement and imbalance of the body. Rush's ideas were similar to those later popularized in Germany by Dr. Daniel Schreber.[45] Rush not only believed these techniques were effective for those who were mentally and physically ill, but also for criminals and for women with hysteria or other "female" ailments. He believed his methods were all-purpose cures for most problems. Tragically, his own son became ill in 1810, possibly with depression, and spent the remaining twenty-seven years of his life living in the hospital ward his father had founded.[46]

Dr. Rush opposed slavery and favored interracial harmony; however, one occasion reveals his underlying attitude of White supremacy. At the celebration of the founding of the first African Episcopal Church of St. Thomas in 1793, Rush noted the public display of Black and White friendship and was effusive in his praise of this accomplishment. The ambiguous subtext, however, spoke of the necessity for Blacks to form separate denominations because of being excluded from full participation in the White churches. Rush "was invariably enraptured by public manifestations of interracial brotherhood and noted with satisfaction the progress of Negroes in letters to his wife. . . . 'And who knows,' he asked, 'but that it may be the means of sending the gospel to Africa, as the American Revolution sent liberty to Europe.' "[47] Later, toward the close of his life, Rush wrote, "It will be much cheaper to build churches for them than jails. . . . "Without the former, the latter will be indispensably necessary for them."[48]

Rush's belief in White supremacy came out in other ways. Important for our purposes is the scholarly paper he delivered on July 14, 1792, to the American Philosophical Society entitled, "Observations intended to favour the supposition that the black Color (as it is called) of the Negroes is derived from the LEPROSY."[49] This speculative proposition was derived from accumulating many of the common White prejudices about "the Negroes."

> The more visible symptoms of leprosy were the Negro's physical features—the "big lip," "flat nose," "woolly hair," and especially the black color of his skin. Negroes, Dr. Rush said, had many qualities which lepers possessed. Like them, Negroes had a "morbid insensitivity of the nerves." As an example of the Negro's ability to disregard pain, Rush cited a Dr. Moseley's claim that he had amputated the legs of many Negroes while they held the upper part of the limbs. Moreover, Rush claimed, like lepers, Negroes had remarkably strong venereal desires. 'This is universal among the negroes, hence their uncommon fruitfulness when they are not depressed by slavery; but even slavery in its worse state does not always subdue the venereal appetite; for after whole days spent in hard labor in a lot sun in the West Indies, the black men often walk five or six miles to comply with a venereal assignation." This was something Dr. Rush could not imagine healthy or white men doing.[50]

We can see a whole set of White male fears in Rush's words: Black, a deviant color in comparison to normative White, could thus be classified as a disease needing treatment; deviancy was invariably connected to sexuality and fear of the instinctual life; and disease and sexuality became attached to physical characteristics such as color and facial features.

Reading this paragraph, we need to remember that Dr. Rush was an Abolitionist, in fact a founder of the Pennsylvania Society for Promoting the Abolition of Slavery.[51] A social and political leader in Philadelphia and the young nation, he believed that assimilation of "the Negroes" into White society could solve the problem of White racism. However, he also believed that "the Negroes" were inferior and should be changed into something resembling White Europeans before integration would work.

In his paper on leprosy, he made three suggestions to solve the race problem: first, that the black skin color of "the Negroes" was a disease which called for compassion from White people; second, that quarantine or segregation of "the Negroes" from the White population would prevent the contagious disease from spreading; third, that medical treatment in one of his asylums would cure "Negroes," that is, make them white and thus acceptable to White society. "The 'diseased' Negro . . . could be spontaneously 'cured,' and his black skin restored to its 'natural' and 'healthy' whiteness."[52]

The tragedy of Dr. Rush's diagnosis and prescription is that in spite of his professed commitment to integration and assimilation, he actually fabricated medical myths of Negro inferiority, which served as compelling arguments for separation and segregation and played into the sexual fears and projections of men of European descent.

In conclusion, Jefferson and Rush were committed to White supremacy. In a society characterized by socioeconomic inequality and injustice between White and Black persons, they rationalized their privilege by focusing on "the problem of the Negro." They concluded that the black color and other physical features indicated inferiority and deficiency. Especially upset about sexuality and their perception that Black women and men were more licentious and animal-like, they were not willing to turn the analysis upon themselves and the White male psyche and spirit. What was the fear in White men that propelled them toward such a hatred of the Negroes? Where did the vicious violence toward Negroes come from? How did intelligent men like Jefferson and Rush fail to analyze the systematic rape of Black women by White men, even when it was brought to their attention through a presidential scandal?

Winthrop Jordan reveals his deeper hunches about the White male imagination in the following passage:

> Perhaps White men sensed how tightly the institution [of slavery] had controlled the pattern of sexual relationships between the races, how handsomely it had afforded them a sexual license and privilege which could be

indulged without destroying their most vital institution of cultural integrity, the family. The controls of slavery were essential not only for curbing the licentiousness of Negroes but, as the "swarms" of mulattoes so eloquently testified, for limiting the license of white men. For if the white man's sexual license were not prudently defined and circumscribed, might he not discover that it was he, as much or more than the Negro after all, who was licentious? Above all, the white man had to sustain his feeling of control: in restraining the Negro he was at the same time restraining and thereby reassuring himself.[53]

Fear of sexuality and its expression, commitment to an economic system based on the exploitation of Africans, and a religious faith that emphasized rationality and control of others became organized into a tight system of ideas, behaviors, and institutions. These characteristics continue to contribute to the maintenance of an evil system that has caused massive oppression against African Americans for 350 years.

In this chapter, we have examined an early nineteenth-century story about courageous resistance to racial and gender evil and have analyzed some of the ways that domination was constructed by prominent leaders of society. Benjamin Rush and Thomas Jefferson publicly opposed slavery as an institution and thus supported the resistance of African American women and men such as Harriet Jacobs. At the same time, their published writings and political actions actually betrayed the communities of resistance by creating the very arguments of Black inferiority that helped maintain the rationale for slavery. Later in the nineteenth century white women were resisting the domination of patriarchy, the story to which we turn next.

WOMEN AND MALE DOMINANCE

The Case of Freud and Dora

When she was eighteen years old, Dora's father, concerned over a suicide note and Dora's loss of consciousness during a family argument, sent Dora to see Sigmund Freud for psychoanalysis. Freud had first seen her two years earlier, when she was sixteen, for medical treatment of a cough and hoarseness. Once again her father handed her over to Freud, requesting that he get to the root of her physical complaints and learn why she was unhappy. Very quickly, Freud discovered reasons for her problems.

The family drama revolved around Dora's relationships to her father and mother (who were unhappily married) and two family friends, Herr K. and Frau K. When Dora was younger, she had become attached to Frau K. while helping with her children. Furthermore, Frau K. had nursed Dora's father back to health, a relationship that led to an affair.

During adolescence, two traumatic events changed Dora's life. When she was fourteen, Herr K. kissed her while they were alone at his place of business. Dora, who was disgusted and fled for safety, told no one what had happened. Two years later, when she was sixteen, Herr K. proposed a sexual relationship to Dora during a walk by the lake. She slapped him, ran away, and left town with her father. Several days later she told her parents what had happened. Freud describes Herr K.'s response.

> Herr K. had been called to account by her father and uncle on the next occasion of their meeting, but he had denied in the most emphatic terms having on his side made any advances which could have been open to such a construction. He had then proceeded to throw suspicion upon the girl, saying that he had heard from Frau K. that she took no interest in anything but sexual matters, and that she used to read Mantegazza's *Physiology of Love* and books of that sort in their house on the lake. It was most likely, he

had added, that she had been over-excited by such reading and had merely "fancied" the whole scene she had described.[1]

Dora's father, who accepted Herr K.'s version of the story, told Freud, "I myself believe that Dora's tale of the man's immoral suggestions is a phantasy that has forced its way into her mind. . . . Please try and bring her to reason."[2] But Freud, who had a commitment to his patients, resolved "from the first to suspend my judgement of the true state of affairs till I had heard the other side as well."[3] When he heard Dora's story, Freud accepted her version, including her perception "that she had been handed over to Herr K. as the price of his tolerating the relations between her father and his wife."[4] These experiences of betrayal and sexual harassment provide Freud's focus for the case.

> The experience with Herr K.—his making love to her and the insult to her honour which was involved—seems to provide Dora's case the psychic trauma which Breuer and I declared long ago to be the indispensable prerequisite for the production of a hysterical disorder.[5]

However, even though Freud accepted Dora's version of the family drama, he focused on her sexual desires rather than the family dynamics. At this point, the case becomes complicated for most readers, because Freud seems to blame Dora for what happened. "[Dora] had made herself an accomplice in the affair, and had dismissed from her mind every sign which tended to show its true character."[6] Why did Freud focus on Dora's complicity rather than the family pathology? Freud's motive for this exploration was his scientific interest in the disease of hysteria, that is, the symptoms and cures of frigidity and physical ailments in women. Commenting on Herr K.'s kissing Dora in his office, Freud said, "I should without question consider a person hysterical in whom an occasion for sexual excitement elicited feelings that were preponderantly or exclusively unpleasurable."[7] In a footnote on this section, Freud also said, "I happen to know Herr K., for he was the same person who had visited me with the patient's father, and he was still quite young and of prepossessing appearance."[8] Freud apparently thought that Herr K. was an appropriate suitor for Dora in spite of her age, his friendship with her father, and the multiple betrayals of fidelity within the family.[9] Freud decided that the therapeutic goal was to help Dora see that her illness was caused by an inner conflict, namely sexual desire for Herr K., and fear of her sexual feelings.

Freud organized his therapeutic work by exploring Dora's sexual conflict and uncovering her love for Herr K. He decided that her physical symptoms were responses to her love for Herr K. She was sick when he was gone and well when he was present. She rejected a governess-maid who tried to expose her father's affair with Frau K. Freud worked on the assumption that Dora must acknowledge her love for Herr K. in order to get well, that is, she must see that saying no to Herr K. actually meant that she loved him.[10]

> If this "No," instead of being regarded as the expression of an impartial judgement (of which, indeed, the patient is incapable), is ignored, and if work is continued, the first evidence soon begins to appear that in such a case "No" signifies the desired "Yes." . . . There is no such thing at all as an unconscious "No."[11]

In his attempts to show that Dora actually loved Herr K., Freud maintains his insistence that her "no" means "yes" through many detours about Dora's sexual fantasies about men and women, about masturbation and bed-wetting, about oral sex and homosexuality. He even defends himself against charges that he was sexualizing Dora through this process.[12]

In his case study of Dora, Freud focuses on two of his patient's dreams. In the first, Dora dreamed that she was rescued from a burning house by her father.

> A house was on fire. My father was standing beside my bed and woke me up. I dressed myself quickly. Mother wanted to stop and save her jewel-case; but Father said, "I refuse to let myself and my two children be burnt for the sake of your jewel-case." We hurried downstairs, and as soon as I was outside I woke up.[13]

Dora had first dreamed this dream just after Herr K's kiss by the lake, and Freud interpreted it as a wish that her father would protect her from Herr K. The jewel-case represented her virginity and drew on her memories of her father waking her as a young child when she had a problem with bed-wetting. Freud interpreted this as a defensive reaction against the underlying love she had for Herr K.

> The dream confirms once more what I had already told you before you dreamed it—that you are summoning up your old love for your father in order to protect yourself against your love for Herr K. But what do all these efforts show? Not only that you are afraid of Herr K., but that you are still more afraid of yourself, and of the temptation you feel to yield to him. In short, these efforts prove once more how deeply you loved him.[14]

Then Freud wrote, "Naturally Dora would not follow me in this part of the interpretation."[15] However, he continued to explore the case using his theory of dream interpretation, with its emphasis on early childhood experiences of bedwetting and masturbation, and continued in his belief that Dora was in love with Herr K.[16]

In the second dream, Dora was informed by her mother that her father was dead. She had trouble finding her way home, and when she finally got there, "The maidservant opened the door to me and replied that Mother and the others were already at the cemetery."[17] Again, Freud explored the dream using a sexual interpretation that led back to Herr K.

Two sessions later, Dora announced that this was her last session. Freud concluded the case holding the same opinion with which he started: "The fact is, I am beginning to suspect that you took the affair with Herr K. much more seriously than you have been willing to admit so far."[18]

At the end of the case, Freud tried to explain why Dora terminated prematurely. Perhaps her father lost interest because Freud did not "bring Dora to reason." Perhaps Freud had not shown enough "warm personal interest in her."[19] Maybe Dora decided to return to her symptoms rather than get well ("Incapacity for meeting a real erotic demand is one of the most essential features of a neurosis").[20] Perhaps, Freud thinks, "I did not succeed in mastering the transference in good time."[21] Perhaps he had underestimated Dora's attachment to Frau K. ("I failed to discover in time and to inform the patient that her homosexual [gynaecophilic] love for Frau K. was the strongest unconscious current in her mental life.")[22]

Fifteen months later, Dora returned to tell Freud that she had confronted Herr and Frau K. with their lies.

> To the wife she said: "I know you have an affair with my father"; and the other did not deny it. From the husband she drew an admission of the scene by the lake which he had disputed, and brought the news of her vindication home to her father. Since then she had not resumed her relations with the family.[23]

Freud tried to disguise his disappointment that Dora terminated therapy before he was finished with her. "I do not know what kind of help she wanted from me, but I promised to forgive her for having deprived me of the satisfaction of affording her a far more radical cure for her troubles."[24] The day after he finished writing up this case, Freud wrote to a friend that this was "the subtlest thing I have written so far."[25] His judgment that this case would turn out to be an important part of his life work was correct, because it has become one of the most widely read clinical cases in the history of modern psychology.[26]

DORA'S RESISTANCE

Freud's case study about Dora belongs in a study of evil, because of its importance in contemporary debates about gender and sexuality and because it provides access to psychoanalytic methods. Although we have no access to anything written by Dora about her experience, Freud's account offers clues about her resistance to patriarchy and to him.

Dora seems to have resisted in silence for many years. In spite of Freud's attempt to manipulate her into revealing her own desires, at the end of the case he confessed that he had underestimated her attachment to Frau K. Dora was silent about her plans to terminate therapy after only three months. Freud could not complete his analysis because she resisted him through silence. At the last session, in which Freud revealed his own view that Dora wanted to marry Herr K., Freud reports that Dora responded with polite silence: "Dora had listened to me without any of her usual contradictions. She seemed to be moved; she said good-bye to me very warmly, with the heartiest wishes for the New Year, and—came no more."[27]

Sometimes Dora resisted through language. During some sessions, Freud became aggressive in trying to convince her that her unhappiness and physical symptoms were caused by her repressed love for Herr K., even though she consistently denied that it was true. "I did not find it easy, however, to direct the patient's attention to her relations with Herr K. She declared that she had done with him." "My expectations were by no means disappointed when this explanation of mine was met by Dora with a most emphatic negative." "Naturally Dora would not follow me in this part of the interpretation." [Dora:] "Why, has anything so very remarkable come out?"[28]

This last comment fits the definition of "sass" we saw in Harriet Jacobs's story. After many hours of psychoanalysis, Dora had the audacity to tell Freud that his interpretation did not impress her very much. Freud seemed confused by this comment, and he ruminated often in the future over his inability to convince Dora of his own brilliance.

Dora resisted through action. She ran away from Herr K. in the first incident of sexual harassment, and slapped him in the face the second time. She told Freud the family secrets, fully expecting him to side with her just claims. But her final victory came when she announced her termination.

She opened the third sitting with these words: "Do you know that I am here for the last time to-day?"—"How can I know, as you have said nothing to me about it?"—"Yes, I made up my mind to put up with it till the New Year. But I shall wait no longer than that to be cured."[29]

Thus Dora acted out her resistance to Freud's mistreatment and abuse.

THE NATURE OF MALE DOMINANCE

The "matrix of domination" is a "system of attitudes, behaviors and assumptions that objectifies human persons on the basis of [socially constructed categories such as race, gender, class, etc.], and that has the power to deny autonomy, access to resources and self-determination to those persons, while maintaining the values of the dominant society as the norm by which all else will be measured."[30]

1. The matrix of domination is "a system of attitudes, behaviors and assumptions that objectifies human persons on the basis of [socially constructed categories such as race, gender, class, etc.]."

What are the clues that Freud had a system of attitudes, behaviors, and assumptions that objectified Dora on the basis of gender? If we rely on Freud's report of Dora's resistance, it appears that she first came to him under pressure from her father. Perhaps she stayed at first because Freud believed her story of family infidelities. She resisted by disclosing family secrets. The first sign of her resistance was her attempt to enlist Freud to take her side and the side of justice. Even after Freud pressured her to accept his fantasy of her love for Herr K., she rejected this interpretation in hope that Freud would believe her again. "She had all these years been in love with Herr K. When I informed her of this conclusion she did not assent to it."[31] When it became apparent that Freud would not change his attitudes and behaviors, she terminated her analysis.

If we follow this line of thinking into Freud's mind, then we begin to find other attitudes, behaviors, and assumptions that objectified Dora on the basis of gender. For example, in the case study introduction, Freud says "that the causes of hysterical disorders are to be found in the intimacies of the patients's psycho-sexual life, and that hysterical symptoms are the expression of their most secret and repressed wishes."[32] Freud decided that Dora must be repressing her sexual attraction for Herr K., because only an abnormal person would respond to "an occasion for sexual excitement" with "feelings that were preponderantly or exclusively unpleasurable."[33] Based on our knowledge of Freud's other theories of sexuality and gender, we can see that, by objectifying Dora so that she would conform to his idea of a "true womanhood,"[34] he himself became her abuser.

Much of the debate about this case focuses on countertransference. Freud, like Dr. Flint in Harriet Jacobs's narrative, held a position of authority. Dr. Flint's power was absolute, allowing him to engage in a crude seduction and attempted rape, whereas Freud depended on overpowering Dora with words. One wonders what might have happened if Dora had been even more vulnerable and had accepted Freud's pressure to believe she was in love with Herr K. Perhaps then the voyeuristic exploitation of Dora would have been more severe and resembled the contemporary sexual abuse by therapists and clergy. Freud's power together with his interest in Dora's being attracted to Herr K. were a dangerous combination for Dora, but, fortunately, she resisted.

2. Domination *"has the power to deny autonomy, access to resources and self-determination to those persons."*

Freud's social power over Dora was not as absolute as Dr. Flint's power over Harriet Jacobs. Yet though his power was constructed much differently—that is, he did not own Dora's labor and her body—Freud's status allowed him to be an oppressor. Not only did he write and publish information about Dora's case, thereby setting the terms for future public discussion of Dora's personal life, but he was male, middle aged, established as a physician, upper class, a published scientific writer, and relatively wealthy. Dora, too, came from a wealthy family, which gave her social status, but she was adolescent, female, and symptomatic. Freud's profession as a physician rested on his responsibility to provide access to resources, in this case insight into the psychological motives of one's life, and education in an emerging scientific anthropology. Many of Freud's students and clients went on to become leaders in the new field of psychoanalytic psychology, and thus gained personal and social power.

Ida Bauer (Dora's real name) was gifted, too, with the potential for personal achievement. Although her brother became a leading intellectual proponent of European socialism, we can deduce, based on the witness of Felix Deutsch many years later, that she did not reach her potential.[35] One can speculate that a more therapeutic and less abusive analysis might have provided her the resolution she needed to make a larger contribution. Instead, she suffered a form of gender oppression that reinforced her subordinate status in her family and in society. Freud went on to become the most famous psychologist of the century without penalty for his mistakes, while Ida Bauer paid for Freud's mistakes with a damaged psyche and spirit.

3. Domination *"maintains the values of the dominant society as the norm by which all else will be measured."*

Many of Freud's followers and critics consider the case study of Dora important for understanding contemporary gender power relations. Although Freud's view of women as deficient and deformed persons persists,

many feminists count Dora among their heroes, because she employed silence, language, and action to resist Freud. Freud's case study exemplifies
the manner in which society maintains the norm of male dominance.
Freud's construction of the Oedipus complex as the basic definition of
gender and sexuality has bolstered patriarchy for almost a century in spite
of the resistance of Dora and other women witnesses to this evil's creativity and persistence.

WHY STUDY FREUD?

There are many reasons not to study Freud. His ideas have been discredited in the minds of many people because of his patriarchal attitudes
toward women; because of his individualistic theories that ignore familial
and socioeconomic realities; because of his obsession with sexuality as the
central drive in human life; and because of his negative evaluation of religious faith and practice. For these reasons many have rejected Freud and
gone on to study and apply other theories such as behaviorism, cognitive
development, family therapy, and humanistic psychology.

However, I believe that the study of Freud is important for understanding the modern psychological age, and especially for understanding issues
of race and gender as ideologies of oppression.

First, in his attitudes about gender, Freud was typical of the European
men of his time. In this sense, he is important in the same way Thomas
Jefferson and Benjamin Rush are important (see chapter 1). Because
Freud's theories reflect gender inequality and the oppression of women,
understanding how Freud's values and ideas are patriarchal gives us insight
into how this evil is created and perpetuated.

> Feminists have been quick to point out that the reasons for Freud's failure
> are clearly sexist: Freud is authoritarian, a willing participant in the male
> power game conducted between Dora's father and Herr K., and at no time
> turns to consider Dora's own experience of the events. That Freud's analysis
> fails because of its inherent sexism is the common feminist conclusion.[36]

Second, Freud has been identified by some feminist scholars as an important dialogue partner because he placed sexuality and gender politics
at the heart of his theory, and thus created the possibility of making
gender thematic for other critical theories.

> I would like to look at this case once again with feminist eyes. . . . I will
> argue . . . that Freud's analysis is only partly true . . . because it is structured

around a fantasy of femininity and female sexuality that remains misunderstood, unconscious if you will. . . . [P]sychoanalysis is not simply the theory of the formation of gender identity and sexuality in patriarchal society but is profoundly ideological as well.[37]

Third, Freud is important because a study of his critical methods can unmask forms of patriarchy of the nineteenth and twentieth centuries. Certain scholars have argued that it is possible to use Freud against Freud, that is, to adopt his methods in a way that explodes the metapsychology reinforcing patriarchy.

There is a difference between Freud's metapsychology and his methodology. Freud's metapsychology includes such powerful constructs as the Oedipus complex, ego-id-superego, and eros-thanatos. His methodology includes such potent analytic concepts as transference, resistance, anxiety, countertransference, counterresistance, and counteranxiety. . . . I accept the judgment that, practically, in the therapeutic situation, it is the analysis of phenomena using methodological concepts that is primary and that allows change while the metapsychological constructs provide supplementary, multidimensional structures of interpretive insight.[38]

INTERPRETATIONS OF FREUD

Freud published his "Fragment of an Analysis of a Case of Hysteria," based on three months of therapy with Ida Bauer in late 1900, in 1905. He originally wrote the case in 1901, one year after the publication of *The Interpretation of Dreams* and four years before *Three Essays on Sexuality*. "[I]t is caught quite literally between . . . the theory of the unconscious and the theory of sexuality. . . . *Dora* would then mark the transition between these two theories."[39] It has become known as "Dora's Case" because of the pseudonym Freud gave the client to protect her privacy. Her true identity was revealed when Felix Deutsch wrote in 1957 that he had seen Ida Bauer for consultation in New York City in 1922. He published her name after she died in 1945.

The following discussion analyzes Freud's interpretation of the case of Dora in three ways: as an example of patriarchal distortion, as a flawed critical theory of gender and sexuality, and as a method to unmask patriarchy.

Dora as a Frigid Hysteric

Until recently, many interpreters of Freud concurred with his view that Dora represents a classic hysteric personality whose fear of sexuality led to frigidity.

"Fragment of an Analysis" . . . is considered a classic analysis of the structure and genesis of hysteria and has the first or last word in almost every psychoanalytic discussion of hysteria. Although some have written addenda to Freud's case study, following up on one or another of Dora's multiple identifications or reconsidering the case from the point of view of ego psychology, or from that of technique, or transference, the essential meaning of the analysis remains unchallenged. Dora's frigidity, so haunting to Freud and to us, is still considered a cornerstone of hysteria and its most profound symptom. And the meaning Freud attributed to it is still considered to be "truth" by psychoanalytic theory and by popular culture.[40]

The case study of Dora defines and illustrates several basic ideas in classical psychoanalytic theory: (a) that hysteria is the repression of sexual desire (frigidity); (b) that dream interpretation confirms unconscious dynamics; (c) that sexuality is formed through Oedipal conflict; and (d) that transference is a phenomenon that forms a basic technique of psychoanalysis.

However, classical interpretations also criticize Freud for misunderstanding Dora. Philip Rieff, translator of Freud, summarizes this viewpoint:

Of course, Freud knew that the girl was right. He had to admire Dora's insight into this intricate and sad affair-within-an-affair. Yet he fought back with his own intricate insights into the tangle of her own motives; that was his error; there is the point at which the complexity of Freudian analysis must reach out, beyond the individual patient, to the entire tangle of motives of all the bad actors—father, mistress, would-be lover, stupid mother. Only then would the analysis have been complete, true and adequately pedagogic.[41]

Dora as a Feminist Hero

Feminists studying Freud's case of Dora have pointed out that, far from representing the typical hysteric whose frigidity is an illness, Dora actually engaged in revolt against the control and oppression of patriarchy. In spite of Dora's being surrounded by men who disrespected her (her father), abused her (Herr K.), and manipulated her in therapy (Freud), she stood against them all and exposed their games. In the end, she told the truth about her father's affair, forced a confession of abuse from Herr K., and rejected Freud's interpretation of her sexual desire. Thus, Dora becomes a hero who rejects male dominance in her life and a model for the resistance of all women to patriarchal oppression.

Maria Ramas gives one of the most forceful presentations of this argument:

> I will argue that at the deepest level of meaning, Ida Bauer's hysteria was exactly what it appeared to be—a repudiation of the meaning of hetero-sexuality. . . . It was an attempt to deny patriarchal sexuality, and it was a protest against postoedipal femininity.[42]

Ramas uses Dora's real name, Ida Bauer, as a way of challenging Freud's control of the patient he wrote about. She also questions Freud's preoc-cupation with Ida's frigidity, so important to his theory of hysteria. As we saw in the previous section, psychoanalytic theory actually helped to create the category of the frigid hysteric, the woman who fears her un-conscious sexual desire and must be forced to acknowledge this desire in order to avoid illness; in other words, in such women marriage and an active sex life could cure hysteria.

These problems, of course, arise out of the theory of psychoanalysis itself, especially the Oedipal complex. Because a girl's first erotic attach-ment is usually with her mother, in order to become heterosexual she must transform this attachment. Accepting heterosexuality as the goal of nor-mative development within a theory that assumes a primitive human bi-sexuality is an internal contradiction of psychoanalysis, and one that is at the root of Freud's treatment of Ida Bauer.

Ramas's interpretation notes the absence of the mother in Freud's study. Freud called Kathe Bauer a neurotic housewife, that is, a woman with an obsessive need for order and cleanliness. Ramas suggests that Kathe Bau-er's fear of contamination, which resulted from having contracted a vene-real disease from her husband, may have contributed to her daughter's negative views of sexuality. Ramas further suggests that, given Ida's moth-er's experience, Ida's disgust with sexuality was a realistic response. Yet "Freud indeed argues here that Ida Bauer was hysterical because she was disgusted by Herr K.'s kiss when she should have felt aroused."[43] So, Ramas asks,

> In the face of such consistent behavior, why should we follow Freud in his assertion that Ida Bauer's attitude toward Herr K. was not what it appeared to be? That her symptoms revealed reversal of affect? Why should we be convinced that her behavior and her desire were at odds?[44]

However, Ida Bauer's forms of resistance were limited. Because she was a child, she had no choice about being a member of this family, with its illnesses and immoralities; but she did have the choice, as she became old enough, of exposing its infidelities. By rejecting Herr K.'s advances, Ida threatened the whole structure of adult liaisons.

When Herr K. demanded that Ida's romantic fantasies succumb to his sexual desire, she blew the whistle, so to speak, on everyone's fantasy, including her own. . . . In a sense, Ida Bauer was an outlaw. As Freud noted, Frau K. was the one person whom Ida spared, while she pursued the others with an almost malignant vindictiveness. In sparing Frau K. Ida spared herself. In this way she denied both her love for Frau K. as well as its futility.[45]

Ida Bauer is a feminist hero because she exposed the sexual abuse in her family even at the expense of jeopardizing her own security.

Dora as Freud's Fantasy

A third interpretation of Freud's case study focuses less on Dora as a patient and a woman and more on Freud as narrator, therapist, and man. In this reading, the case study is less about Dora as a real person and more about Dora as Freud's fantasy.

Freud ended his case study with two astounding acknowledgments: first, that he did not adequately interpret Dora's transference to Freud of her feelings about Herr K.; second, that he failed to understand Dora's homosexual attachment for Frau K. These issues form the basis for much of the feminist debate about Freud.

First, Freud said he misunderstood the significance of Dora's transference. When he interpreted the first dream, Freud said to Dora that leaving the burning house meant that "you have decided to give up the treatment—to which, after all, it is only your father who makes you come."[46] Later, Freud suggested that Dora connected him with Herr K. because they were both smokers, and wondered whether "the idea had probably occurred to her one day during a sitting that she would like to have a kiss from me."[47] He refers to the transference again when she playfully hid an insignificant letter: "I believe that Dora only wanted to play 'secrets' with me, and to hint that she was on the point of allowing her secret to be torn from her by the physician."[48] Later, he comments that the first dream might be about termination: "The dream-thoughts behind it included a reference to my treatment, and it corresponded to a renewal of the old resolution to withdraw from danger."[49] However, Freud did not see that Dora might run from the danger of therapy the same way she ran from the abuse by Herr K.

In the postscript, Freud struggles with Dora's transference to him and wonders about its significance.

> I did not succeed in mastering the transference in good time. . . . At the beginning it was clear that I was replacing her father in her imagination. . . . But when the first dream came, in which she gave herself the warning that

she had better leave my treatment just as she had formerly left Herr K.'s house, I ought to have listened to the warning myself. "Now," I ought to have said to her, "it is from Herr K. that you have made a transference on to me. Have you noticed anything that leads you to suspect me of evil intentions similar (whether openly or in some sublimated form) to Herr K.'s? Or have you been struck by anything about me or got to know anything about me which has caught your fancy, as happened previously with Herr K.? . . .
In this way the transference took me unawares, and, because of the unknown quantity in me which reminded Dora of Herr K., she took her revenge on me as she wanted to take her revenge on him, and deserted me as she believed herself to have been deceived and deserted by him. Thus she *acted* an essential part of her recollections and phantasies instead of reproducing them in the treatment.[50]

Freud's post facto question to Dora about whether he had "any evil intentions similar to Herr K.'s" or whether there was "anything about me which has caught your fancy, as happened previously with Herr K." is fruitful because it raises the issue of countertransference—not simply why Freud was connected with Herr K. in Dora's imagination, but also what Dora meant in Freud's imagination.

Second, Freud failed to understand Dora's homosexual attachment for Frau K. At least five figures appear at various times as Dora's erotic and emotional identification: her mother, her father, Herr K., Frau K., and the governess-maid. At various times, Freud considered each of these figures as Dora's primary identification.

Freud considered and rejected the mother as a figure of identification, saying: "The relations between the girl and her mother had been unfriendly for years. The daughter looked down on her mother and used to criticize her mercilessly, and she had withdrawn completely from her influence."[51] Freud's rejection of the mother is ironic considering that the mother appeared in a central role in both of Dora's dreams, and that psychoanalytic theory itself has always insisted that the mother is the most likely central figure in the object world of patients.

As we have clearly seen, Freud believed that Dora's primary identification figure was Herr K. because of her repressed love for him, and that behind this was her identification with her father. Freud decided, based on the first dream in which her father rescued her from the fire, that the father was an important attachment figure because of her "wish that her father might take the place of the man who was her tempter."[52] This interpretation began to fail when Dora killed off her father in the second dream and Freud was left to scramble for who was left.

Dora's father was dead, and the others had already gone to the cemetery. She might calmly read whatever she chose. Did not this mean that one of her motives for revenge as a revolt against her parents's constraint? If her father was dead she could read or love as she pleased.[53]

But who did she want to love, in her freedom? Freud tried to return to her love for Herr K.: " 'So you see that your love for Herr K. did not come to an end with the scene, but that (as I maintained) it has persisted down to the present day—though it is true that you are unconscious of it.' "[54] The presence of the governess-maid at the end of the dream proves to be very important in some feminist interpretations, as we shall see below.

At the next session, when Dora announced that it was her last, Freud tried to put her in the role of the governess-maid. Just as governess-maids usually gave two weeks notice when they terminated their employment with a family, Dora had decided two weeks earlier to terminate her therapy with Freud. Then, in perhaps the most bizarre episode of the whole case, Freud suggested that Dora wanted to marry Herr K. "I know now—and this is what you do not want to be reminded of—that you did fancy that Herr K.'s proposals were serious, and that he would not leave off until you had married him."[55] But despite this, in his footnotes to the case, Freud acknowledges that he missed the importance of Frau K. "Behind the almost limitless series of displacements which were thus brought to light, it was possible to divine the operation of a single simple factor—Dora's deep-rooted homosexual love for Frau K."[56]

FREUD'S BETRAYAL OF DORA

My thesis in this chapter is that Freud refused to respect and support Dora's resistance to the evil of patriarchy, and thus he betrayed her trust in him as a healer. In this section, I will examine Freud's complicity in patriarchy as a leader of the intellectual debates about gender in Europe and the United States.[57]

Several issues in this case study reveal Freud's complicity with patriarchy. Why did it take so long for Freud to recognize the importance of Frau K. in Dora's desire? Why did Freud refuse to consider Dora's mother important even though she was prominent in Dora's dreams? Why did the governess-maid became a symbolic figure for Freud in the last session with Dora?

Two conclusions about this case are especially relevant to our discussion of the relation of male dominance and evil.

First, Freud did not see the abusive behaviors of the other men in this story because he failed to understand his own mistreatment of Dora. Freud did not adequately interpret Dora's transference from Herr K. and her father because he would have seen that his own abuse of Dora was the similar to Herr K.'s.

Second, Freud's patriarchal worldview prevented him from identifying with Dora's vulnerability and understanding her resistance as a form of active agency. Freud could not see her attachment to Frau K., her mother, and the governess-maid because he did not see women as active agents in their own lives.

Freud and Male Violence

Freud did not see the violence of the other men in this story because he failed to understand his own abusive behaviors against Dora. For many readers, Freud's insistence that Dora's sexual desire was directed toward Herr K. is the most shocking part of the case study. Ignoring the interpersonal and family issues, Freud focused on Dora's so-called frigidity.

In the beginning, Freud seemed to support Dora's protest against the sexual abuse from Herr K., and agreed that it was inappropriate for her father not to protect her. He even called Dora's experience a "sexual trauma."[58] Because he initially seemed to understand her terror and support her wish for safety, Dora may have thought that Freud was different from the other men in her life. Later, she must have been confused to discover that he was more interested in her sexual fantasies than in her safety. True, Dora's fantasies seem to have been sexualized because of the family pathology, but Freud betrayed her trust when he attributed these fantasies to her desire rather than to her best efforts to cope with the family craziness.

We can now see that the burning house in the first dream may have represented Dora's unconscious awareness of the danger of therapy with Freud. Dora was in danger with Freud just as she was with Herr K. Freud himself acknowledged this when he wrote, "But when the first dream came . . . she gave herself the warning that she had better leave my treatment just as she had formerly left Herr K.'s house."[59] Freud's focus on Dora's sexuality was endangering her sexual life.

In spite of his own insight, Freud continued to focus on Dora's sexual desire for Herr K., which led to the second dream, in which Dora killed off her father so she could be free to "read or love as she pleased."[60] In the second dream, Dora indirectly communicated to Freud that she wanted him dead so she could be free to go on with her life. When he was unable to hear that communication, she terminated therapy, thus "killing him off" as a continuing influence in her life. Dora's implicit commentary on Freud's mistreatment was a communication Freud did not hear.

Why did Freud identify with Dora's father and Herr K., and why did he insist that Dora focus on her sexual desire for these men? Why did Freud fail to see that he was acting toward Dora in the same way as her father and Herr K.? The reason is that male sexual violence against women was built into his theories and into relationships between women and men in nineteenth-century Vienna. Freud's developing theories of gender and sexuality included the Oedipus complex, castration anxiety, and the primal scene. At the heart of the Oedipus complex is the idea that, because women are the primary parents, both boys and girls are originally erotically attached to their mothers. Women are their first sexual objects. When boys become aware that the father has a sexual claim on the mother, their impulse is to hate their fathers. But because they fear being castrated by the father's overwhelming power, they repress their desire for Mother, identify with Father, and transfer their sexual feelings to other women. Unfortunately, men also internalize the right of men to possess and dominate women.

However, the theory of the Oedipal complex does not work with girls, because it requires that they comply with the heterosexual norm by denying their sexual feelings for their mothers and developing sexual feelings for men. According to Maria Ramas, psychoanalytic theory offers two solutions to this contradiction for women. In the first solution, the girl hates her mother when she discovers that her mother is already castrated, and transforms her wish for a penis into a wish for a baby. This wish brings her into heterosexual compliance with society. In the second solution, the girl seeks a relationship with her father as a way of freeing herself from the omnipotent mother. Thus in both cases the search for a penis is a form of individuation from the mother.

Ramas rejects both of these theories because of their devaluation of the mother (women and femininity), and because of their failure to acknowledge ambivalence toward the father (men and masculinity).

> Neither theory seriously considers the possibility of an essential ambivalence toward the phallus itself. . . . Psychoanalytic formulations present the phallus alternatively as signifier of desire, as symbolizing protection, invulnerability, potency, or freedom from an all-engulfing, preoedipal mother. The fantasies of castration and of the Father-as-castrator force us to posit other meanings: violence, destruction, sadism. The primal fantasy of castration depends, on the one hand, upon the equation of femininity, masochism, and annihilation and, on the other, upon the sadistic meaning of the phallus/Father.[61]

The Oedipus complex fails for girls as a theory because it cannot explain how the essentially negative attributes of sadism provide adequate energy for heterosexual desire. Identifying with the annihilating mother does not create a positive construction of feminine sexual identity, and idealizing the sadistic, violent image of the father/phallus does not lead to female heterosexual desire.

In psychoanalytic theory sexuality and violence are also related through the primal scene, that is, through the trauma involved when the child witnesses sexual intercourse between her or his parents. Freud believed that most children interpret sexual intercourse as a scene of violence and degradation because they first experience it during the anal-sadistic stage of their own development. Maria Ramas explains:

> Psychoanalytic theory argues that the fantasy of the "primal scene" is in fact a misinterpretation on the child's part. . . . In contrast, I believe it is an accurate perception of the dominant patriarchal sexual fantasy. . . . Embedded most definitively in pornography, the "scene" is one of dominance and submission, and these are its essential erotic components . . . [and] the fantasy is heterosexual; it is a "scene" between a man and a woman. Even when those acting out the fantasy are of the same sex, the "scene" depicts the submission and degradation of whoever is in the feminine position. That is to say, ultimately and always, a woman is being degraded. The fantasy may be mild in content, or it may reach to the extreme other end of the continuum to express a sadomasochistic desire that seeks ultimate satisfaction in the total annihilation of the woman—the feminine.[62]

Freud's attempt to explain away sexual violence by locating sadistic sexual desires in the small child is contradicted by recent research about the prevalence of sexual violence in western society.[63] However, his emphasis on the violence of the "primal scene" accurately describes much adult male sexual fantasy in a patriarchal culture. Because psychoanalytic theory incorporates the violence of the primal scene and considers it central to its theory of sexuality, Freud misinterpreted the sexually abusive behaviors of Herr K. as legitimate sexual overtures. Because Freud believed that it was essential for an adolescent girl to become heterosexual, and also believed that sexual development was always plagued with fears of violence and castration, he was unable to see Dora's legitimate fears of the violation inherent in Herr K.'s proposals. In Freud's fantasies, Herr K. was merely acting as any man would around an attractive woman, and Dora's frigid response was a sign of her illness. Therefore, instead of focusing on Herr K.'s violence toward Dora, he chose awakening her sexual desire for Herr K. as his therapeutic goal, as the way to help her become a healthy woman.

Freud failed to see that his obsession with Dora's sexual desire replicated Herr K.'s abuse. Because his psychoanalytic theory presupposes that gaining a mature sexual identity depends on sexual conflict that is usually sadistic, Freud was blind to the male violence that Dora experienced.

Sexual violence is not only a feature of family relationships, but was built into the economic conditions of nineteenth-century Victorian society.

> During the latter half of the nineteenth century, domestic service became an almost exclusively female profession. Increasingly, domestic servants, who were predominantly young and unmarried, took over tasks involving manual labor and the routine aspects of child care from bourgeois wives. . . . But gender and class, femininity and service, were at the same time conflated—insofar as the question posed was sexuality. Bourgeois sexual fantasy did not distinguish between classes of women. . . . [Ida Bauer's identification with the governess-maid] reveals . . . that femininity was linked with service specifically with regard to sexuality. That is, what lies at the heart of these identifications is a particular fantasy of heterosexuality as service due men, and one explicitly based on submission and degradation.[64]

Therefore, we can see that the presence of the governess-maids in Freud's story was not accidental. All maids were presented by Freud as sexualized figures who fell in love with the master of the house, or actually had affairs with him. Freud feared that Dora might identify too closely with the maids.

> As Cixous points out, the Dora case is punctuated by women being declared "nothing." Both Herr K. and Dora's father say that of their wives. What is true of the wives (mothers) is even more explicit for the two governesses. Dora "sees a massacre of women executed to make space for her. But she knows that she will in turn be massacred." Neither Dora . . . nor Freud . . . can tolerate the position allotted them by the system of exchanges. Neither Dora nor Freud can tolerate identification with the seduced and abandoned governess.[65]

When class is added to gender within a social system that defines human life, the expendability of working-class women, and all women, becomes clear. Freud could not afford to see the violence of the men, including himself, toward Dora, because he could not afford to see male violence against the governesses who were raped and expelled from the

Victorian families of the time. Sexual violence was not a fantasy of children from the anal stage of development, but was an ongoing structure of patriarchal power, in which men of status exploited women from the family and from the "lower" classes. Had Freud been able to see the violence of Dora's father and Herr K., he might have been confronted with the violence of all high-status men in his society. Finally, he would have been confronted with the male dominance of his own theories and practices, which focused on the sexuality of women and ignored the sexual violence of men.

Freud and Women's Agency

Freud's patriarchal worldview prevented him from identifying with Dora's vulnerability and understanding her resistance as a form of active agency. His inability to see Dora, her mother, Frau K., and the governess-maids as active agents in their own lives, as full human beings, is a common patriarchal failing.

Freud admitted his failure to understand the importance of Dora's attachment to Frau K. As we have seen from looking at the two dreams, he also missed the importance of Dora's relationship with her mother. Freud no doubt mishandled the case because his theories did not construct roles for women as full human beings, and because the economic conditions of his society fostered the subordination of women to men.

Freud's theories of sexuality and gender prevented him from seeing Dora's vulnerability and resistance. As we have seen, his Oedipal theory required that the little boy aggressively leave his mother and identify with his father in order to escape castration, but that the little girl identify with her mother and accept a passive role in relation to her father and other men. This developmental difference creates a hierarchy of power that corresponds to the dominance of men in the economic and political order, and makes it difficult for men to identify with women without fearing passive homosexuality and becoming victims of sexual violence.

> Freud . . . systematically refuses to consider female sexuality as an active, independent drive. Again and again he exhorts Dora to accept herself as an object for Herr K. Every time Dora reveals active sexual desires, Freud interprets them away. . . . His position is self-contradictory: he is one of the first to acknowledge the existence of sexual desire in women, and at the same time he renders himself incapable of seeing it as more than the impulse to become passive recipients for male desire. . . . [Freud] fails to see that Dora is caught up in an ambivalent relationship to her mother and an

idealizing and identifying relationship to Frau K., the other mother-figure in this text. Freud's patriarchal prejudices force him to ignore relationships between women and instead center all his attention on relationships with men.[66]

Freud's theory and his social status as an educated White male in a patriarchal society encouraged him not to identify with Dora or any woman. He could "help" Dora by reminding her of her passive role in relationships with men, but he could not join her in her object world and side with her desire. A man in his position could not be a passive nurturer of the desire of another, especially of a woman. But a psychoanalytic principle requires just this kind of identification with the person who comes for treatment. The therapist is a paid helper who offers insights and skills for the needs of the other. Freud avoids this ethical logic of the deep structure of psychoanalysis by engaging in competition with, domination of, and abuse of Dora.

> Since Dora is a woman, and a rather formidable one at that, a young lady who hitherto has had only scorn for the incompetent (and, surely, impotent) doctors who have treated her so far, she becomes a threatening rival for Freud. If he does not win the fight for knowledge, he will also be revealed as incompetent/impotent, his compelling powers will be reduced to nothing, he will be castrated. If Dora wins the knowledge game, her model for knowledge will emerge victorious, and Freud's own model will be destroyed. Freud here find himself between Scylla and Charybdis: if he identifies with Dora in the search for knowledge, he becomes a woman, that is to say, castrated; but if he chooses to cast her as his rival, he must win out, or the punishment will be castration.[67]

Being a man in a patriarchal society and being a therapist whose skills are available for the healing of an "other" are logically contradictory. In order to be a man, Freud must be dominant and win any competition for control. In order to be a therapist, he must engage in a process of mutual transformation with another person. Thus Freud discloses the contradictions of therapy between men and women in a patriarchal society, and a reason violence and abuse by male therapists is so prevalent. A male therapist such as Freud must maintain dominance in order to support the hierarchy of men and women, but he is thus prevented from fulfilling the purpose of his therapeutic vocation. To see Dora as an active moral agent would confront Freud with the violence inherent in his own theories and social location.

Jane Gallop describes Freud's inability to identify with Dora through an analogy to the economic status of the governess-maid. Freud cannot identify with Dora, her mother, or Frau K. because they are women, and he can identify even less with the two governess-maids, who are of a different social class and are sexually abused and rejected.

> What shows in the Dora case that neither Dora nor Freud wanted to see is that Frau K. and Dora's mother are in the same position as the maid. In feminist or symbolic or economic terms, the mother/wife is in a position of substitutability and economic inferiority.[68]

It is this inability to see the interlocking hierarchies of gender and class that prevented therapeutic identification by Freud. Freud's inability to identify with Dora, who represented the less-than-human gender, and his inability to identify with the governess, who represented the less-than-human social class (that of servants), limited his ability to be a healer of the psyche.

At the end of the second dream, which Dora had just before she terminated her therapy "[t]he maidservant opened the door to me and replied that Mother and the others were already at the cemetery."[69] Later, Dora produces "a piece of the dream which had been forgotten: 'she went calmly to her room, and began reading a big book that lay on her writing-table.' "[70] In this dream action, we see Dora's agency. Yet Freud insisted to the last session that Dora would only be fulfilled if she admitted her love for and wish to marry Herr K.[71] He could not imagine other possibilities—that Dora had desires that he would never understand, that men (Dora's father, Herr K., Freud) were not the source of meaning and power for her, that she could find fulfillment in the company of other women (her mother, Frau K., governess-maids), or that her revolt against patriarchy provided meaning in her life even if it did not lead to happiness.

In this case, Freud betrayed his therapeutic contract with Dora. Instead of understanding her suffering and the structure of her unconscious life, he imposed his patriarchal theories and practices upon her, and thus betrayed his commitment to being a healing agent in her life. Paradoxically, feminist analysis of Freud provides a source of hope that patriarchy can be understood and dismantled as both men and women seek to exercise a moral agency that does not need the approval of ideologies and authorities.

In this chapter we have explored the issues of resistance and domination in an important case study by Sigmund Freud and have uncovered some of the ways gender evil is maintained. In the next section, we shall look at the social context in which the same dynamics of resistance and domination between groups and social classes is played out.

CHAPTER THREE

THE REVOLUTION BETRAYED

How Freedom Was Suppressed

During the periods just before and after the Revolutionary War, political and religious leaders made formative decisions about the organization of power and the place of African American women and men and European American women in the new United States. Economic, political, and social exclusion resulting from these decisions led to communities of resistance against evil. In this chapter, we shall look at how communities of African American women and men and communities of European American women have engaged in organized resistance, and how these acts of resistance disclose the existence of social evil. We shall also look at the forms of debate and betrayal that took place.[1]

THE COLONIAL PERIOD

Racial Oppression during the Colonial Period

Winthrop Jordan describes the earliest practice of enslaving Africans in the English colonies as an "unthinking decision."[2] Although European prejudices had previously defined Africans and others as heathens, savages, beasts, and libidinous creatures, and identified their skin color with dirt, stain, and evil,[3] "no one had in mind to establish the institution of Negro slavery."[4] There was no precedent in the definitions of human rights in English law for the form of chattel slavery developed in the United States by 1700, namely lifetime servitude based on color that was passed from generation to generation. How and why were Africans treated in English America "as somehow deserving a life and status radically different from English and other European settlers"?[5]

As early as 1689, Cotton Mather anticipated many of the religious arguments about slavery that would continue through the Colonial period.

According to H. Shelton Smith, Mather advocated Christianizing the Africans but also supported slavery, since he himself was a slaveholder.

> Appealing to [the slaveholders'] self-interest, [Mather] urged that Christianized blacks would make more efficient slaves. He also told the masters that they need have no fear of losing their slaves on account of baptism, since Christianity contained no law forbidding servitude. Mather urged that masters were duty-bound to teach their bondsmen "that it is God who has caused them to be Servants, and that they serve Jesus Christ, while they are at Work for their Masters."[6]

Ideas such as Mather's were common among Quakers in Pennsylvania, Roman Catholics in Maryland, and Anglicans in the South. The Anglican Society for the Propagation of the Gospel, one of the most successful mission movements in reaching African Americans, taught that baptized slaves did not have to be freed.[7]

The Great Awakening of the 1740s, which successfully converted thousands of African Americans, settled the debate over whether Africans should be baptized and still kept in slavery. George Whitefield, a successful evangelist, converted many African Americans to Christianity.

> "I believe," [Whitefield] wrote in his journal, "masters and mistresses will shortly see that Christianity will not make their negroes worse slaves." . . . [H]e himself owned eight slaves whom he used to cultivate his South Carolina plantation for the benefit of his orphanage at Bethesda, Georgia.[8]

Another preacher of the Great Awakening, Samuel Davies, a Presbyterian minister and president of the College of New Jersey (later Princeton University), established churches and converted African Americans to Christianity in large numbers. However, he did not oppose slavery, because God's laws "not only admit, but require, that there should be civil distinctions among Mankind; that some should rule, and some be subject; that some should be Masters, and some Servants."[9]

The choice made by thousands of African Americans to embrace Christianity probably had complex motives, including survival, hope for freedom, deception of White people, and genuine religious fervor. Many scholars have argued that African Americans responded to the promises of access to a transcendent grace that would provide future rewards and also provide support for the daily ordeal of slavery. Riggins Earl forcefully argues that the conversion stories of slaves clearly show that in claiming conversion, slaves were self-consciously resisting bondage.

[S]laves claimed to have encountered the God who empowers the morally impotent of the world to be radically engaged in its moral transformation. . . . If the God of the conversion vision transformed them to be radically engaged as moral agents in the world, this meant that slaves had a new reason for being and doing in the world. We might say theoretically that the slave community's conversion experience language became its means of constructing a metaphysical understanding of the self that was grounded in its own social reality.[10]

Gender Oppression during the Colonial Period

During the colonial period women, although subordinate to men, worked in the agricultural economy of homesteads and cottage industries. The Protestant doctrine of women's inequality, the violence of the witch slaughter, and the influence of the English Reformation firmly established the subordinate social location of women to men. Rosemary Keller shows the conflicted thinking of English religious leaders such as William Perkins, who, while trying to argue gender equality, revealed their own misogyny.

"The duty of the husband is to honor his wife: 1 Peter 3:7 . . . as his companion or yoke-fellow. For this cause, the woman, when she was created, was not taken out of man's head, because she was not to rule over him; nor out of his feet, because God did not make her subject to him as a servant, but out of his side, to the end that man should take her as his mate." However, . . . Perkins wrote six years later . . . "In all ages it is found true by experience that the devil hath more easily and oftener prevailed with women than with men. Hence it was that the Hebrews of ancient times used it for a proverb: the more women, the more witches" (1590).[11]

During the seventeenth and eighteenth centuries, a strong patriarchal ideology enforced by laws and the demands of daily survival kept most women out of public life. However, the human-rights emphasis of the Revolution did not escape the notice of many women, as evidenced in the story of Abigail Adams, who said, "If particular care and attention is not paid to the ladies, we are determined to instigate a rebellion, and will not hold ourselves bound by any law in which we have no voice or representation."[12]

Drawing on the Old Testament story of Deborah, Mary Astell (1666–1731) argued, in *Some Reflections upon Marriage* (1700), that "the Sovereignty of a Woman is not contrary to the Law of Nature; for the Law of Nature is the Law of GOD, who cannot contradict himself; and yet it was GOD who inspir'd and approv'd that great Woman, raising her up to

Judge and to Deliver His People Israel."[13] By starting schools for girls, and by working for change via access to power through their husbands, some White women of the seventeenth and eighteenth centuries challenged gender inequality in colonial society.

Only limited debate seems to have taken place among White men about the role of women in church and society. Apparently, the previous work of the "great theologians" such as Augustine, Aquinas, Luther, and Calvin had adequately fixed the subordination of women so that leading churchmen did not think it merited much discussion. White women of all social classes were subordinate to men of the same social classes. At the end of the eighteenth century, male dominance was firmly established, and female subordination was embedded in theology, social practice, and law. Some historians emphasize the importance of women's prayer groups, sewing circles, and other women's activities as centers for raising women's consciousness about their oppression and developing strategies for survival. But there were not many public organizations in which women could focus their interests as a social class.[14]

> The churches, except for the Quaker, remained male-dominated institutions, and laws were made by males. Holding or willing of property by women was restricted, and what a woman might say, do or learn was delineated by social custom that was at least as binding as the statutes. . . . The decision to limit female education was reinforced by the widespread belief that female capacities were limited.[15]

The most popular advice book for women of the period, *The Lady's New Year Gift, or Advice to a Daughter*, by George Savile, which went through fifteen editions by 1765, gives clues about why gender equality did not make more gains during the colonial period.

> We are made of differing tempers, that our defects might be mutually supplied: your sex wanteth our reason for your conduct, and our strength for your protection: ours wanteth your gentleness to soften, and to entertain us. . . . You have more strength in your looks than we have in our laws; and more power by your tears, than we have by our arguments.[16]

This paternalistic advice to women, which urged them to be content with their inferior position and encouraged them to use their manipulative power to please men, is both troubling and disturbingly contemporary. Buttressed by religious stories of Adam's Rib, the fall of Eve, the temptation of sexuality, and the dangers of the emotional, embodied life, gender oppression was religiously and socially constructed in a way that made effective resistance difficult.

Race and gender oppression were common practices during the early colonial period. However, the human rights debate within the new nation created tensions so that race and gender as economic, institutional, and ideological categories were temporarily threatened.

BETWEEN THE WARS

The Economic and Institutional Context

Changes in economic forces, namely the transition from an agrarian society to industrial capitalism, fueled racial and gender oppression. At a macro level, the economic statistics changed dramatically. From 1815 to 1860 the volume of manufactured goods increased twelvefold, while domestic production, the cottage industries, decreased dramatically from $1.70 per capita in 1840 to $.78 per capita in 1860.[17] Likewise, the percentage of agricultural workers declined from 68.6% in 1840 to 36.8% in 1900, while the percentage of industrial employment increased from 14.5% to 34.7%.

As the need for industrial laborers increased, White women and children began to work outside the home. In New England in 1831, 39,927 women worked in the textile mills, versus 18,539 men. Forty percent of the work force in Pawtucket, Rhode Island, in 1831, were children.[18]

> But what was the reality of mill life? Incredibly long hours—twelve, fourteen or even sixteen hours daily, atrocious working conditions, inhumanly crowded living quarters. . . . The women fought back. . . . In Dover, New Hampshire, for example, the mill women walked off the job in 1828 to dramatize their opposition to newly instituted restrictions. They "shocked the community by parading with banners and flags, shooting off gunpowder." . . . [Women] fought so passionately that "in the 1840's, women workers were in the leadership of labor militancy in the United States."[19]

Industrial capitalism had a profound impact on the construction of gender. By 1830, as factory production grew, the domestic industries declined sharply, undercutting the role of women as economic producers. "[Women's] social status began to deteriorate accordingly. An ideological consequence of industrial capitalism was the shaping of a more rigorous notion of female inferiority."[20] Meanwhile, middle-class White women were told that a "woman's place is in the home," and were pressured to live a new ideal of domesticity.

During the same period that the North was developing industrially, the West was producing foodstuffs for export to the East, and the South was expanding its cotton production. In 1815, cotton exports totaled $17 million (33% of all U.S. exports), and in 1860 totaled $191 million (57% of all U.S. exports).[21] Likewise, the slave population increased from 1,771,656 in 1820 to 4,441,830 in 1860.[22] The average price of a prime field hand increased from about $800 in 1818 to $1,500 in 1860.[23] Scholars estimate that half of the slave population worked on cotton plantations.[24]

> In order to make way for white settlement and the expansion of both cotton cultivation and the market, some 70,000 Choctaws, Creeks, Chero-kees, Seminoles and Chickasaws were uprooted and deprived of their lands, and hundreds of thousands of blacks were moved into the Southwest to work the soil as slaves. . . . The income derived from the export of cotton set in motion the process of accelerated market and industrial develop-ment—the Market Revolution.[25]

Alabama, Mississippi, and Louisiana became the major producers of cotton after the Indian territories were seized and Indian tribes violently removed. Large plantations worked by slaves contributed their stolen wealth to the new capitalism. The slave narratives document the many related forms of hardship, suffering, and impossible choices about health, relationships, family, religion, and every part of the life that the institution of slavery had created.

In the 1850s, pro-slavery advocates in the South argued that the slave trade should be reopened. The purpose was to increase the size of the labor pool. According to Karl Marx:

> "A surplus labouring population . . . forms a disposable industrial reserve army that belongs to capital as absolutely as if the latter had bred it at its own cost. . . . [I]t creates, for the changing needs of the self-expansion of capital, a mass of human material always ready for exploitation. . . . The industrial reserve army, during periods of stagnation and average prosperity, weighs down the active labour-army; during the periods of over-production and paroxysm, it holds its pretensions in check."[26]

In spite of its human and social costs, the economic oppression of Af-rican American women and men under slavery, other native and ethnic groups under industrial capitalism, and White women under "the Cult of

True Womanhood" provided a workable system of exploitation of labor for the emergence of a growing national economy. Controlling the labor of Black women, Black men, and White women maintained a reserve of low-cost labor. Ronald Takaki illustrates how the exploitation of Native Americans, Mexicans, and Chinese enhanced this process by enabling the elite capitalists to pit various ethnic groups against one another.[27]

Powerful economic forces in the hands of northern industrialists and southern slaveholders provided adequate motive for creating the social institutions and ideologies needed to promote racial and gender violence in the mid-nineteenth century. As we focus on ideological debates about race and gender, we must remember the economic forces that defined race, gender, and class oppression and that demanded rationalizations within the market of ideas.

African American Resistance Communities

Memories of the successful slave revolution in St. Domingo (Haiti) in 1804 became a fearful obsession among Whites in the southern states, where African Americans outnumbered Whites. "France had lost the pearl of her empire, hundreds of thousands of people on the island had lost their lives, and millions of white men in other lands wondered what had happened."[28] The Denmark Vesey conspiracy of 1822 in Richmond, Virginia, followed by the Nat Turner rebellion in 1831, the latter of which took the lives of sixty Whites,[29] provided ample evidence that Thomas Jefferson was correct when he said, "Nothing is more certainly written in the book of fate than that these people are to be free."[30]

> Maroon communities, composed of fugitive slaves and their descendants, could be found throughout the South as early as 1642 and as late as 1864. These communities were "havens for fugitives, served as bases for marauding expeditions against nearby plantations and at times supplied leadership to planned uprisings."[31]

The underground railroad, in which Harriet Tubman is probably the most famous participant, assisted women and men fleeing slavery.[32]

Black intellectual leaders, including David Walker, Frederick Douglass, Martin Delaney, and H. Ford Douglas, vigorously debated, often struggling over whether to revolt against or accommodate to the power of White institutions. In some writings, they appealed to Whites to live up to the Constitution's values of equality and freedom by abolishing slavery. In other writings, as in David Walker's *Appeal* of 1829, the leaders called for God's judgment upon "the white American nation," for solidarity with liberation movements in Africa, and for the essential unity of all persons of African descent, whether slave or free.[33]

After the Fugitive Slave Law of 1850 and the Dred Scott Decision of 1857, the latter of which denied the rights of citizenship even to free African Americans, many Black intellectual-activists advocated emigration, self-government, and armed resistance to the United States government. At the Black Convention held in Akron, Ohio, in August, 1854, H. Ford Douglas summarized the view of many Black intellectuals that slavery and racism were endemic to the formation of the United States and not likely to be changed without radical actions.

> You must remember that slavery is not a foreign element in this government nor is it really antagonistic to the feelings of the American people. On the contrary, it is an element commencing with our medieval existence, receiving the sanction of the early Fathers of the Republic, sustained by their descendants through a period of nearly three centuries, deeply and firmly laid in our organization, completely interwoven into the passions and prejudices of the American people. It does not constitute a local or sectional institution as the generous prompting of the great and good [Charles] Sumner would have it, but is just as national as the Constitution which gives it an existence.[34]

According to Vincent Harding, Black resistance leaders often struggled between appealing to the Constitution for relief and appealing to the Black community for organized revolt. The conflict can most clearly be seen in the difference between the 1853 National Black Convention in Rochester, New York, at which Frederick Douglass addressed resolutions to the White community, and the 1854 National Black Convention in Cleveland, at which Martin Delany drafted a call to revolutionary action by all African Americans, slave and free.[35] Thus, the debate in the 1960s between Martin Luther King and Malcolm X over appropriate strategies of resistance had a long history of debate within the African American community.

Laws developed after the Revolutionary War and in the early nineteenth century give clues about Black resistance. Slave codes outlawed the harboring of fugitive slaves, restricted religious meetings of slaves, and virtually eliminated "hiring out" (the practice of collecting wages when slaves worked for someone else).[36] Other laws created a second class of citizenship for "free Negroes."

> Free Negroes might lawfully possess only one gun; they were not allowed to testify against white men in a court of law; no free Negro, on pain of

thirty lashes, was to "at any time lift his or her hand in opposition to any person not being a negro or mulatto" unless in self-defense against wanton assault; and by a separate act which placed a seal on existing racial arrangements, "No Negro, mulatto, or Indian, shall at any time purchase any servant, other than of their own complexion."[37]

Many northern and southern states passed laws barring Blacks from the militia, depriving them of the vote, outlawing interracial marriage, and stripping away their civil and human rights.[38] We can assume that laws were passed because people were engaging in just those activities, that is, exercising their human rights in a way that only violently enforced laws could control.

Black churches and informal religious movements became forms of resistance to slavery. Many laws regulated the gathering of groups, especially without White supervision. Harriet Jacobs referred to the presence of White preachers and others who ensured that the religious activities of slaves properly focused on submissive obedience to masters.[39] Indeed, as Franklin Moss points out:

> In most states Negro preachers were outlawed between 1830 and 1835, and thereafter Negro religious services were presided over by some white person. . . . This ambivalent attitude toward autonomous Negro religious activity reflected whites' fears that it would be difficult, if not impossible, to control and monitor the belief and practices of slaves who were devout Christians. Such fears proved accurate, for many of the most pious and influential slaves had a keen understanding of the difference between the gospel of proslavery preachers and the Christian scriptures' messages of divine punishment for oppressors and liberation for the faithful.[40]

Scholars such as Patricia Hill Collins and Angela Davis point out that Black women resisted slavery in many ways: by simple survival, protecting their families, participating in churches, and starting schools in the North. The full story will never be told, but the figures of Sojourner Truth, Jarena Lee, and many others symbolize the Black women's resistance.

Riggins Earl has identified four kinds of resistance that became organized among the slaves in the nineteenth century: conversion stories, spirituals, autobiographies, and Br'er Rabbit trickster stories. Each of these genres helped African Americans communicate with one another the myriad forms of creative resistance. Earl's argument is that in the presence of the radical evil of slavery and extreme violence, African Americans created alternative ways of being and acting that did not depend on the negative images given them by the White slaveholders.

Slaves wove out of the fabric of their own experience of slavery and their escape from it what I would term a mosaic portrait of the self, which shaped their complex views of self, God and community—and vice versa. Our theoretical claim here is that four ideal types of narrative self can be derived from the responses—testimonies or conversion stories, song lyrics, autobiographies, and trickster stories—that the slave community made to the soul and body and mind problems. The four idea types are: the soul narrative self; the rational narrative self; the playful narrative self; and the dialogical narrative self.[41]

Each of these creative forms of resistance enabled African Americans to partially transcend the brutality of their everyday existence and reenter life with definitions of the self that did not depend solely on how they were defined by evil structures.

Women's Resistance Communities

After the Revolution, Lerner observes, women were encouraged to see themselves as "mothers of the republic" as the "Cult of True Womanhood" shaped and controlled their lives. "As men institutionalized their dominance in the economy, in education, and in politics, women were encouraged to adjust to their subordinate status by an ideology which gave their maternal function higher significance."[42]

Angela Davis agrees with Lerner to the extent that all women were oppressed in various ways by the changing patriarchal ideas and structures.

As the ideology of femininity—a by-product of industrialization—was popularized and disseminated through the new ladies' magazines and romantic novels, white women came to be seen as inhabitants of a sphere totally severed from the realm of productive work. The cleavage between the home and the public economy, brought on by industrial capitalism, established female inferiority more firmly than ever before. "Woman" became synonymous in the prevailing propaganda with "mother" and "housewife," and both "mother" and "housewife" bore the fatal mark of inferiority.[43]

However, Davis challenges statements by White feminists who attempt to speak for all women, because African American women have experienced gender oppression much differently. The slavery of Black women, enforced by both racial and gender violence, differed from the oppression of White women.

The slave system defined Black people as chattel. Since women, no less than men, were viewed as profitable labor-units, they might as well have been genderless as far as the slaveholders were concerned. . . . Judged by the evolving nineteenth-century ideology of femininity, which emphasized women's roles as nurturing mothers and gender companions and house-keepers for their husbands, Black women were practically anomalies. . . . Seven out of eight slaves, men and women alike, were field workers. . . . Where work was concerned, strength and productivity under the threat of the whip outweighed considerations of sex. In this sense, the oppression of women was identical to the oppression of men. But women suffered in different ways as well, for they were victims of sexual abuse and other barbarous mistreatment that could only be inflicted on women.[44]

The exclusion of African American women from the Cult of True Womanhood led to a different articulation of resistance. "Among Black female slaves, this vocabulary [of domesticity] was nowhere to be found. The economic arrangements of slavery contradicted the hierarchical sexual roles incorporated in the new ideology. Male-female relations within the slave community could not, therefore, conform to the dominant ideological pattern."[45] The Cult of True Womanhood also did not apply to the lives of working-class women who could not stay at home, and poor women whose survival needs took precedence.

The revival movements of the nineteenth century created new space for White women's resistance to patriarchy. The theology of individual conversion and spiritual empowerment provided a ready-made framework in which women could assume leadership. "Women's evangelical work was a natural result of their conversions. New converts—male or female—characteristically felt a strong desire to share their experience with others and spread the 'good news' of the Lord."[46] As a result, some women began preaching and teaching in churches and in public places in new ways, and others lectured on social issues that were fueled by religious faith, namely temperance, women's rights, and the abolition of slavery.

> In their evangelical work women occasionally attained fame and often gained a new forum for their talents. They also won a sense of solidarity with other women. The "Cult of True Womanhood" had separated women into their own sphere, but their evangelical faith provided a common understanding of life that united women with bonds far stronger than gender alone could furnish. It made them sisters in the Spirit as well as in the flesh. At the same time that their religiosity united women, it enhanced their world. The dominance of women in evangelical religion transformed their sphere into an *ecclesia in ecclesiolae*, a church within a church, and endowed it with a spiritual significance which the male realm entirely lacked.[47]

After Elizabeth Cady Stanton and Lucretia Mott were excluded from participation in the 1840 World Anti-Slavery Convention in London, they helped organize the first women's rights convention in Seneca Falls, New York, in 1848. In the decades before this, White women had been active in abolitionist activities, often alongside their husbands.

> As they worked within the abolitionist movement, white women learned about the nature of human oppression—and in the process, also learned important lessons about their own subjugation. In asserting their right to oppose slavery, they protested—sometimes overtly, sometimes implicitly— their own exclusion from the political arena.[48]

Some of the earliest connections between the abolition movement and women's rights came from the Grimké sisters, Sarah and Angelina, who were often prevented from their abolitionist activities on the grounds that women should not speak in public. In 1837, Angelina Grimké resisted this injustice using religious arguments.

> And can you not see that women could do, and would do a hundred times more for the slave if she were not fettered? Why! We are gravely told that we are out of our sphere even when we circulate petitions; out of our "appropriate sphere" when we speak to women only; and out of them when we sing in the churches. Silence is our province, submission our duty. . . . But we are actuated by the full conviction that if we are to do any good in the Anti Slavery cause, our right to labor in it must be firmly established, not on the ground of Quakerism, but on the only firm basis of human rights, the Bible. . . . Women are regarded as equal to men on the ground of spiritual gifts, not on the broad ground of humanity.[49]

White women analyzed their oppression in systematic ways and agitated for changes in laws and customs. By contemporary standards we judge such discrimination against women as blatant violations of human rights. Women were forbidden to vote, hold property, inherit capital in their own names, or obtain custody of their children. Elizabeth Cady Stanton summarized her complaints in a speech at the 1848 convention.

> We are assembled to protest against a form of government, existing without the consent of the governed—to declare our right to be free as man is free, to be represented in the government which we are taxed to support, to have such disgraceful laws as give man the power to chastise and imprison his wife, to take the wages which she earns, the property which she inherits, and, in case of separation, the children of her love; laws which make her the mere dependent on his bounty. It is to protest against such unjust laws as these that we are assembled today, and to have them, if possible, forever

erased from our statute-books, deeming them a shame and a disgrace to a Christian republic in the nineteenth century.[50]

Sojourner Truth, an ex-slave and minister, delivered speeches that helped to strengthen the resolve and resistance of White and Black women. In her now-famous speech given in 1851, "Ain't I a Woman?", Sojourner Truth challenged the distortions of the biblical creation story and misinterpretations about Jesus' maleness that kept women subordinate.

> Then that little man in back there, he says women can't have as much rights as men, 'cause Christ wasn't a woman! Where did your Christ come from? Where did your Christ come from? From God and a woman. Man had nothing to do with Him. If the first woman God ever made was strong enough to turn the world upside down all alone, these women together ought to be able to turn it back, and get it right side up again! and now they is asking to do it, the men better let them.[51]

The women's rights movement grew quickly, and Stanton and Susan B. Anthony traveled all over the country analyzing women's oppression, agitating for changed laws concerning women, and arguing especially for women's right to vote. At first, issues related to women's rights, temperance, and abolitionism overlapped. After the Civil War, however, White women and Black women split along class lines. We will examine racism in the White women's movement more closely in chapter 4.

The resistance movement's strength during the nineteenth century represented a significant threat to power arrangements. In response, White men, to maintain White supremacy and male dominance, engaged in vigorous debate.

Debate and Betrayal

In the North, the churches were the first institutions to segregate Blacks from Whites. Because these churches also denied membership to Blacks, Absalom Jones founded the Negro Episcopal Church in 1793 and Richard Allen founded the African Methodist Episcopal Church in 1794.[52]

The story of the antislavery debates among the mainline denominations is one of both courage and disappointment. In December, 1784, the Methodists, at their founding conference in Baltimore, passed minutes expelling any member who bought a slave. However, by June 1, 1785, the church decided "to suspend the execution of the minute on slavery" until some future date. However, no discussion took place for ten years. "Thus while the new church grew in membership from 18,000 in 1785 to 56,664 in 1796, its doors remained open to slaveholders,"[53] who became active leaders and major contributors. The power of this group prevented the approval of antislavery proposals. In spite of agitation by James O'Kelly and others, Methodists rejected any firm action against slavery in 1800, 1804, and 1820. One Bishop wrote his own pragmatic solution in a journal: "Would not an amelioration in the condition and treatment of slaves have produced more practical good to the poor Africans, than any attempt at their emancipation? . . . What is personal liberty of the African which he may abuse, to the salvation of his soul; how may it be compared?"[54] Such rationalizations prevented the issue of slavery from interfering with the expansion and influence of the Methodist Church. The denomination's compromises helped seal the fate of African Americans until the Civil War.

The Baptist emphasis on local congregational autonomy allowed the Virginia and Kentucky conventions to pass actions against slavery in 1785 and 1787 but shortly thereafter "to drop the divisive question on the claim that . . . it fell within the political rather than the religious sphere."[55] Kentucky Baptists discussed, with many conflicts and schisms, antislavery for a longer time than Baptists in other states, and continued to do so until the antislavery movement disintegrated.[56] In the deep South, Baptists took no positions against slavery, which was not surprising, given the social class of some of its leading preachers.

> "Of the 100 preachers or licentiates of 1780–1800 listed in the 1790 census, one had 55 slaves, one 19, one 17, and thirty-seven from one to 11, a total of 40 slave owners, or two-fifths of the whole." These facts become all the more significant when it is noted that the most influential preachers, such as Richard Furman, Peter Bainbridge, and Edmund Botsford, were among the largest slaveholders. They generally owned sizable plantations as a means of supplementing their salaries.[57]

Presbyterians likewise failed to take a strong antislavery position.

H. Shelton Smith summarizes the actions of the mainline churches during the post–Revolutionary War period:

> It is certain, that no communion in the South except the Society of Friends succeeded in disentangling itself from human bondage. The Baptist, Methodist, and Presbyterian bodies seriously compromised with domestic bondage from the outset of their antislavery efforts. They passed laudable resolutions against slavery, but at the same time continued to receive into membership owners of Negroes, and even to ordain slaveholders to the ministry. Inevitably this compromising process undermined their antislavery witness. . . . Within the next three decades, more than one million blacks were added to the region's population. In the meantime, however,

neither the churches nor the manumission societies offered effective resistance to the growth of human bondage.[58]

The antislavery impulses of the Quakers and others just before and after the Revolutionary War were based on an analysis of the evil effects of slavery for Whites rather than on the merits of spiritual and political equality of White and Black men. (Women were excluded by gender oppression.) This was shown even in the Quaker experience; Friends agitated successfully against slavery among their own membership, and encouraged other Christians to work against slavery, but they did not accept African Americans as equals within their own fellowship. By 1800, the antislavery movement, both within the church and without, had collapsed.

Meanwhile, scientists debated White superiority and male dominance. In the early nineteenth century, according to Winthrop Jordan, the argument for slavery among White men hinged on the theory of The Great Chain of Being. Such a concept preserved confidence in order and rationality for the young republic trying to create its identity in the midst of chaotic and contradictory conditions.

The Great Chain of Being postulated that everything in creation stretched in an unbroken line from the perfection of God down through the different gradations of the human races to the animals with their bestiality and on down to the plants, rocks, and seas. The location of each species on this line in some manner combined divinity and earthliness, human rationality and animal impulses. In the White male imagination, Africans represented an inferior combination of human rationality and animal impulses. In 1774, historian Edward Long expressed the sentiments of many southerners:

> The Negroe race (consisting of varieties) will then appear rising progressively in the scale of intellect, the further they mount above the Oran-outang and brute creation. The system of man [i.e., slavery] will seem more consistent, and the measure of it more complete, and analogous to the harmony and order that are visible in every other line of the world's stupendous fabric.[59]

Northern abolitionists developed the ideology of the Great Chain in another direction. Although they opposed extreme racist interpretations of the Great Chain, they accepted the premise that the Chain existed, and the assumption that European Americans were superior. They agreed that the United States was meant to be a pure, White nation and that intermixing of the races would be a violation of God's natural law. And they

believed that emancipation would result in race war and probable genocide for African Americans because of White prejudice.

In order for the slaves to be freed in a way that preserved White
America, the abolitionists organized efforts for Blacks to be saved by
sending them to Africa or South America. In 1801, Virginia governor
James Monroe and President Thomas Jefferson corresponded on detailed
plans for colonization; however, economic commitment to slavery and the
lack of commitment to the costs of colonization made such planning
moot. In 1816 through 1817, northern abolitionists formed the American
Colonization Society. For a time, the idea of colonization allowed abolitionists to oppose slavery without jeopardizing their vision of a homogeneous White society. In the twentieth century, Marcus Garvey, An African
American activist, transformed the idea of colonization into a genuine interest in African culture and history.[60]

The rise of science provided support for those wanting to preserve slavery and White supremacy.

> During the 1840's and 1850's the conclusions of scientists on the nature and
> extent of racial diversity came for the first time to play an important role in
> the discussion of black servitude. In educated circles in the South as well as
> in the North, there developed, especially among those who wished to
> expose the "errors" of their opponents, a growing belief that Jefferson had
> been right in anticipating that science would eventually decide once and
> for all whether Negroes were biologically equal to whites or were ever
> likely to be.[61]

Two theories of creation formed the background for the scientific debate
and the resulting conflict. Samuel Stanhope Smith, president of the College
of New Jersey (later Princeton University),[62] presented the argument for
monogenesis, or the belief that all "races of man were members of the same
species and had common remote ancestry" (published in 1787 and 1810).[63]
Smith, who was a dedicated environmentalist, argued that the inferiority of
Africans was caused by climate and "savagery." He believed that exposure to
White civilization would cure black inferiority, and that Whiteness was the
norm by which Black equality would be judged.

Charles Caldwell, prominent southerner and founder of two medical
schools in Kentucky, proposed the theory of polygenesis, "or the separate
creation of the races as distinct species" (1830).[64] He argued that the inferiority of Blacks was not their fault and should lead to benevolent paternalism in Whites. However, more dedicated proponents of slavery
quickly saw the benefit of devaluing the Blacks, because it justified more
brutal and effective control of the slave population.

The new science of ethnology entered the argument at about this point. Dr. Samuel George Morton of Philadelphia published his *Crania Americana* in 1839. Based on collections of skulls that purported to represent the Great (unbroken) Chain of Being in terms of brain size and angle of forehead, he concluded that Whites and Blacks did not come from the same species, that the original Egyptians and their civilization were Caucasians, that "Negroes were permanently inferior to whites . . . and that only Caucasians were authentic descendants of Adam."[65] Additional "proof" for the theory that Whites and Blacks were different species came from the widespread belief that mulattoes were a weak hybrid of the species that would die out in a few generations.[66]

His view widely accepted in the South, Morton became a friend of John C. Calhoun of Charleston, South Carolina, a senator and leading proslavery politician. Morton's ideas were adopted and expanded at his death in 1851 by Dr. Josiah Nott, a scientist who argued that Negro improvement from domestication would reach its peak in one or two generations.[67] He concluded that permanent Negro inferiority was a fact.

[Nott] described the Caucasians as having "in all ages been the rulers"; their destiny therefore is "to conquer and hold every foot of the globe where climate does not interpose an impenetrable barrier. No philanthropy, no legislation, no missionary labors can change this law; it is written in man's nature by the hand of his creator." As for the "inferior races," they would serve their purposes and become extinct.[68]

Fredrickson concludes: "Nott was arguing less from the supposed facts of craniology or Egyptology than from a dogmatic white-racialist view of history, of the kind then coming into fashion all over the Western world as a justification not only for slavery but also for imperial expansion."[69]

That a scientific view challenging the biblical doctrine of a single creation of humankind could be so popular in the South indicated this doctrine's ability to support the prejudices and economic structures of White supremacy. However, a spirited debate ensued about the conflict between science and the Bible, because the southern elite wanted support from the Bible and from science, in spite of their conflicts and contradictions.

Meanwhile, in the North, ethnology and the theory of polygenesis provided support for White supremacy and led to the constitutional amendments restricting or eliminating Negro suffrage in New York in 1821 and in Pennsylvania in 1838. In 1857, the Dred Scott decision of the Supreme Court was written; it denied United States citizenship to all Blacks, and was partially based on the new "scientific" proofs of Black inferiority.[70] Dr. John H. Van Evrie of New York articulated the northern version of White supremacy in a pamphlet in 1860.

> God has made the negro an inferior being . . . not in most cases, but in all cases. . . . There never could be a negro equalling the standard Caucasian in natural ability. The same almighty creator made all white men equal—for idiots, insane people, etc., are not exceptions, they are the result of human vices, crimes, or ignorance, immediate or remote.[71]

As George M. Fredrickson caustically points out, "All white shortcomings, in other words, had environmental explanations, while Negro frailties were inherent."[72] Van Evrie expressed many northern prejudices accurately, and emerged "as a major spokesman for racist opposition to emancipation."[73] Such northern racist "scientific" ideas created the climate that led to White draft resistance and race riots in northern cities, and opposition to emancipation elsewhere.

As scientists coopted The Great Chain of Being to support slavery, northern Republicans and abolitionists, the liberal thinkers of their day, began developing arguments that glorified Anglo-Saxons and romanticized African Americans. Nevertheless, according to Fredrickson, the glorification of Anglo-Saxons as the inventors of individual liberty and democratic ideals led to "a tendency to make America's virtues racial rather than historical or environmental in origin."[74] Theodore Parker, "liberal Unitarian minister and militant abolitionist," was critical of certain aggressive tendencies in Europeans, yet concluded that Anglo-Saxons were "a good hardy stock for national welfare to grow on. . . . I look with great pride on this Anglo-Saxon people. It has many faults, but I think it is the best specimen of mankind which has ever attained great power in the world."[75] From this lofty position of White superiority, it was not difficult to move toward the romanticization of the inferior, primitive peoples of the world.

> The biological school saw the Negro as a pathetically inept creature who was a slave to his emotions, incapable of progressive development and self-government because he lacked the white man's enterprise and intellect. But those who ascribed to the priority of feeling over intellect sanctioned both by romanticism and evangelical religion could come up with a strikingly different concept of Negro "differences." Whereas scientists and other "practical" men saw only weakness, others discovered redeeming virtues and even evidences of black superiority.[76]

The romantic school helped to make racialized thinking acceptable in the North and was a major move toward acceptance of race as an idea.[77] For example, northern abolitionists developed the "child stereotype" as an antidote to the "savage stereotype" being developed in the South. That these two stereotypes actually worked together to reinforce the belief in white supremacy was apparently beyond the awareness of many intellectuals at the time.

The view of the "Negro as child" was most fully developed by Alexander Kinmont in Cincinnati (1839). He believed that God had created Whites and Blacks as complementary races, and that aggressive industriousness, with its tendency to violence, in Whites must be tempered with Black love and its tendency to passivity in order to find a true balance of Christian virtues.

The popularized expression of the romantic viewpoint came from Harriet Beecher Stowe in her novel *Uncle Tom's Cabin*. Stowe was probably influenced by Kinmont, because she lived in Cincinnati in 1839 and could hardly have been unaware of his opinions. "In the novel, Uncle Tom speaks for this simple childlike religious faith; and in this he is abetted by the angel-child, Little Eva, who manifests an identical simplicity."[78] In Stowe's writing, the connection of race with the Cult of True Womanhood also becomes clear.

> [In *The Minister's Wooing* (1859)], Mary, as a woman, performs much the same function for members of what Mrs. Stowe called "the coarser sex." It becomes clear from this novel, therefore, that women and Negroes are almost interchangeable when it comes to their natural virtues. According to Mrs. Stowe, "women are burdened with fealty, faith, and reverence, more than they know what to do with," and hence they can serve as mediators between the overly intellectual male and a God who responds to simple devotion.[79]

This view was echoed by Theodore Tilton, editor of the *Independent* newspaper in New York:

> In all the intellectual activities which take their strange quickening from the moral faculties—which we call instincts, intuitions—the negro is superior to the white man—equal to the white woman. It is sometimes said . . . that the negro race is the feminine race of the world. This is not only because of his social and affectionate nature, but because he possesses that strange moral, instinctive insight that belongs more to women than to men."[80]

The binary opposition of White and Black applied equally well to male and female, and both supported the "natural hierarchy" of White supremacy and male dominance.

To be fair, there were abolitionists who rejected this argument in favor of black revolt and supported John Brown's revolt.[81] In spite of the moral arguments of these people, who included William Lloyd Garrison, Theodore Weld, and Wendell Phillips, the romantic racialism in the North defined the predominant version of United States culture, with its view of inherent White supremacy and male dominance. As Fredrickson interprets:

> The inability of the abolitionists to ground their case for the black man on a forthright and intellectually convincing argument for the basic identity in the moral and intellectual aptitudes of all races weakened their "struggle for equality" and helps explain the persistence of racist doctrines after emancipation."[82]

Takaki reminds us that these stereotypes were driven by the economic and institutional forces of industrial capitalism during the presidency of Andrew Jackson and "the Market Revolution—extension of the suffrage, cultivation of new farms, erection of factories, construction of canals and railroads, expansion of the market, and accumulation of money and material goods."[83]

> Images of blacks as children and savages did far more than buttress segregation in the North and slavery in the South: promoted by white culture-makers and policy-makers, these images also constituted a "persuasion" which gave whites direction and identity in Jacksonian society. What is significant is how whites defined blacks *vis-à-vis* themselves. . . . The black "child/savage" defined deviancy and served in effect to discipline whites, especially working-class and immigrant groups, into republican conduct.[84]

In short, the class system desired by capitalism, together with a view of White male dominance constructed to justify such a system, fueled the debates among White men about the inferiority of Negroes and women. By inventing racial and gender oppression through economic, institutional, and ideological structures and systems, White men ensured that their class, race, and gender would remain dominant, not only in "autonomy, access to resources and self-determination," but also by maintaining White supremacy and male dominance as "the norm by which all else will be measured."[85]

The Cult of True Womanhood functioned as an ideology of male dominance and economic exploitation by constructing the category of "woman" so that women were defined as inferior and thus became a surplus population that could be forced to work at low wages or kept at home under the control of men. This ideology was enforced by laws about property, voting, parental custody, and by restrictions on most jobs, including church leadership. However, it applied differently to Black and White women, because of racial theory and the needs of capitalism. The Cult of True Womanhood served to keep White middle-class women subordinate and often imprisoned in an isolated domestic sphere, while many White working class women were deemed inferior because they worked in factories. For Black women under slavery, the ideology perpetuated racist stereotypes of inferiority by denying them the possibility of conforming to the ideals of womanhood.[86]

In her discussion of "controlling images and Black women's oppression,"[87] Patricia Hill Collins shows how these racial and gender stereotypes worked their evil intent. Because of the development of the "child/ savage" stereotype by southern proslavery intellectuals and northern romantic abolitionists, "Black women emerged from slavery firmly enshrined in the consciousness of White America as 'Mammy' and the 'bad black woman.' "[88] Within the Cult of True Womanhood, White women were idealized for their "piety, purity, submissiveness and domesticity," while Black women were negatively defined by their presumed inability to aspire to these virtues.[89]

> The first controlling image applied to African-American women is that of the mammy—the faithful, obedient domestic servant. Created to justify the economic exploitation of house slaves and sustained to explain Black women's long-standing restriction to domestic service, the mammy image represents the normative yardstick used to evaluate all Black women's behavior. By loving, nurturing, and caring for her white children and "family" better than her own, the mammy symbolizes the dominant group's perceptions of the ideal Black female relationship to elite white male power. Even though she may be well loved and may wield considerable authority in her white "family," the mammy still knows her "place" as obedient servant. She has accepted her subordination.[90]

Thus the "child" stereotype functioned to define the mammy as happy to be submissive to her benevolent White masters and as without desires of her own, including that to nurture her own children. In addition, this false image created the fantasy that even though she had physical household chores, Black women were asexual and harmless, thus fulfilling the demands of the Cult of True Womanhood by severing the ties of "sexuality and fertility." The image also reinforced class oppression by providing a rationale for economic exploitation that kept Black women in low-paying jobs.

Opposite the mammy was Jezebel.

> Jezebel's function was to relegate all Black women to the category of sexu-
> ally aggressive women, thus providing a powerful rationale for the wide-
> spread sexual assaults by white men typically reported by Black slave
> women. Yet Jezebel served another function. If Black slave women could be
> portrayed as having excessive sexual appetites, then increased fertility
> should be the expected outcome. By suppressing the nurturing that African-
> American women might give their own children which would strengthen
> Black family networks, and by forcing Black women to work in the field or
> "wet nurse" white children, slaveowners effectively tied the controlling
> images of Jezebel and Mammy to the economic exploitation inherent in the
> institution of slavery.[91]

In the stereotypes of Mammy and Jezebel as "child/savages," race and
gender come together as structures of evil. During the antebellum period,
the White mind constructed the Black woman as an asexual child happily
subordinate to her masters, or as a hypersexual savage tempting White
men to violate their moral standards. Such sexist and racist rationalizations served to project the fears of the White community onto African
Americans and deflect the blame for the economic and sexual exploitation
that was built into the personal and social behaviors of White men. Winthrop Jordan, in commenting on the social function of slavery at the beginning of the nineteenth century, focuses on the importance of racial and
gender stereotypes not only for exploiting African American women and
men and White women, but also for controlling and explaining White
male fears of their own sexuality and violence.

> Perhaps white men sensed how tightly the institution [of slavery] had con-
> trolled the pattern of sexual relationships between the races, how hand-
> somely it had afforded them a sexual license and privilege which could be
> indulged without destroying their most vital institution of cultural integrity,
> the family. . . . Above all, the white man had to sustain his feeling of con-
> trol; in restraining the Negro he was at the same time restraining and
> thereby reassuring himself.[92]

In this chapter, we have reviewed some of the history of resistance
movements against racial and gender oppression within the socioeconomic context, and have critically examined the debates that reconstructed these evil systems. In 1861, these ideas fueled the Civil War,
which dramatically changed the identity of the United States. In the next
chapter, we will review the resistance following the Civil War and the violent reassertion of white supremacy and male dominance by 1900.

EMANCIPATION FOR WHOM?

How Racism and Sexism Survived Reconstruction

Prior to the Civil War, resistance movements gained strength during the time of debate among liberal and conservative White men about the nature of their economic and political control. After the Civil War, Reconstruction created new possibilities for African American women and men and White women. Our goal in this chapter is to discover how, despite some reforms, the resistance movements were suppressed so that African American women and men and White women were kept in subordinate and vulnerable social locations.

ECONOMIC AND INSTITUTIONAL SETTING

Capitalism made great strides after the Civil War. In the North and West, railroads were built (the transcontinental line was completed in 1869); northern technology was booming, and the United States entered into imperialistic expansion in Cuba and Puerto Rico (1898) and in the Philippines (1899–1902).

"Transportation was the key [to economic expansion]. There were 35,000 miles of steam railroad in the United States in 1865; more than five times as much in 1900, more than in all Europe."[1] Improved transportation led to settlement of the West and rapid increases in corn, wheat, and meat production. "The wheat crop increased from 152 to 612 million bushels between 1866 and 1891 . . . [corn from] 868 million bushels in 1866 to 2000 million bushels in 1891. The greater part of the corn was converted into meat" and processed in Chicago.[2]

In the Midwest and the East, the change could be measured in the increase in industry and manufacturing. "The ship tonnage passing through the 'Soo' (Saulte Ste. Marie) canal between Lakes Superior and Huron [increased from] roughly 100,000 tons in 1860 [to] half a million in 1869 and 25 million in 1901. Wheat and iron ore formed the bulk of these cargoes."[3]

In the 1880's the iron and coal beds of the southern Appalachians began to be exploited, and Birmingham, Alabama, became a Southern rival to Pittsburgh and Cleveland. American steel production, a mere 20,000 tons in 1867, passed the British output with 6 million tons in 1895 and reached 10 million before 1900.[4]

These changes in production correlate with drastic changes for workers.

In 1869 there were two million wage earners in factories and small industries, producing goods to the value of $3,385 million; in 1899 there were 4.7 million wage earners in factories alone, producing goods to the value of $11,407 million. In 1870 there were 6.8 million workers on farms, and the value of farm productions was $2.4 billion; in 1900 the number of farm workers was 10.9 million, and the value of their products $8.5 billion.[5]

In the "New South," cities were growing. Atlanta grew from 14,000 in 1865 to 89,872 in 1900; Birmingham grew from 3,086 in 1880 to 38,415 in 1900.

The pride of the "New South's" manufacturing was located in textile and iron production. The number of spindles jumped from 600,000 in 1860 to nearly 175,000,000 in 1890; the number of mills increased from 161 in 1880 to 400 in 1900. By the late 1880's southern pig-iron production surpassed the total output of the entire country in 1860. Jefferson County, in which Birmingham was located, had only 22 manufacturing establishments in 1870; thirty years later, it had almost 500 plants with 14,000 workers.[6]

Some freed slaves became workers in the new mills and plants.

In 1890, 6 percent of the total black work force was employed in manufacturing compared with 19 percent of the total native white work force. Between 1890 and 1910, the number of black male workers in nonagricultural occupations increased by two-thirds, or to 400,000, due mainly to expansion in saw mills, coal mining and railroad construction and maintenance. In 1880, 41 percent of Birmingham's industrial workers were black; the Immigration Commission reported in 1907 that blacks made up 39.1 percent of all steelworkers in the South.[7]

To keep wages low and break any attempts by White workers to organize as their northern counterparts were doing, Southern industrialists employed and exploited Black workers as cheap labor. Furthermore, a form of slavery continued through the convict lease system, in which government leased out thousands of Black women and men prisoners as labor to plantations and other work projects. According to DuBois, "Since 1876 Negroes have been arrested on the slightest provocation and given long sentences or fines which they were compelled to work out."[8]

We can see the effect of these economic changes in the statistics about Black women.

According to the 1890 census, there were 2.7 million Black girls and women over the age of ten. More than a million of them worked for wages: 38.7 percent in agriculture, 30.8 percent in household domestic service, 15.6 percent in laundry work; and a negligible 2.8 percent in manufacturing.[9]

The 38.7% in agriculture labored as sharecroppers, tenant farmers, or workers earning subsistence wages. Through exorbitant interest rates and unchallenged control of all aspects of the agricultural business, land owners and bankers were able to keep most Black families in debt, in poverty, and landless.

During the post-slavery period, most Black women workers who did not toil in the fields were compelled to become domestic servants. Their predicament, no less than that of their sisters who were sharecroppers or convict laborers, bore the familiar stamp of slavery. Indeed, slavery itself had been euphemistically called the "domestic institution" and slaves had been designated as innocuous "domestic servants." In the eyes of the former slaveholders, "domestic service" must have been a courteous term for a contemptible occupation not a half-step away from slavery. While Black women worked as cooks, nursemaids, chambermaids and all-purpose domestics, white women in the South unanimously rejected this line of work. Outside the South, white women who worked as domestics were generally European immigrants who, like their ex-slave sisters, were compelled to take whatever employment they could find.[10]

Domestic service included poverty-level pay, fourteen-hour days with a half-day off every two weeks, and sexual abuse.

From Reconstruction to the present, Black women household workers have considered sexual abuse perpetrated by the "man of the house" as one of their major occupational hazards. Time after time they have been victims of extortion on the job, compelled to choose between sexual submission and absolute poverty for themselves and their families.[11]

In summary, as capitalism expanded after the Civil War, oppressed groups provided cheap labor. Although economic expansion is often promoted as an unqualified good, we see here some of its destructive consequences.

THE RESISTANCE COMMUNITIES

Resistance to 250 years of slavery exploded immediately after emancipation, as thousands of African Americans left their homes in search of family members who had been sold or had escaped, formed institutions of survival such as businesses and schools, and entered politics. Black soldiers provided protection for thousands of Black families as they claimed the right to own land, to travel, to obtain education, and to self-defense.[12] Reconstruction offered opportunities for resistance as African Americans took advantage of new economic, political, and social avenues to express their freedom and "uplift the race."

> Black people were hardly celebrating the abstract principles of freedom when they hailed the advent of emancipation. As that ". . . great human sob shrieked in the wind and tossed its tears upon the sea—free, free, free," Black people were not giving vent to religious frenzy. They knew exactly what they wanted: the women and the men alike wanted land, they wanted the ballot and ". . . they were consumed with desire for schools."[13]

In the South, massive violence tried to destroy this resistance. As soon as the war was over, violent suppression of Black freedom began, in spite of Federal troops and Radical Reconstruction (the attempt of northern states to reconstruct the southern states after the Civil War). Jim Crow laws were passed to enforce segregation and justify White supremist violence.

> Beginning in Tennessee in 1870, white Southerners enacted laws against intermarriage of the races in every Southern state. Five years later, Tennessee adopted the first "Jim Crow" law, and the rest of the South rapidly fell in line. Blacks and whites were separated on trains, in depots, and on wharves. After the Supreme Court outlawed the Civil Rights Acts of 1875, the Negro was banned from white hotels, barber shops, restaurants, and theatres. By 1885 most Southern states had laws requiring separate schools. With the adoption of new constitutions the states firmly established the color line by the most stringent segregation of the races; and in 1896 the Supreme Court upheld segregation in its "separate but equal" doctrine set forth in *Plessy v. Ferguson.* . . . [14]

Yet the resistance continued. Prevented from working through public channels, the Black community focused on self-help by forming and sustaining educational institutions, women's clubs, and strong churches.

> By 1890 it had become preeminently clear that the black community would have to devise its own strategies of social and political advancement. . . . During the "nadir" [of Jim Crow, lynchings, etc.], black communities turned increasingly inward. . . . African Americans, looking now to themselves to educate the masses of their people, care for the needy, facilitate economic development, and address political concerns, tapped their greatest strength from the tradition of their churches. . . . In the decades following Reconstruction, the church's autonomy and financial strength made it the most logical institution for the pursuit of racial self-help. It functioned not only as a house of worship but as an agency of social control, forum of discussion and debate, promoter of education and economic cooperation, and arena for the development and assertion of leadership.[15]

The story of Ida B. Wells illustrates African American resistance to violent White supremacy at the end of the nineteenth and early twentieth centuries. Born into slavery in 1862, Ida B. Wells obtained an education because of the gains for African Americans during Reconstruction. In 1883, she filed and won a suit against the Chesapeake, Ohio, and Southwestern Railroad for refusing her a seat in a so-called White car. However, the judgment was overturned by the Supreme Court, which said, "We think it is evident that the purpose of the defendant was to harass. Her persistence was not in good faith to obtain a comfortable seat for the short ride." This case was the first heard in the South after the death of the Civil Rights Act of 1775.[16]

Ida B. Wells's account of this and other experiences in a local newspaper cost her her teaching job in 1891. When a close friend, Thomas Moss, was lynched in Memphis, Tennessee, in 1862, she launched a campaign that brought her international notoriety. Ida B. Wells did research and writing to prove her thesis that lynching had nothing to do with White fears of rape of White women, but was a terrorist activity aimed at destroying economic and political leadership in the Black community. Her statistics proved the truth of her own experience. As Emilie Townes summarizes:

> As one of the growing number of Blacks who began to make economic gains in the South, Moss and his business partners opened a grocery store and sold at prices competitive to the white store owner across the street. Their crime was that they were successful, Black, and chose to defend their store against attack by whites rather than allow it to be ransacked and de-

stroyed. The lynching of these three men who were leading citizens in the city of Memphis, was not carried out by a few lower class whites. Members of the white establishment of Memphis comprised the lynch mob. Wells wrote, "The more I studied the situation, the more I was convinced that the Southerner had never gotten over his resentment that the Negro is no longer his plaything, his servant, and his source of income."[17]

Southerners invented the false rape charge to justify economic and political acts of terror, knowing that idea of rape by Black men provoked fear in both North and South. When Ida B. Wells published her research on June 5, 1892, "it contained names, dates, places, and circumstances of hundreds of lynchings for alleged rape."[18] In Wells's opinion, "[l]ynching was an act of political and economic repression"[19] directed against the leadership of the Black community. It was also an attack against voluntary relationships between Black men and White women.

> Well's attack on the rape myth was an attack against southern sexual mores. The South contented itself with the illusion that any liaison between an African-American man and a white women must be an involuntary one for the woman. Wells was quite clear that such liaisons were ill-advised, but she was candid about the willingness of white women. . . . Meanwhile, white men seduced and raped Black women and girls with impunity.[20]

The following responses of a White southern newspaper was typical: "The [Memphis, Tenn.] Appeal-Avalanche has time and again recorded itself as against lynch law, no matter where the lynchings occurred, but so long as negroes or whites either, commit rape, there will be lynchings."[21] Some of Ida B. Wells's most vicious opposition came from White women in the North, who were counting on White support in the South as a part of the suffrage and temperance movements. White opinions, like the following by Frances Willard, president of the Women's Christian Temperance Union in 1890, in Wells's view supported the terrorism of disfranchisement and illegal lynchings:

> The colored race multiplies like the locust of Egypt. The grog-shop is its center of power. . . . The safety of women, of children, of the home is menaced in a thousand localities so that men dare not go beyond the sight of their own roof-tree.[22]

Ida B. Wells was unrelenting in her responses to such uninformed opinions.

> Miss Willard has . . . put herself on record as approving the Southerner's methods of defying the constitution and suppressing the negro vote; has

promised that "when I go North there will be no word wafted to you from pen or voice that is not loyal to what we are saying here and now"; has unhesitatingly sown a slander against the entire negro race in order to gain favor with those who are hanging, shooting, and burning negroes alive.[23]

Ida B. Wells was probably the most militant and public of the antilynching resistance, but she was not unusual in her views.

It is important to recognize that black women like Frances Harper, Anna Julia Cooper, and Ida B. Wells were not isolated figures of intellectual genius; they were shaped by and helped to shape a wider movement of Afro-American women. This is not to claim that they were representative of all black women; they and their counterparts formed an educated, intellectual elite, but an elite that tried to develop a cultural and historical perspective that was organic to the wider condition of black womanhood.[24]

Because of the terroristic violence of lynching and segregation in the late nineteenth century, "black communities turned increasingly inward"[25] and learned they could not count on coalitions with White groups and institutions. As they turned inward, they found the church a source of strength for their continuing resistance.

The black church represented the realm where individual souls communed intimately with God and where African Americans as a people freely discussed, debated, and devised an agenda for their common good. . . . The church connected black women's spirituality integrally with social activism.[26]

Meanwhile, the labor movement and the White women's movement were active in the North, resisting the exploitation of workers and the domestication and exploitation of women. Angela Davis recounts the largely unknown story of Black women's leadership in the socialist and Communist parties at the turn of the century, groups that were aligned with the labor movement and also supported the resistance of Black women and men as workers and advocated the vote for women.[27] The Industrial Workers of the World, the Knights of Labor, and other groups suffered much violence as they attempted to organize workers and improve their working conditions. The social gospel movement joined in the agitation to end some of the worst forms of exploitation of children and other workers.

Another bold act of resistance was the publication in 1898 of the Women's Bible under the leadership of Elizabeth Cady Stanton. The authors sought to "revise all texts and chapters directly referring to women or excluding women."[28] This project was part of an effort to challenge the arguments that women could not be ministers because Eve was created after

Adam, because Eve sinned against God first, because Jesus and the disciples were men, and because Paul said women were subordinate in the New Testament. In spite of strong opposition, women began to preach and write in growing numbers.

In summary, the resistance movements continued their work in whatever public space was available, but oppression became more violent and effective by the end of the century. We will next explore the story of how this evil was organized and maintained.

DEBATE AND BETRAYAL

The Debate about Race

It was no accident that some of the most vicious racist violence in the history of the United States occurred after Emancipation and the failure of Reconstruction, that women's suffrage was delayed for fifty years, and that male dominance and White supremacy survived. In addition to economic and institutional factors, the work of reconstructing racial and gender evil solicited unrelenting work by both liberal and conservative intellectuals.

Before the Civil War, both liberal and conservative White men shared the view that African Americans were an inferior race. Furthermore, they believed that the end of slavery would preserve the United States as a White nation, either "through planned colonization, unplanned migration, or extermination through 'natural' processes."[29] President Lincoln, like Jefferson more than half a century earlier, apparently favored colonization as the best solution and actually made contact with Haiti for such a purpose. Lincoln told a delegation of Black leaders in 1862:

> "You and we are different races. We have between us a broader difference than exists between almost any other two races. . . . [T]his physical difference is a great disadvantage to us both, as I think your race suffers very greatly, many of them by living among us, while ours suffers from your presence." He recommended colonization in Central America, "especially because of the similarity of climate with your native land—[it] thus being suited to your physical condition."[30]

Many northerners believed that "natural" migration would solve "the Negro problem" and maintain a White nation, that "the blacks would migrate to the tropics, leaving the Whites to occupy the more temperate regions." Such persons were often "opposed to discrimination against Blacks but 'looked forward to the separation of the races.' "[31] Under the influence of the new theories of Darwin (*The Origin of Species* was published in 1859), some leaders believed the survival of the fittest would lead to the natural extermination of the Black race.

> As early as 1839, Horace Bushnell, a Congregational clergyman and the North's most distinguished theologian, had predicted that the black race would not survive emancipation because it would then be placed in direct competition with the whites. . . . In 1860, in a sermon on "The Census and Slavery," he returned to this happy theme and envisioned the free white population of the North pushing down on the South and setting off a Malthusian struggle for existence which would end in the disappearance of the blacks. "I know of no example in human history," Bushnell told his congregation, "where an inferior and far less cultivated stock has been able, freely intermixed with a superior, to hold its ground. . . . [I]t will always be seen that the superior lives the other down, and finally quite lives it away.[32]

This theory was supposedly a liberal argument favoring the abolition of slavery, but its White supremist assumptions reveal a fatal weakness in the northern progressive view of race.

Post–Civil War scholars watched for signs of Black population growth or decline in the census figures. In 1870, the report of a small decline led some to predict that "the African race will go on to extinction."[33] However, in 1880, there seemed to be a 30% increase, which created panic among some and "could be accounted for only by 'the remarkable fecundity of the African.' "[34]

> This dark, swelling, muttering mass along the social horizon, gathering strength with education, and ambitious to rise, will grow increasingly restless and sullen under repression, until at length, conscious through numbers of superior power, it will assert that power destructively, and, bursting forth like an angry furious crowd, avenge in tumult and disorder, the social law broken against them.[35]

Thus, White racism shows its adaptability. White people were willing to believe that a decrease in population meant that Blacks were weak and therefore inferior, while also believing that an increase in population meant that Blacks were more animal-like and therefore inferior.

However, by 1890, "General Francis Walker, a leading Northern economist and a former superintendent of the United States census, used the latest figures on the Black population to demonstrate that the racial nightmares . . . were pure fantasy." He concluded that "the apparent increase between 1870 and 1880 . . . had been due to the fact that the census takers had overlooked many Blacks in 1870."[36] Walker's conclusions confirmed predictions from before the Civil War that an inferior race of African Americans would diminish in numbers, thus validating Darwin's theory. This discussion resulted "in an unparalleled outburst of racist speculation on the impending disappearance of the American Negro."[37]

> Racial Darwinism . . . was a philosophy appropriate to anti-Negro thinkers during . . . the postemancipation "competitive" stage of race relations. Its function was to justify a policy of repression and neglect. Coming in the wake of the supposed "failure" of blacks during Reconstruction, it not only served to underline the alleged futility of the kind of policies that radicals had espoused but even raised doubts whether the blacks should receive any help at all from paternalistic white philanthropists and reformers. Further-more, it constituted a convenient rationale for new and more overtly op-pressive racial policies. If the blacks were a degenerating race with no future, the problem ceased to be one of how to prepare them for citizenship or even how to make them more productive and useful members of the community. The new prognosis pointed rather to the need to segregate or quarantine a race liable to be a source of contamination and social danger to the white community, as it sank even deeper into the slough of disease, vice and criminality.[38]

Such arguments provided the intellectual rationalization for terrorism and genocide against the Black population. Being this explicit about racism created discomfort among some White male intellectuals because it so contradicted the ideology of equality under the Constitution.

Claiming the middle ground between these two options—Radical Re-construction, which held out the possibility of full economic and political citizenship for African Americans, and, alternatively, the construction of an apartheid society through the violence of lynching, Jim Crow laws, legal segregation, and disfranchisement—lay the benevolent paternalism of the "New South," a myth that was very attractive to northern business leaders.

> When the last Federal occupation troops were withdrawn from the South in 1877, Northern Republicans took comfort from the fact that spokesmen for the triumphant Southern conservatives disclaimed any intention of depriv-ing blacks of their recently won rights as citizens.[39]

The leading spokesperson for this view was Henry W. Grady, editor of the *Atlanta Constitution.* Considered a moderate leader, he was enthusiastically welcomed by northern industrialists such as J. P. Morgan and Andrew Car-negie. In his view, the South had two problems.

"What shall the South do to be saved?" asked Grady in an 1887 Dallas speech, "The South and Her Problems." The South, he explained, had a twofold problem—its "race problem" and its "no less unique and important industrial problem." In Grady's judgment, to solve the first problem the South must have home rule, and to have home rule the South must have industrial progress and economic development.[40]

Grady believed in White supremacy. "The line has been drawn just where it should be. Just where nature drew it and where justice commends. The negro is entitled to his freedom, his franchise, to full and equal legal rights. . . . Social equality he can never have. He does not have it in the north, or in the east, or in the west. On one pretext or another, he is kept out of hotels, theatres, schools and restaurants, north as well as south."[41]

Emilie Townes illustrates the truth of Grady's claim that racial segregation enjoyed a broad consensus among the White population in both North and South.

> Racial segregation had its roots in the North, where it matured before moving to the South. Although slavery was near nonexistent in the North by 1830, a strict color line was in place. . . . By 1860 nearly every phase of Black life in the North was segregated from whites. All railroad cars, stagecoaches, steamboats, had special Jim Crow sections designated for Blacks alone. This segregation extended to theaters, lecture halls, hotels, restaurants, resorts, schools, prisons, hospitals, and cemeteries. In white churches, Blacks sat in "Negro pews" or in "nigger heaven" and had to wait to receive communion after the whites. Until Massachusetts permitted Black jurors in 1855, Blacks could not serve on juries throughout the North.[42]

Grady was also an advocate of industrial capitalism as a way of ensuring that the south would no longer be a "virtual colony of the North."[43]

> Clearly, Grady was not only proclaiming a "New South" but also promoting a new industrial order based on black labor and class control. His message contained a class criticism of labor unions, and an implied invitation to northern capitalists to utilize the reserve army of black labor in the South. No wonder northern businessmen like Carnegie who were locked in combat against white labor applauded Grady, and even began transporting black workers into East St. Louis, Detroit, Chicago, and other northern cities within two decades after Grady had given his speech in New York. . . . [H]e helped capitalists of both sections become conscious of their common identity and interests.[44]

Grady was opposed from two directions. "At one extreme were the pessimists and die-hard racists who denied the possibility of black progress, except under slavery, and who favored a more openly repressive system. At the other extreme were lonely spokesmen—most notably the novelist George W. Cable—who argued in effect that the "New South" advocates could not realize their own professed goal of a prosperous and progressive region unless they implemented a policy of genuine public equality."[45]

The crowning achievement of Grady and his so-called "moderate" views was the 1895 Atlanta Exposition, to which the elite leaders from the South invited Booker T. Washington as a main speaker. In his speech, Washington promised to support a racial hierarchy and social segregation in exchange for economic opportunities for the Black workforce during southern industrial expansion. Washington said, "In all things that are purely social we can be as separate as the fingers, yet one as the hand in all things essential to mutual progress."[46] A working coalition was in place: a consensus of northern White progressives, southern White moderates, and accommodating African Americans. "White men of power and progress could feel confidence in their technology; and as they looked at the interracial scene around them, they could affirm their superiority over peoples of color."[47] Andrew Carnegie was one of Washington's bankrollers.

W. E. B. Du Bois emerged as Washington's strongest critic and a challenge to White male control of Black workers. "Is it possible, and probable, that nine millions of men can make effective progress in economic lines if they are deprived of political rights, made a servile cast, and allowed only the most meagre chance for developing their exceptional men? . . . NO."[48]

The White debate of this time returned to the discussion of whether the Negro was more childlike or beast-like. The Southern moderates adopted the Negro-as-child that had been developed earlier by Northern Abolitionists.

> "I am convinced," [Grady] wrote in the New York *Herald*, "that the great masses of negroes in South Carolina, as well as elsewhere, are perfectly peaceable and harmless. It is only when their leadership stir up their passions and appeal to their prejudices that they are vicious and dangerous."[49]

The weakness in this argument was easily exploited by conservatives more honest about their White supremacy.

> The proslavery theorists had argued that the "brute" propensities of the blacks were kept in check only as a result of the absolute white control made possible by slavery and that emancipation in the South would bring

the same "reversion to savagery" that had allegedly taken place after the blacks had been freed in Haiti and the British West Indies. Many Southerners of the Reconstruction era professed to find confirmation for this theory in the behavior of the freedmen under Radical leadership.[50]

In 1889, Philip Alexander Bruce argued that there was a rise in Negro crime and sexual immorality because of emancipation. Generally accepted among southern Whites, Bruce's argument interpreted the resistance of African Americans as proof of their rebelliousness and danger to the White population. By the end of the century, a theory of "the black peril" had generated a new genre of literature.[51] Fueled by fears about the economic difficulties of the time, the labor disputes, the possibility of wars, and expansion, this more virulent theory of racism gives clues to the White male imagination.

> The psychology of Southern colonizationism or expulsionism would appear to be similar to a characteristic attitude of European colonialists toward the native populations they exploit. At times, Albert Memmi points out, the colonialist is "fed up with his subject, who tortures his conscience and his life. He tries to dismiss him from his mind, to imagine the colony without the colonized. A witticism which is more serious than it sounds states that 'Everything would be perfect . . . if it weren't for the natives.' "[52]

By the 1890s, the moderate-progressive approach to the Negro problem—that Blacks were harmless children, that they would not be able to compete, that their numbers would dwindle—had collapsed. Most White leaders of the North and South agreed that the Negro was a beast who had to be forcefully controlled. Moderate ideology had served its purpose of cloaking the evil forces of manipulation and violence, so that now the elite White economic leaders had firm enough control to express their White supremacy in the open. "They discarded their paternalistic rhetoric and adopted the slogans of White equality and Black proscription."[53] With economic agreements between northern and southern leaders in place, the myth of racial paternalism and moderation could be dropped in favor of overt racial violence.

"The Black image in the White mind" in the 1890s reveals itself in the myths of the Black male rapist and the Black female prostitute. To justify the violence of lynching, terrorism, and rigid segregation, a new literature arose at the turn of the century, literature that revived images of African American bestiality, evolutionary and sexual relations to apes, and large sexual organs. One example was the work of Thomas Dixon, "a prominent Baptist minister before he became a sensationalist novelist, [who] thought of his work as an evangelical effort to transform the stereotype of the Negro,"[54] to challenge the "child" images of *Uncle Tom's Cabin* with "the truth."

> In his most popular novel, *The Clansman*, published in 1905 (a decade later the basis of the highly successful film "The Birth of a Nation"), Dixon intensified his efforts to demonstrate the bestial propensities of the blacks. The character who speaks most directly for the author describes the Negro as "half child, half animal, the sport of impulse, whim, and conceit. . . . a being who, left to his will, roams at night and sleeps in the day, whose speech knows no word of love, whose passions, once aroused, are as the fury of the tiger." The climax of the book is the rape of a young White virgin. As Dixon described this event, before discreetly lowering the curtain: "A single tiger spring, and the black claws of the beast sank into the soft white throat." The act results in the suicide of the victim and her mother, following by a solemn, portentous lynching by the Ku Klux Klan. Dixon's fictional glorification of such vigilante action during Reconstruction served to justify similar retaliation by white mobs in his own time.[55]

These fictions of the White male imagination effectively organized the fears and prejudices of Whites, who not only accepted horrifying violence against Black communities, but also tolerated the sexual exploitation of Black women. Entrenched notions about African American women and men allowed White men to maintain control of White women, who thought they had to depend on White men for protection. Patricia Hill Collins connects this White construction to the experience of Black men and women.

> Depicting African-American men as sexually charged beasts who desired white women created the myth of the Black rapist. Lynching emerged as the specific form of sexual violence visited on Black men, with the myth of the Black rapist as its ideological justification. The significance of this myth is that it "has been methodically conjured up when recurrent waves of violence and terror against the Black community required a convincing explanation." Black women experienced a parallel form of race- and gender-specific sexual violence. Treating African-American women as pornographic objects and portraying them as sexualized animals, as prostitutes, created the controlling image of Jezebel. Rape became the specific act of sexual violence forced on Black women, with the myth of the Black prostitute as its ideological justification.[56]

After the Civil War, the churches, too, reflected the racism and sexism of the time. According to Smith, prominent leaders of the major denominations developed explicitly racist policies that encouraged Black members to leave in order to form their own denominations. By 1867, 150,000 Black members of the Southern Baptist Convention, 90,000 Black Methodists, and 10,000 Black Presbyterians had left.[57] Jeremiah Jeter, a Southern Baptist leader,

> argued that God had implanted in man an instinct which set apart blacks and whites, and that social mingling between them violated the divine plan, since such mingling would result in miscegenation, and thus "degrade our noble saxon race . . . to a race of degenerate mongrels."[58]

The churches played a crucial role in "the triumph of racial orthodoxy" in both North and South.[59] While rigid forms of racism extended the interests of the former slaveholding elite, an accommodationist stance in northern and southern progressives was based on paternalism and belief in Negro inferiority, which had always been the trademark of White supremacy. Washington Gladden, a leader of the social gospel movement, said, "The ballot was given to the Negro . . . in the expectation that it would protect him, educate him, and make him an element of strength, rather than of weakness, in the state. Neither of these results has been realized."[60]

The Southern version of racist theology had a different sound, but very similar outcome. In 1883, Henry Holcombe Tucker, a minster of the Southern Baptist Convention who had also served as president of Mercer University and the University of Georgia, wrote,

> We do not believe that "all men are created equal," as the Declaration of Independence declares them to be; nor that they will ever become equal in this world. . . . We think that our own race is incomparably superior to any other. . . . We believe that fusion of two or more of these races would be an injury to all, and a still greater injury to posterity. We think the race-line is providential, and that . . . any . . . great intermingling [of races] must have its origin in sin.[61]

Notice Tucker's explicit appeal to White supremacy, as well as an implicit reference to White fears of miscegenation and a theological appeal to intermingling as sin. Smith summarizes the principles that became part of southern theological orthodoxy:

> 1) [The] human races are unequal, and will remain unequal to the end of history; 2) the Negro is far inferior to the Caucasian; 3) the racial fusion or amalgamation of black and white peoples is injurious to both races; 4) free social intermingling of blacks and whites "must have its origin in sin."[62]

The predominance of these racist ideas helps to explain the silence of the church after 1877, when segregation was legalized and enforced with terrorism and violence.

> C. Vann Woodward credits the South's embrace of extreme racism to the relaxation of significant opposition to racism by the liberal North, the decline in power and influence of the southern conservatives, and a corollary decline of the influence of the ideals of the southern radicals. When the liberal North agreed to the Compromise of 1877, this signaled the beginning of the North's retrenchment on race. Eventually the North and South differed little on their race policies. Northern liberals and abolitionists began to voice the "shibboleths of white supremacy regarding the Negro's innate inferiority, shiftlessness, and hopeless unfitness for full participation in the white man's civilization."[63]

The response of Reverend Percy Stickney Grant is typical of the northern White liberals from the social gospel movement at the beginning of the twentieth century:

> Grant called for a new philosophy of race relations, based on a recognition of the inadequacy of the idealism of the Reconstruction era. According to the theory of evolution, Grant argued, the Negro was not entitled to equal rights, because he had not yet developed sufficiently to share fully in the privileges of the more advanced race.[64]

Liberal leaders such as Washington Gladden and Walter Rauschenbusch shared these views. However, as Fredrickson shows,

> Benevolent and progressive Northerners, who thought they had learned a "tragic" lesson from Reconstruction, were not prepared to intervene in the South in order to ensure that the blacks had an environment conducive to "the progressive awakening of race pride and race ambition," nor were they ready to deny the popular belief in the Negro's inferiority; but they did try to reconcile this posture with social optimism and humanitarian concern. . . . In a sense, then, Southern paternalism lost the South to the extremists but won the North, or an articulate segment of it, to its way of thinking.[65]

The betrayal of the principles of equality and justice by White male progressives ensured that the evils of racial oppression would continue until by the Civil Rights Movement of the 1960s.

When we study these theological ideas alongside the debates between Black women and White women in the North—for example, those that took place between Ida B. Wells and Frances Willard over lynching and

rape—we can see that the belief in White supremacy among both northern and southern White men and women contributed to the betrayal of
the resistance movement's ideals of emancipation and equality. Although
northern and southern Whites disagreed on issues such as slavery and especially violent forms of racial violence, they agreed on the underlying
assumption of White superiority. Thus the charges of degeneracy that
made Blacks seem unfit for citizenship in the state or the church, the false
rape charges that seemed to justify lynching, and the withholding of economic and political support for Black efforts at "race uplift" all seemed reasonable in a White supremist culture.

As a result of White apartheid and northern betrayal, African American
women and men increasingly withdrew into their own churches and clubs
for survival and for preserving the strength needed for the endless battles
that lay ahead.[66] Thus the foundation was laid for the formation of the
NAACP and the legal suits that by 1955 would successfully challenge segregation laws.

The Debate about Gender

Through religious and theological support for the "Cult of True Womanhood," and by fostering conflict and alienation between White and Black
women, White male religious leaders betrayed the movement for women's
rights. In this discussion, "male dominance" refers to the economic exploitation of working-class women and general subordination of women in all
social classes.[67]

In the South, the Cult of True Womanhood worked differently because
of slavery:

> The myth of southern womanhood in the antebellum South was an exag-
> gerated version of the romantic, inspirational aspects of the Cult of True
> Womanhood—conceding to women command of worshipful attention but
> no real responsibility. William Taylor has described the South's exaggerated
> chivalry to white women as a way of buying them off, an offer of "half a loaf
> in the hope they would not demand more." . . . The false elevation of the
> white woman matched the degradation of the slave—both conditions far
> from the conception of moral and spiritual equality.[68]

The role of women in church and society was heavily debated during
parts of the nineteenth century, largely because of the women's rights
movement and because of the powerful cult of domesticity then being
constructed. An article in the *Congregational Review* of 1868 is, according to
Barbara Brown Zikmund, "a good example of the 'separate but equal' argument that denied women the right to preach."[69] The article states:

Man is made the head of the woman. The place of woman, in the family and in society, is one of subjection to man. Man was first formed . . . to have dominion of the earth. Woman was formed out of the man . . . to be a 'helpmeet for him' (Gen 2:18). . . .[70]

The article acknowledges the resistance of women to this view by chiding them for their rebelliousness:

We find at the present time the 'strong-minded' leaving the teachings of Scripture, and trying to reason out the duty and mission of woman; and they are quite confused by the acknowledged fact that she is the equal of man, and the unquestioned fact that she is differently organized. . . . She is the equal of man, and his help; in some qualities she is his inferior, in other qualities his superior. . . . They are not equal, in the sense that they have both equal rule and authority, but equal in their respective spheres.[71]

By appealing to the biblical letters of Paul, the article identifies the central problem: women's power in competition with that of men.

The Apostle insists that, as compared with man, she must be "in subjection," she must not "usurp authority over the man," she must "learn in silence," "be in silence." . . . The reason is given why the woman should not teach or speak in the church. It is because this would be usurping authority over the man; and her place is "to learn in silence in all subjection." It is because "the head of the woman is the man"; and "the woman is the glory of the man."[72]

If salvation, according to the author, comes to women through subordination to their husbands and bearing and nurturing children in the home, how sinful it must be to seek leadership in church and society, or to agitate for change in God-given and natural gender roles. Such articles demonstrate how religious arguments supported and reinforced the gender oppression that imprisoned women in the home and subjected them to violence from men.

Augustus Hopkins Strong, president and professor of theology at Rochester Theological Seminary, Rochester, New York, typified northern White liberal male attitudes about women. While trying to reconcile his view of equality before God and his view of women's subordination, he developed the following ideas on "Woman's Place and Work. . . . This doctrine may be summed up in three particulars: 1st, equality with man in nature; 2ndly, subordination to man in office; 3rdly, union with man in life and work."[73] In explaining the second point concerning subordination, Strong said,

> And what shall we say to the claim to the suffrage which is made for woman? . . . If I am not mistaken, the whole argument for suffrage rests upon the unconscious assumption that a woman is a man. . . . We have seen that while woman can claim equality with man in nature, she misses her true place and work when she forgets that she is different from him and in office subordinate to him. She gains most herself, and does most for others, when she recognizes this divine order and accepts the place of man's helper, without aspiring to fill that of man himself.[74]

Imagine—the president of a nationally known seminary preached this sermon in the city where Susan B. Anthony lived, forty years after the beginning of the women's rights movement. No wonder it would be more than thirty years before the United States passed the Nineteenth Amendment. Such attitudes on gender also typified the nineteenth-century missionary movement, which imported attitudes of male superiority into other cultures. Women in Nicaragua, for example, struggled against patriarchal prejudice to follow their calls to ministry.

White liberal men were not the only ones who betrayed resistance movements. Two resistance communities that had reason to be in solidarity with each other divided along class/racial lines. The suffrage movement, controlled by middle-class White women, appealed to class and race prejudice to strengthen its coalition with White men in power. Susan B. Anthony and Elizabeth Cady Stanton, as well as other suffrage leaders, increasingly argued that White women were more qualified to vote than Black and immigrant working-class men or women. Stanton wrote in 1882:

> In view of the fact that Freedmen of the South and the millions of foreigners now crowding our shores . . . are all in the progress of events to be enfranchised, the best interests of the nation demand that we outweigh this incoming pauperism, ignorance, and degradation, with the wealth, education, and refinement of the women of the republic.[75]

To some extent, White women eventually won their right to vote by promising to support the class hegemony of the White male elite. This was happening at the same time that literacy and property laws were being passed in the South to disfranchise Black men and deprive them of any political or economic protection. If literacy and property laws prevented African Americans and other poor people from voting, educated White women would use their votes to assure the political and economic hegemony of the elite social classes of both North and South. White women opted for class solidarity rather than choosing gender or anti-racism as criteria for political identification.[76]

The debate after the Civil War about the wisdom of allowing Black men *or* White and Black women to vote was an effective means of preventing either group from exercising political and economic power. Black men lost the right to vote less than twelve years after passage of the Fifteenth Amendment, and the vote for women was delayed until White women had promised class and racial solidarity more than fifty years later.

> White women who felt that caste was their protection aligned their interests with the patriarchal power that ultimately confined them. . . . [Ida B.] Wells . . . was able to reveal how a patriarchal system which lost its total ownership over black male bodies used its control over women to attempt to completely circumscribe the actions of black male labor. . . . Racism led to segregated organizations and, outside the antilynching movement itself, to a resounding silence about and therefore complicity in the attempt to eliminate black people politically, economically, and literally as a presence in North America.[77]

George Francis Train, a southern White politician, subsidized Susan B. Anthony and Elizabeth Cady Stanton in order to encourage their increasingly White supremist arguments for women's suffrage. Train, Anthony, and Stanton traveled together throughout the United States, and Train financed a journal called *Revolution* that bore the motto, "Men, their rights, and nothing more; women, their rights, and nothing less."[78] Train and other politicians obviously had little interest in women's suffrage, except to counter the Republicans who were sponsoring Black male suffrage.

Thirty years later, northern White male theologians were developing White supremist arguments in anticipation of the "Christian Century" of progress. In 1885, Josiah Strong, a leading promoter of the social gospel, General Secretary of the Evangelical Alliance for the United States, and one of the founders of the Federal Council of Churches, published *Our Country*, of which 148,000 copies were sold. The incredible ideological compatibility between his position and the positions of Anthony and Stanton can be seen in the following, taken from his chapter "The Anglo-Saxon in the World's Future."

> It seems to me that God . . . is training the Anglo-Saxon race for an hour sure to come . . . when the pressure of population on the means of subsistence will be felt here. . . . Then will the world enter upon a new stage of its history—the final competition of races, for which the Anglo-Saxon is being schooled. . . . If I read not amiss, this powerful race will move down upon Mexico, down upon Central and South American, out upon the is-

lands of the sea, over upon Africa and beyond. And can any one doubt that the result of this competition of races will be the "survival of the fittest?" . . . Whether the extinction of inferior races before the advancing Anglo-Saxon seems to the reader sad or otherwise, it certainly appears probable. . . . We of this generation and nation occupy the Gibraltar of the ages which commands the world's future.[79]

Strong's book discloses the depth of the northern liberal betrayal on the issue of racial oppression, as well as its interlocking connection with issues of gender. In the midst of the worst years of lynching, apartheid, and segregation, and other forms of racist oppression and violence, Strong was advocating White supremacy at the expense of "the extinction of inferior races," and United States imperialism against Latin America, the Philippines, and Africa. He was advocating a masculinist invasion and destruction of other cultures and languages—a complement to the common view of the need to subordinate and domesticate women. Such racial and gender prejudice had a profound effect on the new churches of Latin America, Asia, and Africa that continues till today.

In summary, White male fantasies and fabrications about race, gender, sexuality, and violence led to potent ideologies that served the interests of the economic elite. Such ideas and practices were supported by acts of violence and exploitation, especially against people of color and White women. Oppressed by evil forces, African American women and men and White women have engaged in creative forms of resistance. At times, conflicts between liberals and conservatives over who would dominate have led to periods of debate. Sometimes, when the power structure has been divided, there has been increased opportunity for resistance movements to bring their claims. When resistance movements seem to have gained too much power and have threatened to bring about significant social change, liberals and conservatives have reunited on the basis of White supremacy and male dominance: conservatives have turned to more overt racist and sexist ideologies, and liberals have collapsed into ineptitude and survival mechanisms. The result has been a harsher environment for the oppressed that corresponds with the consolidation of economic power. The main losers have always been oppressed groups.

We see this pattern over and over: conflict between liberals and conservatives, the rising strength of resistance groups, the return of racial and gender violence, and the collapse of liberal support for real social change. In the following chapter, we shall look at contemporary resistance and betrayal.

CHAPTER ◆ FIVE

CONTEMPORARY RESISTANCE AND BETRAYAL

After the Revolutionary War, the ideas of freedom and equality opened a brief time offering opportunities for African American women and men and European American women to engage in active resistance. Slavery was abolished in the North, manumission laws were passed in the upper South, and some educational and organizing opportunities emerged for White women. But within thirty years, segregation laws had been passed in the North, and the legal codes restricting slaves and free Blacks became much more repressive in the South. Antislavery social action nearly stopped as slavery became firmly established as an economic and political system. The Cult of True Womanhood made it more difficult for White women to assume public leadership roles.

Before the Civil War, Black resistance, women's rights, and abolitionist activity created a lively public debate about freedom, civil rights and suffrage for women and men. The end of the Civil War and the beginning of Reconstruction ushered in a brief time of hope and change. However, reactionary forces promoted terrorism, lynching, and legal manipulation that disfranchised Black citizens and instituted apartheid. The cause of women's rights was set back when women were not included in the constitutional amendments and civil rights acts of the 1870s. Liberal organizations betrayed the cause of freedom by invoking class arguments for women's suffrage and used White prejudices to promote Anglo-Saxon supremacy.

During the early part of the twentieth century, the public resistance of African American women and men and White women began building again, this time through labor unions, educational endeavors, and the legal challenges made by the NAACP. The social disruption caused by World War II created possibilities for change. In Brown v. Board of Education (1954), the NAACP won a crucial victory in the Supreme Court that provided a legal foundation for the beginning of the modern civil rights movement. The

Montgomery bus boycott in 1955 began more than a decade of massive, nonviolent resistance by the Black population. The civil rights acts of 1965 and 1968 not only struck down most legal segregation laws, but also provided a legal platform for agitation on gender injustice.

The feminist movement became a force in the 1960s, bringing about significant change and opening many opportunities, especially for educated, professional women. Although the Equal Rights Amendment was not ratified, civil rights laws against sex discrimination provided a legal platform for challenges to inequality in jobs and to sexual harassment, and opened up some professions to women.

However, by 1980, political backlash against racial and gender justice coincided with economic recession and institutional retrenchment. The economic gains of African American workers and White women were reversed, poverty for single parents and children increased, and financial support for liberal causes diminished. By 1990, explicitly racist and sexist ideologies had become effective political tools for controlling votes and money.[1]

What was the role of the church in this dynamic between the resistance communities and liberal betrayal? Three developments have influenced the church's theology and programs: Black male theology, White feminist theology, and Black womanist theology.

BLACK MALE THEOLOGY

In 1965, Black theology emerged as a part of the larger social debate about Black power. Black men emerged as significant public figures in the culture and as an influence on White churches. Malcolm X and Martin Luther King, Jr., represented to the African American community viable modes of resistance. The Student Nonviolent Coordinating Committee and the Black Panthers represented the radical wing of Black power in the culture, and their words and actions captivated the public through media notoriety. Charles Farmer confronted the White church with demands for reparations for the years of slavery and racism. James Cone developed the beginnings of Black theology for a new generation of Black male theologians.[2] These events had a major impact on the development of many young persons, both Black and White, who were entering church leadership at that time. Many denominations restructured their educational and social programs to focus on equal rights, housing, education, poverty, and community organization. With new opportunities for advanced education, many African American women and men felt a spirit of optimism about fundamental changes in the economic and political situation.

During the federal War on Poverty, the poverty rate for all children decreased from 17.3% in 1957 to 14.0% in 1969.[3]

James Evans summarizes the origins of Black male theology.

> The most profound contribution of the black power movement to the development of black theology was its challenge to black people to show how they could be black and Christian at the same time. . . . Black theologians viewed the history of black resistance to white oppression, and the fact that the leaders of that resistance were more often than not black Christians, as evidence that the black liberation struggle was rooted in black religion.[4]

After 1980, economic gains for poor people declined. For all children, the poverty rate increased from 16.4% in 1979 to 21.8% in 1991. In 1994, according to the Children's Defense Fund, 39.8% of African American children, 32.2% of Hispanic children, and 38.8% of Native American children lived below the poverty level.[5] A percentage of the Black community was able to enter the middle class through improved job and educational opportunities; however, for more than one-third of the Black community, poverty increased, health care quality decreased, and inner-city schools worsened.

The "Black image in the White mind"[6] became mixed. The White media promoted positive images of some Black men: sports heroes Michael Jordan and Magic Johnson; political leaders Jesse Jackson, Andrew Young, Vernon Jordan, David Dinkins, and Douglas Wilder; intellectual leaders Cornel West and William Julius Wilson; and artists Spike Lee and Bill Cosby. But the White media also promoted ambiguous images of other Black men: Clarence Thomas, Michael Tyson, O. J. Simpson, and Marion Barry all were associated, fairly or not, with crime, drugs, and sexual violence. At the same time, White society appropriated Black music, art, and images in what Cornel West calls "the Afro-Americanization of American youth."[7] By appropriating Black culture, the White community detached itself from the issues of justice in the Black community. Symbols of Black culture became consumer trends.

Within the media, "violent crime and drugs" has become a euphemistic term for White fear of Black men. Increasingly harsh crime bills have been passed; in 1994, 48 persons were executed under the Texas capital punishment law. Black men as of that year made up 50% of the United States prison population, even though they made up only 5% of the total population. In New York State, there was a fourfold increase in the prison population between 1970 and 1994. Since, according to many criminal justice scholars, only 1% of violent crimes result in actual time in jail, the overrepresentation of Black men in prison is a clear result of White fear, prejudice, and discrimination.[8]

What did the White churches do during this time? During the 1960s and 1970s, many liberal White churches[9] courageously engaged in social action programs to change the political and economic situation, and instituted education and mission programs on poverty and racism. But, more recently, liberal, progressive churches have experienced one of the most serious internal crises in centuries, namely a 25% decrease in membership, correspondingly drastic cuts in finances and programs, and increasingly divisive internal conflicts. As a result, liberal, progressive churches have curtailed cooperative interracial and ecumenical programs and withdrawn into survival attitudes and postures. At the same time, conservative churches have experienced a dramatic increase in influence and power. The Christian right and many fundamentalist churches seem to have set the goal of restoring the White church as the moral center of Western culture. The conservative churches have emphasized a number of concerns that seem directed specifically against Black men: law and order, more prisons for criminals, support of private schools at the expense of public schools, and seeking exclusion from affirmative action programs for colleges and employers. All of these issues depend on latent White racism and increase racist fears.[10]

Perhaps the decline of the progressive churches and the rise of the religious right relates to White fears of Black Power and the continuing effectiveness of White racism as a way of consolidating White power. If so, then strengthening coalitions between African American resistance communities and the liberal White churches is important for justice.

In a time of increasing racial oppression, Dwight Hopkins suggests the role of Black male theology:

> We hear the painful but powerful voices of the state of Black America and the cries of our unborn demanding to know what preparations we have made for their births. Basically, the second generation has to integrate a gospel of full humanity, a critical acceptance of African-American religious history, and an understanding of theological, cultural, and political power in the United States today. . . . Black theology has a calling to organize itself at the service of silenced voices.[11]

WHITE FEMINIST THEOLOGY

The development of White feminist theology and the increasing numbers of women in church leadership have corresponded with dramatic changes for women in the society: an increase in economic opportunities; the increased freedom that comes from birth control, abortion, divorce, and sexual choices; more work options, as the professions slowly open up for women's participation; better protection from sexual and domestic violence, as issues of abuse gain a public hearing. Many professional graduate schools for lawyers, doctors, ministers, and psychologists are reporting 50% enrollment of women, and there are more women than ever in most of the professions.

Out of this social ferment has come feminist theology as a critical examination of the role of religion in promoting patriarchy. Elisabeth Schüssler Fiorenza summarizes the assumptions of white feminist theology.

> Feminism . . . is not just concerned with gender inequalities and marginalization. Rather, feminism is a movement of those women and men who seek to transform patriarchal structures of subordination. . . . Christian feminism engages in the struggle to transform the *ekklesia* understood as a discipleship of equals. Therefore, it seeks to expose and to redress women's subordination, exploitation, and oppression in society and church.[12]

After improving in the 1960s and 1970s, the economic situation for poor and working-class women has worsened, as the economy has shifted toward low-paying service jobs and unemployment has increased.[13] The Federal poverty line for a three-person family in 1993 was $11,890, but the annual salary for a full-time year-round worker at minimum wage ($4.25 per hour) was $8,840.[14] A single working mother with two children could easily spend 50 to 75% of her income for the lowest monthly rent available.[15]

Some conservative rhetoric gives the appearance of blaming women themselves for their worsening economic situation. By trying to make divorce and welfare more difficult to obtain, conservatives would force women to stay in relationships with men, even if the men were abusive. So-called liberal politicians often support cutbacks in welfare, favoring the creation of work and education requirements for receiving welfare, regardless of the effect on children. In some ways, these political debates are based on an implicit assumption that women's increased freedom is the cause of their poverty rather than economic exploitation.

What has been the church's response to changes in women's situation? The conservative churches have led the backlash against the change in women's status and opportunities. Through campaigns against the Equal Rights Amendment and against sex education that includes birth control information, abortion rights, and liberalized divorce laws, conservative churches have opposed some of the basic reforms that have improved women's lives. At the same time, conservative churches have promoted a "family values" discussion that advocates the two-parent, heterosexual couple and their children as the ideal family. Single women and homosexuality are seen as threats to the future of White culture and society. Some religious leaders even use the phrase "religious war" to describe their rage at feminist and other liberation theologies that advocate gender and racial equality.

After the 1960s, the liberal churches slowly came to support many issues raised by feminist theologians, such as the ordination of women to ministry, inclusive language in worship, equal representation on governing bodies, improved education on sexuality, and a willingness to review basic theological doctrines about God, Christology, and ecclesiology. However, the decline in the size, coherence, and influence of the liberal churches has undermined its commitment to gender equality. As conservative caucuses have organized within all of the liberal denominations and fought for their "right" to use masculine language for God, to exclude women from church leadership, and to reject new thinking on sexuality—including that on abortion, sexual abuse, and homosexuality—liberal leadership has offered compromise and accepted a moratorium on the discussion of controversial "social issues." Increases in sexual harassment, abuse complaints without effective response, and "glass ceilings" that limit women's power to small areas of church life also represent a lack of support for women's issues. The liberal churches seem on the brink of betraying their support for the issues of importance to women and thus losing many of the gains that have been made.[16]

Carter Heyward writes in response to the challenges that White feminist theologians face in church and society today:

> I understand our work as feminist theologians to be that of explorers, diggers, artists, re-formers. . . . We are coming to realize that God is present, acting, moving, creating, here and now among us—revealing Godself to us, compelling us to act and speak, to live and sooner or later to die, on the basis of God, just as surely as God is living and acting among those who penned, compiled, and canonized holy scripture.[17]

BLACK WOMANIST THEOLOGY

In recent decades, Black women have emerged as a significant influence in society and in the larger church. Alice Walker, Toni Morrison, Maya Angelou, and Audre Lorde have written popular novels and poetry from the Black woman's perspective. Angela Davis, bell hooks, and other Black female intellectuals have written about the constructions of race, class, and gender that dominate the lives of Black women. The churches are more aware of the virtues Katie Cannon has attributed to Black women—"invisible dignity, quiet grace, and unshouted courage"[18]—because of centuries of survival and resistance to racist and sexist oppression.

Although Black men, taking center stage in the 1960s through promoting slogans of Black Power, influenced the White churches by direct confrontation, Black women also led. Rosa Parks and Fannie Lou Hamer were heroes of the early civil rights movement; Angela Davis and Ella Baker were key leaders of the Black Power movement.

Black womanist theology is a response to the creativity of Black women and an attempt to face the racism of White feminists and the sexism of Black male leaders. Jacquelyn Grant summarizes the origins of Black womanist theology:

> Black feminism grows out of Black women's tridimensional reality of race/sex/class. It holds that full human liberation cannot be achieved simply by the elimination of any one form of oppression. . . . It must be based upon a multi-dimensional analysis. Recent writings by secular Black feminists have challenged White feminist analysis and Black race analysis, particularly by introducing data from Black women's experience that has been historically ignored by White feminists and Black male liberationalists.[19]

However, since 1980, Black women have suffered economically as much or more than any ethnic group in the United States. Some studies indicate that two-fifths of Black children live in families with income under the poverty level. This translates, for Black mothers and their children, into substandard housing, inadequate health care, and troubled inner-city schools.

During this time of rising creativity and public leadership by Black women, what has the White church done? The backlash of the religious right has directed barely disguised racism against Black women. We have seen in the previous section how violent crime and drugs are often euphemisms for White fear of Black men. In a similar way, abortion, welfare, lack of "traditional family values," and sexual promiscuity are often euphemisms for White fear of Black women. White rage is directed against mythical Black women who are on welfare, don't care for their children, and use abortion as birth control. Although many conservative religious leaders would deny it if confronted, these social constructions are appeals to what Patricia Hill Collins calls "controlling images" used against Black women: images of mammies, matriarchs, welfare mothers, and Jezebels.[20] For many religious conservatives, these images are threats to the so-called

Christian values including White, two-parent families with two children who go to church, work hard, and obey the law. The negative images of Black women in the White imagination have been effective in increasing the political influence of the religious right during a time of racist and sexist backlash.

Recent years have brought increased contact between Black women and liberal White women and men, with periods of cooperation and mutual mission. However, tensions have developed as Black women have spoken forthrightly about the long history of betrayal and oppression supported by progressive White churches. Soul-searching conversations have occurred between Black womanists and White feminists about the many ways that White women have ignored, trivialized, and tried to destroy the needs and desires of Black women. Out of this struggle have come some new forms of solidarity.[21]

However, as their leaders have focused on institutional survival, progressive churches have withdrawn from many forms of interracial cooperation. In trying to consolidate their power, most liberal churches compromised with conservative factions, allowing "controversial social issues" to be set aside. The result has been less attention to the life-and-death issues facing Black women and children in our society and a willingness to be distracted by debates about biblical authority, abortion, and world mission.

Delores Williams has written,

> The great hope of womanist theology is for Christians to come together and work in concert to alleviate the sin of devaluation and defilement threatening the lives and spirits of Black women as well as the life of the natural environment that sustains all life.[22]

RESISTANCE, BACKLASH, AND BETRAYAL

In our survey of recent history, we have uncovered a pattern of resistance by oppressed groups, liberal support, conservative backlash, and liberal betrayal. In the next section, we shall examine two contemporary situations that illustrate how the vacillation of liberals between their coalitions with resistance communities and with conservatives maintains racial and gender oppression. In each situation, when coalitions between resistance communities and liberals brought an important justice problem to the public arena for debate, some change usually occurred. However, in response to conservative backlash, liberals have betrayed these coalitions, resulting in significant damage to the cause of justice.

The White Debate about the Black Family[23]

In a 1990 speech to the Republican National Convention, President George Bush stated that the problem of poverty in the inner city is caused by the breakdown of the family, a conclusion that now seems to be accepted by both Democrats and Republicans. Serious attempts are being made to abolish welfare or to limit families to two years of support and to require mothers to work in order to receive welfare. Some politicians have even suggested that single mothers should be ineligible for welfare because of their sexual irresponsibility, and that only the threat of poverty will reverse the trend of increasing numbers of single mothers with children. Even though the Black resistance communities have their own critique of the welfare state and its racism, Black leaders are clear about the racist motives of the current debate. Racism and sexism compose the background for this discussion, although, as one would expect from any evil rhetoric, euphemism and claims to legitimacy mask the truth.[24]

Daniel P. Moynihan, author of *The Negro Family: The Case for National Action* (1965), established the terms of the debate about Black families, single women, and poverty.[25] His research provided an analysis of poverty that informed the federal government's programs for equal economic opportunity. Drawing on the research of E. Franklin Frazier on the history of the Black family, which suggested that the traumatic history of slavery and racism had created deviant family structures,[26] Moynihan concluded that the dysfunction of the Black family was a major cause of poverty in the Black community. According to his argument, because it was the slaveholders' practice to divide families as a way of maintaining control, to impregnate Black women, and to exclude Black men from family participation, a matriarchal pattern of family life emerged that put the Black family at a disadvantage in normal American culture.

> The Negro community has been forced into a matriarchal structure which, because it is out of line with the rest of the American society, seriously retards the progress of the group as a whole and imposes a crushing burden on the Negro male and, in consequence, on a great many Negro women as well.[27]

This statement is important for two reasons. First, Moynihan's analysis shifts the blame of poverty in the Black community from "the racial discrimination that produced unemployment, shoddy housing, inadequate education and substandard medical care"[28] to the family structures and behaviors of the Black community itself.[29] Instead of an environmentalism that traces problems to the socioeconomic realities, this analysis "blames the victims" for a deficient and deviant organization of family life.[30] The modern form of the old argument for Black inferiority can serve as either an environmental or genetic argument.[31]

Second, Moynihan's analysis assumes the validity of the patriarchal, male-dominant family as the norm against which all families should be measured, and then faults the Black family for its maladaptation. In effect, the report blames Black women for being too aggressive in their leadership of the family (for being too "matriarchal") and laments the plight of the Black men who are excluded from family leadership (with resulting trauma to self-esteem). These ideas have led to strange recommendations: a reordering of the Black family along traditional patriarchal lines, military service for Black men, and withdrawal of government programs, such as welfare and other family supports, to "encourage responsibility."

> The document (the Moynihan Report) had important strategic implications, for it attempted to justify the withdrawal of government measures that had been specifically designed to counter the racist edge of the social crisis that seemed destined to hurl the Black community into the throes of permanent impoverishment. . . . As far as government programs were concerned, those that directly intervened in Black family life were deemed most desirable. Once the Black family began to reflect the prevailing nuclear (male-supremist) model, problems such as unemployment and the decline in the quality of housing, education, and health care, would eventually be solved.[32]

Some of the worst policies to emerge from this analysis were implemented during the Reagan administration of 1981 through 1989. Extending the argument that the Black family was dysfunctional because it was matriarchal and that men had lost their rightful place as heads of families meant that welfare was a cause rather than a cure for Black poverty.

> [George Gilder argues] . . . "In the welfare culture money becomes not something earned by men through hard work, but a right conferred on women by the state. Protest and complaint replace diligence and discipline as the sources of pay. Boys grow up seeking support from women, while they find manhood in the macho circles of the street and the bar or in the irresponsible fathering of random progeny." Moreover, Gilder maintains AFDC "offers a guaranteed income to any child-raising couple in America that is willing to break up, or to any teenaged girl over sixteen who is willing to bear an illegitimate child."[33]

The fact of Black poverty was turned into the deception that government welfare programs create an artificial economy that is not subject to the values of free markets and male domination.

> Robert B. Carlson, Reagan's advisor for social policy development, put forth similar arguments, holding existing government social programs responsible for the increasing number of single-parent, female-centered households. Moreover, he asserted that the main problem is the failure in the Black community to form families at all.[34]

This ideological approach to poverty among Black families has been convincing to both Democratic and Republican politicians, so that today "single-parent" families are euphemistically understood to mean sexually active single women, especially women of color, who violate the dominant sexual ethic of United States society.

One can see in this brief case study how historic ideas about race, gender, and sexuality come together to benefit the status quo. Thomas Jefferson's words sound strangely up-to-date in this context: "I advance it therefore as a suspicion only, that the Blacks, whether originally a distinct race, or made distinct by time and circumstances, are inferior to the whites in the endowments both of body and mind."[35] A perverse form of environmentalism has won the day by suggesting that past history has so distorted the values and family structure of African Americans that their inferiority can be taken for granted. This is racism as surely as it was in 1784, when Jefferson's *Notes on Virginia* was published. The connection of race and sexuality in the White mind is firmly established by the view that sexually active single women and men who "find manhood . . . in the irresponsible fathering of random progeny" are the real causes of poverty in Black families.

The social science research about White and Black families, single parents, and poverty is much more complex than the political rhetoric portrays. Even the definition of "single parent" is contested. With a 50 to 60% divorce rate among all marriages, a majority of all children now live in single-parent homes at some time in their lives. More never-married single White women are having children, but fewer never-married Black women are having children. Although a majority of children in poverty live in single-parent homes, most children in single-parent homes do not live in poverty. This means that the political rhetoric about race, gender, and economics serves certain political agendas without being connected with the realities of actual families struggling against discrimination.[36]

The attack on matriarchy as a form of family dysfunction assumes that the rightful place of women is in a submissive relationship to men within a nuclear family. When Cornel West suggests that racism and sexism are built into our language, he is referring, among other things, to the use of phrases like "single parent" to evoke a false image of a promiscuous African American single woman. When President Bush said in 1990 that the cause of poverty in the inner cities is the breakdown of the family, he was implicitly referring to 350 years of racism and sexism in United States history. And he did this because racism and sexism remain politically effective ideas for organizing White power and distracting public attention from economic and social problems.

> The hidden issue in this election [1994] is race. A Martian would not know it, since the word itself is almost never mentioned. But crime and welfare, taxes, and immigration, are often code words for "them." After all, in the popular imagination, it is not whites who have children out of wedlock, spend a lifetime on welfare and shoot up themselves with dope and the neighborhood with lead. It's "them."[37]

Just as the debate about "the Negro" served the White male interests of both slaveholders and abolitionists, so the debate today about single-parent families and crime serves the interests of White men in power.

Debates about Sexual Abuse

In response to the ferment of the civil rights movement in the 1960s, White women began to gather in "consciousness-raising groups" to talk about their experiences as women. As Hester Eisenstein puts it, "To raise one's consciousness was to become aware of knowledge one would have preferred to keep hidden or unconsciousness, of one's own subordination or oppression as a woman, and the impact that this had on one's life."[38] As women talked with one another within the safety of same-gender groups, stories about rape, sexual abuse, sexual harassment, and physical violence emerged as important themes. Crimes against women had been committed with nothing done about them. Suddenly, women's personal experiences took on political significance. Why were violent crimes against women considered less serious than similar crimes against men?

> Once spoken aloud, women's private experience could become the stuff of public campaigns. . . . First, the facts of individual oppression came to be perceived as political and social, that is, as the effects of forces operating in the society at large to perpetuate the subordination of women as a class. Second, these facts could then become elements of political organizing. They could become the substance of the politics of the women's movement.[39]

Feminist thought and organization thus created a base for political action to support women who were victims of sexual and physical abuse and exploitation. Survivors of child sexual abuse, battered women, rape victims, and others brought criminal and civil charges against the perpetrators of the violence against them. The Civil Rights Act of 1968, which made sex discrimination illegal, provided support for sexual harassment suits. Many judges and juries agreed with the women who brought charges about these violations and awarded damages to the survivors. Gradually, male violence against women became an issue of public moral debate.

Professional sexual abuse of women by doctors, therapists, and ministers was one of the issues identified during this time.[40] The following case study illustrates the growing resistance of women to professional abuse, as well as the debate and betrayal that occurred in response.

In her 1989 book, *Is Nothing Sacred? The Story of a Pastor, the Women He Sexually Abused, and the Congregation He Nearly Destroyed*,[41] Marie Fortune describes sexual abuse by a clergyman. It is an actual case study with names changed to protect the vulnerable.

In 1980, Peter Donovan, a thirty-six-year-old divorced pastor, was called to First Church of Newburg. Personally charismatic, an effective preacher, and a good administrator, Donovan provided energetic pastoral care. New members joined the church and new programs were initiated. The congregation seemed to be surging forward.

Joan Preston, a twenty-one-year-old single woman, started dating Peter Donovan soon after his arrival in town. They became serious very quickly, talking of marriage and becoming sexually involved. When Preston discovered that Donovan was also involved with another woman, Jackie Randell, she broke off the relationship, feeling hurt and rejected.

After her husband died, Marian Murray went to Peter Donovan for counseling, seeking help for one of her children. In less than two weeks, he proposed that they go to bed together. When she hesitated, he said that "he would not suggest anything that was not for her well-being."[42] A few months later, discovering that Donovan was also involved with Joan Preston, Marian Murray ended their sexual relationship.

Donovan asked Kristin Stone, a twenty-one-year-old college student, to be the volunteer leader of an after-school children's program. Six months later, she went to him to talk about her feelings about the death from cancer of a former dance teacher. During the session, Donovan forced her onto the floor and raped her. It was "her first experience of genital sexual contact."[43] Over several months, he raped her two more times before she told him she didn't want to see him again. But she told no one about her experience.

Katie Simpson, a young pastor in the area, saw Donovan at various ministerial functions. Several times he proposed a sexual relationship to her, then attempted to rape her in his office. After fighting him off and escaping, she told her husband, "The pastor at Newburg jumped me in his office today."[44] She did not use the term "attempted rape" and wasn't sure what she had experienced.

Eventually, the six women found each other, began talking about what they had experienced, and decided to do something. The exact number of women whom Donovan abused is uncertain, but it may have been as high as forty-five during his four-year tenure as pastor.[45]

The women who brought complaints differed from each other—married, single, younger, older, professional, volunteer—but they shared one thing in common: they had all had abusive and exploitative experiences with Donovan. They were each strong enough to end their relationship with him in some way, and several had confronted him about his behavior toward other women. He had denied their charges, admitted mistakes that were in the past, threatened them with exposure if they didn't keep quiet, and ignored their pleas to stop. Nothing they had done made any difference in his behavior.

Several of the women went to Dan Lawson, president of the church council, and waited for something to be done. It was obvious to the women that Donovan should be forced to resign, and they believed that Lawson was a good person who would protect the church and women. But after several months, they received a vaguely worded letter saying that the charges were unfounded or hard to prove, that Donovan was in therapy, and that everything was taken care of. Donovan had controlled the interpretation of what had happened, assured Dan Lawson and other church leaders that nothing serious was going on, and continued his behavior. Lawson had apparently accepted Donovan's deception that a single, attractive pastor often was a victim of the desires of troubled women.

Finally deciding to act as a group, the six women went to the District leaders in the governing body that held Donovan's ordination. Marie Fortune was called in as pastor and advocate for the women. Initially, the District leaders pledged to do something quickly and effectively, but they had no policies or procedures and no experience with such a situation. Its members tried to negotiate with Donovan, pressuring him to resign and spare the congregation and the district a major scandal. He used the same techniques he had used with congregational leaders—stalling, promising to do better, denying that anything had happened, blaming the women, and threatening to sue or take the congregation out of the denomination. Through these methods he prolonged his stay.

Eventually, after the local paper published a version of what was happening, the congregation met and pressured Donovan to resign. He did resign, but only after the congregation promised that the record would be sealed. Barred from taking another pastorate in the denomination, he nevertheless was allowed to keep his ordination. Because of the secrecy of the process and the lack of reliable information, the congregation itself became polarized between those who believed the women and those who maintained their loyalty to the pastor. The damaged relationships were not quickly healed.

During the last ten years, most denominations have adopted policies and procedures that deal explicitly with the sexual misconduct of clergy. However, because male dominance is so pervasive in United States churches, sexual abuse by clergy continues.

The analysis of Freud's case of Dora in chapter 2 provides guidance for understanding sexual abuse by clergy and why churches have so much difficulty dealing with it. We must see sexual abuse by clergy as an abuse of power based on the inequities of profession and gender. Freud could not see the violence of the other men in this story because he failed to understand his own abuse of Dora. Because he could not see women as agents, he could not identify with Dora's vulnerability in a patriarchal world, nor could he understand her resistance as a form of active agency. Likewise, male clergy who sexually abuse women fail to understand male violence and women's resistance in a patriarchal culture and religion. By discussing these issues, we can learn how individuals, societies, and religions collude to create ideologies of evil such as male dominance, which make women vulnerable to acts of violence.

This discussion will be organized around two questions. First, why do men fail to see the sexual misconduct by clergy as an issue of male violence against women? Second, why do men fail to identify with the vulnerability and resistance of women? As we have learned from the previous discussion of Freud, the answers center on gender inequality as an intrinsic part of traditional theology and of the church's life.

Male church leaders at First Church in Newburg did not see Donovan's behavior as abuse of power, even though he had manipulated, lied to, and physically coerced some of the women into sexual intercourse. When Joan Preston first talked to Dan Lawson, president of the congregation, he was sympathetic, seemed to believe her, and said he would take care of the problem. But nothing happened. Seven months later, the women received the following letter from Mr. Lawson.

Suggestions that there have been pastoral indiscretions have led me to several months of investigation, and many hours of consideration of the courses of action available to me. I believe mistakes have been made, but that it is also apparent that there are many evidences of excellent leadership during that time. It may be that the mistakes, which, of course, cannot be corrected, are now behind us, and will not be repeated in the future. It must be said that some of the reports of indiscretions were not supported, or were based upon inaccurate information. Any further reports of unprofessional conduct should give the person involved the opportunity to meet with the dissatisfied party, before some kind of forum, with opportunity to respond to the charges. I believe that such a confrontation at this time would not result in any agreement, and would only be a traumatic experience for all involved. There is no question in my mind that the Church would be severely damaged. It is my opinion that we should take steps to prevent any future indiscretions, but that we should also recognize and encourage the positive leadership for the betterment of the church program. Professional counseling will be secured to identify and correct any faults which would tarnish such leadership.[46]

In this letter Donovan's violence toward and violations of women are hidden beneath euphemisms—"pastoral indiscretions," "mistakes," "unprofessional conduct," "faults which would tarnish such leadership." The abusive acts of Peter Donovan are not concretely identified and described. In fact, Peter Donovan as a perpetrator of abuse is not identified by name and only indirectly alluded to in the term "pastoral indiscretions." "Indiscretion" implies that one may have given an appearance of wrong whether one did anything wrong or not. A mistake is "an error or fault resulting from defective judgment, deficient knowledge, or carelessness."[47] All of these terms give a vague picture of what happened and characterize Donovan's behavior as a problem that, although unfortunate, certainly was not a crime or misconduct that should lead to job termination. Rather, these terms imply that the problems in Donovan's behavior are hard to understand and better left alone.

As a man, Dan Lawson identified with Peter Donovan; he felt threatened by the sexual powers of women, and tried to cover up what happened because otherwise "the church would be severely damaged." Why couldn't people see Donovan's behavior as acts of abuse and violence? Because the theologies of church have sexualized gender relationships as inherently conflictual, problematic, and violent. Male sexual violence against women is built into the church's theology and into the inequitable relationships between women and men, issues that will be discussed in greater detail in chapter 8.[48]

Likewise, the women disappeared in Dan Lawson's letter. Language such as "suggestions that there have been pastoral indiscretions," or "some of the reports of indiscretions were not supported, or were based upon inaccurate information," or "the dissatisfied party," hides the fact that there were real people who were hurt. But there is no clear statement such as, "Six women have brought serious charges of professional sexual misconduct against Peter Donovan that must be investigated and resolved so that the church can continue its ministry." Just as Freud was unable to see Dora as an active agent in her own life, Dan Lawson fails in this letter to identify with the women as persons who suffered abuse and who resisted that abuse by bringing complaints to the leaders of the church.[49]

In later chapters, we will explore the theological assumptions for the failure of the patriarchal imagination that lead to gender violence. For now, it is sufficient to see that Freud's attitudes toward Dora and her family are only possible within an ideology of male dominance, and that the same worldview produces sexual misconduct by clergy. Male dominance is an evil ideology that makes it difficult to see male sexual violence as an ethical problem and that makes the vulnerability and resistance of women "disappear."

In this chapter we have briefly reviewed themes in the contemporary historical situation to illustrate the pattern of resistance, backlash, and betrayal. Since the 1960s, African American women and men and European American women have resisted racial and gender evil in many ways, including political action and intellectual critique. Liberal Christians have engaged in coalitions that have helped to keep the moral claims of resistance groups in the public domain. However, conservative Christians have led the backlash against racial and gender justice, and in recent years liberal Christians have betrayed their coalitions in order to protect their institutions and professional status. In the next section, we shall turn to theological reflection on case studies and historical accounts in order to search for forms of faithful Christian response.

RESISTING EVIL
IN THE NAME
OF JESUS

CHAPTER SIX

UNDERSTANDING RESISTANCE TO EVIL

Resistance to evil is a form of liberated and critical consciousness that enables persons and groups to stand against evil in silence, language and action.[1]

Harriet Jacobs resisted evil by silence, by talking back, by hiding and escaping. Ida Bauer resisted evil by telling family secrets, disagreeing with Freud, and leaving therapy. Slaves sabotaged, revolted, and escaped. White women marched and spoke out. The women abused by Peter Donovan told the church's secret and pressed for justice. Black womanists have criticized the assumptions and policies of our government about and against Black families. Wherever there is evil, there will be resistance to it. Understanding resistance is crucial to demystifying racial and gender oppression.

THE DYNAMIC OF RESISTANCE AND EVIL

Often society attributes flaws and pathologies to oppressed groups and individuals. White women are blamed for their passivity in violent relationships with men ("Why doesn't she leave?"), and African American women are blamed for being too aggressive ("Welfare matriarchs destroy the self-esteem of their children.") According to Cheryl Townsend Gilkes, "Black women's assertiveness . . . [has] been a consistent, multifaceted threat to the status quo. As punishment, Black women have been assaulted with a variety of negative images."[2] I am suggesting we make a reversal in our usual understanding of power by emphasizing the hermeneutical priority of the oppressed and by questioning the legitimacy of dominant powers. I want to counter the way in which evil ideologies maintain their power in our personal and corporate spirituality.

Violence or the threat of violence is always an aspect of evil. Slavery and racial evil were and continue to be enforced by systematic and sustained violence directed against the people, and by deliberate attempts to destroy any semblance of support, community, or organized power.

> Black women did not willingly submit to their exhibition on southern auction blocks—they were forced to do so. Enslaved African women could not choose whether to work—they were beaten and often killed if they refused. Black domestics who resisted the sexual advances of their employers often found themselves looking for work where none was to be found. Both the reality and the threat of violence have acted as a form of social control for African-American women.[3]

Laws and customs backed by police and militia have enforced subordination and oppression of White women. Elizabeth Cady Stanton demanded that legislatures abolish "such disgraceful laws as give man the power to chastise and imprison his wife, to take the wages which she earns, the property which she inherits, and in case of separation, the children of her love; laws which make her the mere dependent on his bounty."[4]

Oppression tries to stifle people's ability to resist systematic evil. Therefore, those who would resist must construct a double consciousness that attends not only to their own human needs and desires, but also to the danger that is poised to destroy their resistance.

> "In order to survive, those of us for whom oppression is as American as apple pie have always had to be watchers . . ." [Audre Lorde]. This "watching" generates a dual consciousness in African-American women, one in which Black women "become familiar with the language and manners of the oppressor, even sometimes adopting them for some illusion of protection" [Audre Lorde] while hiding a self-defined standpoint from the prying eyes of the dominant groups. . . . Behind the mask of behavioral conformity imposed on African-American women, acts of resistance, both organized and anonymous, have long existed.[5]

We can best understand resistance within the context of the extreme evil of violence and death. By studying extreme situations, we can begin to see the more subtle forms of domination that control and distort everyday life. Ellen Wondra summarizes one definition of resistance developed by Emil Fackenheim as a response to his reflections on the Jewish Holocaust.

> Within this world *in extremis*, resistance is properly defined as "the maintenance by the victims of a shred of humanity." To retain, to recreate a

shred of humanity in the midst of the radical, systemic dehumanization of the Holocaust world is itself an act of resistance by those who felt themselves "under orders to live" in the midst of confronting the overwhelming horror which entrapped them. Such resistance is an Ultimate beyond will or nature; it is a way of being indistinguishable from life itself.[6]

During the Holocaust, in which the coercive power of the government itself was aimed at the physical extermination of a people, the forms of resistance to this evil were "the maintenance by the victims of a shred of humanity." We can best understand the massive evil perpetrated by the Nazis by studying their victims' efforts to survive and maintain their humanity. Likewise, we can understand the evils of racism and sexism by studying the victims' efforts to survive and maintain their humanity.

Within African American women's communities, resistance has taken the form of survival and activism. The will to survive is a form of resistance against evil violence that attempts to dehumanize and even destroy the victims' lives.

> The struggle for group survival is the first dimension. Consisting of actions taken to create Black female spheres of influence within existing structures of oppression, this dimension does not directly challenge oppressive structures because, in many cases, direct confrontation is neither preferred nor possible. Instead, women engaged in creating Black female spheres of influence indirectly resist oppressive structures by undermining them.[7]

At other times, whenever possible, oppressed groups engage in active opposition to evil.

> The second dimension of Black women's activism consists of the struggle for institutional transformation—namely those efforts to change existing structures of oppression. All individual and group actions that directly challenge the legal and customary rules governing African-American women's subordination can be seen as part of the struggle for institutional transformation. Participating in civil rights organizations, labor unions, feminist groups, boycotts, and revolts exemplify this dimension of the Black women's activist tradition.[8]

The form resistance takes depends largely on the nature of the domination. In certain periods—for example, during the southern White violence of 1877, after the northern White betrayal of African Americans—survival was often the only possible goal of resistance. In other periods—for example, during the civil rights movement of the 1960s—African Americans organized nonviolent resistance for institutional change. The kind of resistance depends on the kind of domination.

THE NATURE OF RESISTANCE

Resistance to evil is a form of liberated and critical consciousness that enables persons and groups to stand against evil in silence, language, and action.[9]

Patricia Hill Collins identifies the resistance of African American women as arising from "a distinctive, collective Black women's consciousness":

Black women intellectuals have long explored this private, hidden space of Black women's consciousness, the "inside" ideas that allow Black women to cope with and, in most cases, transcend the confines of race, class and gender oppression.[10]

A consciousness that supports survival and activism requires liberated and critical perspectives, that is, resisting the dominant ideology's pressure to internalize oppression.

A system of oppression draws much of its strength from the acquiescence of its victims, who have accepted the dominant image of themselves and are paralyzed by a sense of helplessness.[11]

Such a consciousness must be collective, that is, it must be rooted in a community of dialogue, empathy, and mutual empowerment.[12] Mutual support creates a perspective that liberates the consciousness of the oppressed and provides a basis for criticizing of evil ideologies and institutions.

Resistance takes the forms of silence, language, and action. "Silence is not be to interpreted as submission."[13] In situations of evil oppression,

To be silent is to refuse to speak when evil cannot be spoken about without perpetuating it.
To be silent is to refuse words that have no power.
To be silent is to be angry without gestures.
To be silent is to be sad without tears.
To be silent is to join the eternal silence of God when evil cannot be defeated by words.

> I am silent concerning the evil that has invaded my life, so that when I speak, my words will be swords of truth that cut through the conspiracy of silence.[14]

Silence does not consent to evil, although it is often interpreted that way by dominant powers. Often it points to the presence of threats of spiritual and/or physical violence. Therefore, silence can be a form of resistance.

However, Audre Lorde challenges those who are silent to be self-critical, and thus provides insight into "the transformation of silence into language and action," the title of an essay in Lorde's *Sister Outsider*.[15]

> In the cause of silence, each of us draws the face of her own fear—fear of contempt, of censure, or some judgment, or recognition, of challenge, of annihilation. . . . For to survive in the mouth of this dragon we call america, we have had to learn this first and most vital lesson—that we were never meant to survive. Not as human beings. . . . Because this machine will try to grind you into dust anyway, whether or not we speak. . . . We can sit in our safe corners mute as bottles, and we will still be no less afraid.[16]

Shawn Copeland reminds us of the terrible suffering that results from organized and systematic evil and the powerful forms of faith and resistance that can emerge from the struggle.

> Suffering always means pain, disruption, separation, and incompleteness. It can render us powerless and mute, push us to the borders of hopelessness and despair. Suffering can maim, wither, and cripple the heart; or, to quote Howard Thurman, it can be a "spear of frustration transformed into a shaft of light."[17]

This definition of resistance to evil thus leads to a definition of domination. The following has been adapted from the work of The Cornwall Collective and from Patricia Hill Collins:

> The "matrix of domination" is a "system of attitudes, behaviors and assumptions that objectifies human persons on the basis of [socially constructed categories such as race, gender, class, etc.], and that has the power to deny autonomy, access to resources, and self-determination to those persons, while maintaining the values of the dominant society as the norm by which all else will be measured."[18]

I use this definition with its adaptation because it identifies the personal dimension of evil ("attitudes, behaviors and assumptions"), the social location of evil ("the power to deny autonomy, access to resources and self-determination"), and the propensity of evil to reductively project its own normative definitions onto all Others ("the norm by which all else will be measured").

In chapters 1 and 2, I used the structure of this definition to understand the forms of domination in the stories of Harriet Jacobs and Ida Bauer. The evil in their lives was possible because persons in power, through their attitudes, behaviors, and assumptions, objectified these women on the basis of race and gender. James Norcom and Sigmund Freud had the power to deny autonomy, access to resources, and self-determination to them, and chose to do so. Jacobs and Bauer struggled to survive in a context in which the values of the dominant society were unquestioningly accepted as the norms by which all else was to be measured. As a result, Jacobs and Bauer experienced violence and suffered the loss of potential love and work that God might have called them to. The matrix of domination functioned as an evil force in their lives.

PERSONAL REFLECTIONS

Since I am personally implicated in racial and gender evil because I am White, male, and middle class in the United States, a key question is whether my own consciousness can be liberated and criticized so that I can stand against the evil of my social class in silence, language, and action. By social location, I am a member of multiple dominant groups, for which I need to be held accountable and around which I need to engage in active resistance. I have inherited a moral responsibility for centuries of oppression that continues to be perpetrated by those of my race, class, and gender. I believe it is possible to defect, in part, from conscious moral support of these systems of domination.[19] I am supported by Patricia Hill Collins's insight that the dialectic of resistance and domination is complex. Resistance is not easy for anyone, and solidarity among groups of many social locations is necessary for real change.[20]

At the same time, structures of evil have damaged significant parts of my experience. My relational capacities, my sensitivities and empathies, my sexuality—these aspects of myself have been devalued as my commitments and work are coopted for the benefit of systems. Suffering is a part of my experience, even though its deeper causes have been hidden from my awareness for most of my life. I believe that as I work on both aspects of my life—my moral culpability as a member of a dominant class, and my suffering as one who is oppressed by evil systems—I can come to new forms of forgiveness, healing, and shared action for justice. I can be a part of the communities of resistance in my own life, and thus defect from some of the ways I participate in evil.

I believe that strengthening the coalitions of liberal Christians with communities of resistance is important for the cause of racial and gender justice. When liberals act in solidarity with oppressed groups who have moral claims against the dominant social classes, they also fulfill their own principles of freedom and equality. Developing an analysis of resistance to evil provides the hermeneutical perspective from which we can begin to define evil—our task for the next chapter.

DEFINING EVIL

Genuine evil is the abuse of power that destroys bodies and spirits; evil is produced by personal actions and intentions which are denied and disso-ciated by individuals; evil is organized by economic forces, institutions and ideologies, but mystified by appeals to necessity and truth; evil is sanc-tioned by religion, but masked by claims to virtue, love, and justice.[1]

Discussion of evil is a problem for many Christians because it sounds like an ultimate judgment of persons and groups. We would rather educate and encourage individuals than threaten them with hell for origi-nal and individual sin. We would rather reform social and political systems than condemn them as irredeemable. We would rather form ecumenical councils for religious dialogue than define fundamental doctrines that separate false and true religions. The Christian spirit often abhors the judgment involved in calling something evil.

At the same time, our openness to God's future has strong roots in the prophetic tradition of Jesus and the Hebrew prophets. Favorite scriptures exemplifying this tradition include Matthew 25 (doing justice to the oppressed and separating the sheep from the goats); Luke 10 (the Good Samaritan and the evil religious leaders); Matthew 2 (Mary's Magnificat—how the poor will be raised up and the rich brought down); Luke 4 (the year of Jubilee, when society's oppressed will be freed); Jeremiah 31 (having a new heart for God's justice); Amos 5 (justice rolling over the country like a river). These scriptures have inspired church programs for social action that depend on firm judgments about the evils of society and the evil behaviors of individuals.

However, many Christians have not reconciled their openness to God's future and their implicit judgments about evil in the world. One way this tension has been handled is to separate social and personal evil, as Reinhold Niebuhr did in *Moral Man and Immoral Society*. He assumed that human beings are likely to be compassionate in interpersonal relationships, but he believed that people in large groups such as government bureaucracies and capitalistic businesses are willing to follow policies detached from human values, even when these policies cause enormous suffering.[2] A favorite folk saying has been, "I hate the sin, but I love the sinner."

In recent decades, liberation, African American, and feminist theologians have criticized Christian churches for underestimating the depth of evils such as racial, gender, and class oppression—for example, the amount of institutional racism present in employment and education, or the amount of physical and sexual abuse that occurs against women in families. They have criticized the churches for being too optimistic about progress in situations of massive poverty. Many Christians have an underdeveloped understanding of personal, social, and religious evil. In this chapter, I join with the many writers who have recently addressed the problem of evil in Christian theology.[3]

THE HIDDENNESS OF EVIL

Whenever evil is the subject of discussion, its hiddenness creates an immediate problem. In his study of radical evil and sin, Ted Peters says, "Sin is not clear. It cannot be. No matter how much effort we invest, sin and its accompanying evil will remain unexplainable. Why? Because of the lie. Because of the deceit. Inherent in sin is the denial of the truth."[4] Evil survives because of the lie.

In my earlier work, I discussed evil in this way: "Social injustice and individual abuse of power are evil. They harm the power of life itself within the relational web. Power so used stifles the possibility of mutuality and interdependence. Abuse of power not only is destructive to individuals, it also is destructive to the web of relationships on which all life depends. [Evil] is denial of communion and denial of freedom for self, others and God."[5]

In these sentences, I was struggling to understand discrete examples of evil in which the more powerful damaged or diminished vulnerable individuals, and I also wanted to understand the structures of society that create the conditions within which groups of persons are vulnerable to violation. Both situations exemplify the abuse of power. The parent who beats his or her child is committing an evil act, and the social institutions of family, church, school, law, and so on that fail to protect the child from such violence are engaged in evil. Thus there is both a personal and a social dimension to evil; both dimensions must be explored and understood before justice can be done.

Since writing the earlier book, my thinking has changed. Research has led me to understand evil not only as the discrete result of individual and social behaviors, but also as a complex web of power and violence that is carefully constructed over a long period of time and maintained through the actions and intentions of many individuals and groups. Evil is more than the impulsive and largely unconscious action of individuals, or unintended flaws in institutions and ideologies. Evil has a personal and social history and existence. Evil is systemic and organized at every level of human life, including the religious level.

GENUINE EVIL

I have borrowed the term "genuine evil" from David Griffin and others who argue that certain kinds of losses cannot be explained away by appealing to the limits of human understanding.

> The issue then becomes whether the reality of such evil should be affirmed. That is, should we affirm that some things happen which really do not "turn out for the best"? Do events occur without which the universe would have been a better place, all things considered?[6]

Evil is something other than the good that appears evil, or the suffering that good sometimes requires. In the Hebrew scriptures, Job's friends argued that he falsely perceived evil because of his sin and pride. If Job could see from God's perspective, his friends argued, what appeared evil to him would have a good purpose, and suffering that seemed evil would turn out to have good consequences. Job refused to give up his idea that he had suffered evil or his idea that God existed. The writer of Job leads us to struggle with the contradiction between God and evil. Theologians have long debated the question of theodicy, namely whether evil can exist if God is good and whether God can exist if evil is real. Some theologians argue that evil is not real because God is all-powerful and all-loving. Some philosophers argue that the profound reality of evil proves that God does not exist. This theological discussion is important, and will inform our exploration at several points.[7]

However, as a practical theologian, I start first with human experience rather than with logical argument. Along with Job, I believe in genuine evil, because I know of children who have been killed by their parents, of adult survivors of sexual abuse who died after many years of drug addiction, of Black and White women murdered by a psychopath while they were being prostituted. I believe there is genuine evil in the world because I have seen it with my own eyes, and because I have experienced it in my own life. Part of my quest to understand evil comes from a religious intuition that genuine evil, which is not adequately explained by much Christian theology, exists. The violation and destruction to the human body and spirit that leads to loss for which there is no adequate justification or larger purpose is evil.[8] And I also believe in God, for whom evil is a practical problem because it opposes creativity and value.

Several factors lead to everyday confusion about the nature of evil. First, persons with power refuse to acknowledge the evil they have done, and effectively disguise their evil behavior as necessary and/or benevolent. For example, abusive parents frequently argue that their violence is for the child's own good. Second, good sometimes appears to be evil. For example, the rebellion of a child can seem dangerous to a possessive parent, but actually provides the potential for transformation of the parent-child relationship. Third, actualizing values sometimes requires suffering, which may seem evil. Although suffering itself is not good, the consequences may be worth the chosen suffering. For example, Marie Fortune distinguishes between involuntary and voluntary suffering. Involuntary suffering such as that inflicted by child abuse serves no useful purpose and cannot be justified. Voluntary suffering, such as that involved in acts of civil disobedience for a just cause, may lead to suffering that is not desired, but that some persons choose to endure for a larger purpose.[9]

Evil is also confusing because it is usually taboo to identify evil in an immediate situation. We know that evil exists, but usually it exists "over there" in someone else, or "back there" in the past. Perhaps we fear being moralistic and judgmental and therefore wrong, or perhaps we lack a language for discussing evil in everyday terms. Evil always involves deception and lies that mystify and hide the truth. When children and women suffer injustice, community leaders often deny that the institutions and customs are evil. They tend to explain such events as unique, unfortunate, and unrelated to the particular situation. The community needs a language in which to speak of evil that is not narrowly moralistic and bigoted, so we can identify and debate the existence of evil in everyday life. As I will suggest later, perhaps religion can help people acknowledge the ambiguity of good and evil in themselves, and abandon the myth of personal innocence that so often serves as a defense against responsibility for human actions.[10]

EVIL AS THE ABUSE OF POWER
THAT DESTROYS BODIES AND SPIRITS

In my previous work, I defined the good in this way: "Loving power un-distorted by evil in human experience is interaction characterized by sensitivity which moves toward communion with self, others, and God and by creativity which moves toward enlarged freedom for self, others and God."[11] Loving power is characterized by sensitivity, the ability to internalize our relationships with others, and give value to the interconnectedness of the relational web. Loving power is also characterized by creativity or the ability to contribute value to other persons and to the relational web itself.[12] The constant rhythm of internalizing value from others and contributing value to others creates the relational web. Loving power seeks to enhance relationships with particular others and to enlarge the quality of life of the relational web, including the experience of God.

However, the rhythm of sensitivity and creativity in human interaction and the interconnectedness of the relational web also create the possibility of genuine evil.

> Sin is the denial of loving sensitivity, the turning away from communion with self, others, and God. Sin is the willful decision of the individual to value down the relational aspects of life with its consequences of smaller size for all individuals and the totality of the world. . . .
>
> Sin is the denial of loving creativity, the rejection of enlarged freedom for self, others and God. Sin is the willful decision of the individual to value down the freedom of life with its consequences of smaller size for all individuals and God.[13]

In terms of this discussion, decisions to deny loving sensitivity and loving creativity are abuses of power, and the consequence is destruction of bodies and spirits. God has given us personal and social power for the purposes of enhancing value for individuals and for the relational web. When this power is instead used for destruction to individuals and to the relational web itself, those actions are evil.[14]

Evil is holistic, that is, it affects the total experience of persons and communities. I have tried to capture this totality by the phrase "bodies and spirits."

Understanding evil as an abuse of power that is destructive to the physical bodies of persons is particularly important because of the relationship of violence and evil. Violence is a form of evil, although not all evil is physically violent. Much evil has direct impact on the physical body—hunger, lack of resources during illness, injury from war, physical and sexual abuse, torture and murder, and more. Both racial and gender oppression abuse the body.

In the construction of racial oppression, White theologians chose black skin as the focus on inferiority that included the whole person. Benjamin Rush decided to understand black skin as a disease that should be medically treated until Blacks were white, just like Europeans. Thomas Jefferson's racism focused on sexuality and racial intermixture. Riggins Earl analyzes the theological roots of the White supremist ideas of the black body.

> Ideal Christian-type masters believed that the souls of slaves satisfied the norm of biblical anthropology, but at the same time had ambiguous concerns about whether the slave's body, because of its blackness, met these same norms. . . . Whites readily concluded that the dilemma of the external blackness of slaves' bodies gave them the right to be God's viceroys of slaves' souls and ultimately the rulers of their bodies on earth. It was conceded that while the blood of Jesus could not change the blackness of the slave's body, it would transform the status of the slave's soul.[15]

We must recall the story of Harriet Jacobs and other slave narratives in order to understand the impact of this theological construction. Separating the soul and the body and deciding that black bodies could not be redeemed by Jesus' blood resulted in the mistreatment of African Americans—violence justified by the theologians of that time. This abuse of power destroyed people's bodies.

In an analogous way, a theology of male dominance devalues the female body. In her study "Religious Imagination and the Body," Paula Cooey focuses on state torture in Latin America, especially as it is directed toward women. She concludes that the human body must be understood as a "testing ground for values in struggles for power." That is, whoever controls the definitions of the body in a culture also determines its values and its power arrangements. Throughout history, patriarchal culture has controlled the definitions of the female body, with massive violence as a consequence: rape, murder, and sexual and physical abuse. Thus, to stop the violence, we must reconstruct the definitions of the gendered bodies of men and women. Cooey has chosen to use the term "body" in her study, even though it is problematic. She rejected the terms "physicality" and "embodiment" because they seemed to reinforce jargon and dualism, which she wanted to avoid. "Body" most adequately picks up the multiplicity of meanings necessary for an adequate study of how male dominance has distorted female bodies.[16]

I have chosen the word "spirit" to refer to the personal energy of individuals in their relationships with others. Daniel Day Williams discusses the relationship of body and spirit in the following way:

> The guiding conception which informs our understanding of all love is that love is spirit taking form in history. Love is an expression of spirit. It is spirit seeking the enjoyment of freedom in communion with the other. Spirit is the best word we have to indicate the concrete personal expression of living creative beings. God is spirit. [Human beings], created in God's image, [have] spiritual existence, not as something added to [their] bodily substance, but as the expression of that concrete *body-mind unity* which [they are as persons.] The freedom of spirit is the freedom of God as the ultimate form-giving and life-giving reality. The freedom of [human beings] is also the freedom of spirit, but within the conditions of finite existence.[17] (Emphasis added; text changed to reflect inclusive language)

The term "body-mind unity" describes an incarnational view of human and divine life. Jesus was the incarnation of God who could not be divided into two substances, divine and human. Rather, God was in Christ as both human and divine, the embodiment of God's love for all creation.[18] "Body" points to the importance of one's physical location in a particular body with particular relationships. "Spirit" clarifies the relationship of the Holy Spirit or energy of God with the particular energy of spirit in individuals and groups. Spirit is the image of God in persons and communities as freedom seeking communion. Spirit is the totality of a person or community as an expression of God.

Bernard Meland defines spirit as the goodness of relationships in human life.

> Spirit connotes a depth of sensitivity that forms the matrix of relations in which all life is cast. This depth of sensitivity is not so much known as lived in. It is a kind of womb or matrix out of which the waking life of individual persons emerges and in which individuals participate, knowingly or unknowingly, as living creatures. We may say that spirit is a quality of being which arises out of a particular depth of sensitivity in relations. It is, in other words, a goodness in relationships.[19]

"Spirit" is a word for the relational web that includes the particularity of individual persons in all aspects of their existence and also includes all the relationships within which individuals live and move and have their being. Spirit is a word for the relationality that connects individuals, communities, and God in one interconnected web of interaction and value.

My use of body and spirit is very similar to definitions of "experience" found in feminist theory. Ellen Wondra summarizes the feminist epistemology of Teresa de Lauretis:

> [Human] subjectivity is constituted "by one's personal, subjective engagement in the practices, discourses, and institutions that lend significance (value, meaning, and affect) to the events of the world." Experience is then defined as "a complex of habits resulting from the semiotic interaction of 'outer world' and 'inner world', the continuous engagement of self or subject in social reality." The human subject is thus understood to be socially and historically constituted, and human consciousness develops and changes within the limits of historical identity and concrete situation.[20]

"Bodies and spirits" refers to the personal, social, and religious dimensions of historically and socially constructed consciousness found in individuals and groups, and which also refers to the consciousness of all, which is sometimes called God.[21]

The phrase "destructive to bodies and spirits" describes the abuse of power that diminishes the sensitivity and creativity of individuals and groups. I want to offer at least two caveats concerning what destruction does not mean.

First, this phrase points to the fact that not all destruction is evil. There is "a time to be born, and a time to die . . . a time to kill, and a time to heal; a time to break down, a time to build up" (Eccles. 3:1,3). Life has its rhythms and transitions, its beginnings and endings, which involve adjustment and difficulty. Such transitions may even create occasions for evil, just as life itself creates occasions for evil. But the destruction of form is not itself evil.[22] For example, when a person moves from adolescence to young adulthood, dramatic changes in the person and the family are required, and these changes involve some loss of what has existed. But such loss is necessary in order for the young adult to achieve an education, to serve the community, and to form other intimate relationships. Also, some systems deserve to be destroyed because they have become centers of chronically evil patterns. A community must engage in a complex evaluation of whether a particular pattern of events constitutes destruction of spirit. In our definition of evil, we must not use destructiveness per se in an essentialist way in our definition of evil.

A second caution to recall when using the phrase "destructive to bodies and spirits" is that setting limits and boundaries in relationships is not in itself evil. In other words, love does not require an uncritical and naive openness to all aspects of all relationships. In fact, love requires decisions about value and integrity. In process thought, it can be loving to "exclude data from feeling" by way of "negative prehension;"[23] for example, to set limits on relationships that have destructive potential. Such decisions can actually decrease the amount of evil in the world. A decision to devalue some aspects of an abusive relationship is not evil, because it protects the self, challenges the other to growth, and creates the possibility of more loving relationships in the future. It is important that we not confuse the "appreciative awareness"[24] of the relational web with a naive openness to relationships regardless of their quality.

> [The human] spirit is subject to the distortions, estrangements and perversity of its finite freedom. Thus we use the term spirit for many kinds of human expression. We speak of a mean spirit, a prideful spirit, an artistic spirit, a courageous spirit, a perverse spirit. [The human] spirit can express love or the opposite of love.[25]

Evil is persistent. There is no "end of evil"[26] within human life as we know it. Whenever creative good emerges and survives, potential evil also emerges. Bernard Loomer has perceptively interpreted Reinhold Niebuhr on this point:

> [Niebuhr's] insight that every advance in goodness brings with it the possibility of greater evil entails the caveat that there is no progressive conquest of evil. On the contrary, the forms of destruction or diminution take on a character and a strength that are proportional to the character and strength of the advance. In this fashion every creative advance may give rise to its contrary or to some condition that either negates or qualifies the advance.[27]

For example, the rise of the western, bureaucratic, industrial nation-state created the potential good that every citizen could receive adequate food, health care, and education. But when Germany committed itself to exterminating the Jewish people and other perceived enemies, institutional power that could have been used for good turned into a death machine.

As Loomer reminds us, evil is not a foreign force outside the life of bodies and spirits, but arises from life itself. Evil is life turned against itself, organized into historic patterns and institutional forms that seem to have their own lives, even though they arise from the same spirit. Bernard Meland summarizes this point well.

> Human evil is the dissolute and destructive turn of events which arises from human nature itself and from the accumulative results of human behavior. What [human beings are and do create] conditions in existence which are not only destructive of good and of the creative intent, but productive of

rival forces that turn power and structure into aggressive agents of evil doing.[28]

THE STRUCTURE OF EVIL

Based on the foundational insight that evil is destructive to bodies and spirits, we now turn to a discussion of three levels of interlocking systems necessary for genuine evil to be fully actualized—personal, social, and religious evil. Understanding each of these three complex systems requires attention to how evil is organized and maintained, and how its existence is hidden so resistance to it can be defeated.

Evil always has a double character—its existence and its hiddenness. Since evil has no other source of power than the power of life and love, its existence is parasitic. It is essentially a perversion of spirit and not an independent spirit of opposition. This characteristic has led some theologians, such as Karl Barth, Paul Tillich, and others, to the conclusion that evil has no being and is therefore non-being.[29] Although there is truth in this analysis, it gives a false impression that evil is not real. The power of spirit is not dualistic, that is, there are not good and evil spirits at the level of metaphysical principles. In this sense, Tillich and Barth are correct in defining evil as non-being. Rather, the power of spirit itself is ambiguous and has potential for both good and evil. Evil is destructive to bodies and spirits; it is a form of spirituality that is real and powerful because of the commitment of persons, economic forces, institutions, ideologies, and religions to the existence of evil. Rather than debate evil, we will discuss how it organizes and maintains itself, and how it remains hidden and legitimate in the eyes of other powers and principalities.

Evil is a chameleon that maintains itself by remaining intertwined with the good and masking itself as good.[30] Judging the nature of a particular ambiguous situation (whether the amount of evil is so great that a system should be destroyed, or whether good and evil are so intertwined that destruction of evil would necessarily entail too much destruction of the good, or whether the amount of evil is trivial in comparison to the amount of good) is one of the most difficult ethical tasks of the church and of individuals. It is important to realize that the ambiguity of value and the deviousness of evil do not exempt persons and communities from analyzing and evaluating it in their lives. This project assumes that genuine evil is real, that it is organized and powerful, that it is destructive to bodies and spirits, and that it is always hidden under some claim to goodness and legitimacy.

Personal Evil

Evil is produced by personal actions and intentions that are denied and dissociated by individuals.

The issue of personal actions and intentions has been one of the most difficult aspects of my study of evil. Because of my formation in the liberal, progressive tradition, I am more comfortable locating evil in social institutions and ideologies and have often excused individuals from the same level of responsibility. I believed there were few people who were intent to do evil. In 1980, I defined sin as "the willful decision of an individual" to devalue the relational and creative aspects of human life for self, other, and God.[31] I believed that the decision to participate in evil was active and/or intentional. However, my understanding of personal actions and intentions has changed. The issue of personal responsibility for evil hinges on what we mean by actions and intentions and by the distinction between conscious and unconscious personal intentionality.

That evil requires personal action seems obvious at first, especially if we focus on violence as a defining moment in our understanding of evil. For a child to be physically or emotionally abused, someone has to act. The action can be a direct one—such as hitting, which we call physical abuse—or it can be a pattern of actions such as restricting a child to her room instead of going to school, thus depriving her of resources she needs to develop, which we call emotional abuse. The action can be neglect, as when an alcoholic parent abandons three preschool children for five days during a binge; we also call this deprivation. It can even be a parent's refusal or inability to get medical treatment for depression, which undermines the bonding a child needs. All of these forms of abuse and neglect against children require personal actions by adults. We may disagree about the level of conscious intentionality in various decisions, but most people would agree that personal actions are required.

However, evil actions can also take the form of systematic violence through political decisions about policies. For example, the government may require that, to receive her check, a mother on welfare work twenty hours a week as a volunteer doing office work. If something prevents her from fulfilling this requirement, the social worker may not be able to give her money. In this scenario, no clear individual actions and intentions are causing evil. We have to move from an individualistic analysis of actions and intentions to the realization that every personal decision occurs within a web of decisions that have good and evil consequences. In a situation of physical violence, we can see that evil would be diminished if the perpetrator ceased the violence, so an analysis of individual actions and intentions seems adequate. In situations of systematic violence, however, it is harder to see the role of personal actions because of the complexity of the web of decisions. To deprive a parent of financial support for a family, many people must make decisions, making it impossible to trace the cause of the injustice to a single decision.[32]

However, in order to exist, individual and systemic evil depend on personal actions. In a situation of interpersonal violence, one person must decide to engage in the physical abuse of another. In a situation that deprives a parent of financial support, many people must help design and maintain the system. Although no individual can easily change the system, evil systems are more difficult to maintain when many people resist them. Thus, it is fair to say that every instance and system of evil requires personal actions to make it work.[33]

Philosophers and theologians have long debated the nature of the will, that is, whether people are free to choose good and evil. Part of the tradition has suggested that because of original sin, the will can do nothing but evil. Eighteenth-century philosophy suggested, however, that the will could be enlightened by faith and reason and therefore could choose to create good instead of evil. Challenging the traditional authority of the church and of the empires of the past, the Enlightenment view opened a new faith in the authority of the individual conscience. Its emphasis on reason as a reliable aspect of will, however, has led to overconfidence in the conscious mind and its reasonable processes, and to the view that, for the individual to be guilty of sin, the conscious decision to commit an act accepted as evil is necessary. Otherwise, the individual is merely the object of social and historical forces for which he or she cannot be held responsible. Such rationalization is a standard defense given by those of power and privilege. The way to change an evil situation, according to the Enlightenment view, is not to convict individuals of sin, but to educate the public and engage in social action designed to change the institutions and ideologies that make evil possible.

This definition of the will, of course, articulates the classical position of liberal and progressive theologies. Conservatives, on the other hand, tend to believe that the corrupted will of the individual is the primary source of human sin and evil and that the road to change is individual conversion, repentance, justification, and sanctification. The debate between liberals, who believe that most evil is social, and conservatives, who believe that most evil is individual, has served to obscure the underlying reality, namely that evil can only exist when it is real both in individuals and in social structures.

Discussion since Freud, Marx, and other critical philosophers has moved the debate in new directions. Part of this debate changes our understanding of personal actions and intentions. "Habermas and the critical school of Frankfort have been leaders in showing how personal and social interest determines the knowledge that comes from analysis of experience."[34] Marx showed that individuals are embedded in economic interests that shape the language, assumptions, and ideas of persons and communities and justify the dehumanization of other groups that might threaten these interests. Elaborately constructed ideologies of social class serve to justify and legitimate these economic interests. Freud showed that individuals are influenced by sexual interests they deny. To preserve sexual access for those with the most privilege and power, strict definitions of gender, race, and class are maintained as structures of power.

Marx, Freud, and others showed that actions and intentions are both conscious and unconscious, both social and personal. Post-Enlightenment thought defines intentionality as the total force of an individual life, the telos or goal of personal decisions. Regardless of whether individuals can articulate all their economic, sexual, or other interests, an individual does construct a trajectory of decisions for which that person bears relative accountability. Intentionality or will is not just the rationalized intent of the conscious mind, but the drive of the whole person. This description of the conscious and unconscious mind has had a powerful influence on the modern imagination. Human beings repress their sexual and economic interests because their disclosure would create intrapsychic and social conflict and lead to a loss of social power.[35]

Let us examine a real case. George was a respected man in his community, an active and serious church leader and the father of five children, four of whom were adopted. I knew him after he was arrested for molesting his fourteen-year-old daughter. Remarkably, George had no conscious sexual interest in his daughter before, during, or after the incidents, which he confessed and for which he was convicted. This lack of awareness became a focus of his healing as he worked to discover the desires that led to such destructive behavior and that were so contradictory to his self-understanding. He reached a significant point in his therapy when he could identify his internal conflictual needs and impulses and begin to take some responsibility for his conscious and unconscious intentionality. He was personally responsible for molesting his daughter, even though he had no conscious desire to hurt or sexualize her.

Personal actions and intentions remain obscure partly because of the dynamic of denial and dissociation, two psychological (and spiritual) defenses identified by psychoanalytic theory.

> *Denial* may be manifested as a complete lack of concern, anxiety, or emotional reaction about an immediate, serious, pressing need, conflict, or danger in the patient's life, so that the patient calmly conveys his cognitive

awareness of the situation while denying its emotional implications. Or an entire area of the patient's subjective awareness may be shut out from his subjective experience, thus protecting him from a potential area of conflict.[36] (his, him, *sic*.)

Dissociation is viewed as an unconscious defense mechanism where threatening attitudes, ideas, and feelings become distinctly separated from the rest of the psyche. This "splitting" of mental processes may result in the display of wandering behavior, multiple personalities, and memory loss.[37]

These definitions depend on a theory of unconscious intentionality, that is, that "threatening attitudes, ideas, and feelings" of the self can be repressed from the conscious to the unconscious mind, where they become even more powerful motives for behavior than before. In both denial and dissociation, there can be total amnesia about these attitudes, ideas, and feelings, as well as about traumatic past events. In fact, the nature of personal evil is that such facts, feelings, and consequences are always denied and dissociated to some extent.

Denial and dissociation are not distinct categories, but I use them both for emphasis. In denial, the individual believes that an attitude, idea, or feeling no longer exists or has importance. The individual attempts to banish memories and feelings connected with past events and pretends they have no reality or consequences. Dissociation implies that an attitude, idea, or feeling can be put away someplace in the psyche where it will no longer create a problem. Its existence is, in the words of one client, "behind us, in the past, we can't do anything about it now." Therefore, it does not need attention in the present even though it may be remembered in vague outline.

Denial and dissociation are important in our discussion of evil because they are defenses that protect the conscious self from knowledge of evil. For a survivor of evil, these defenses protect the self from fragmentation so that the person can continue living. For perpetrators of evil, these defenses defend the self against identification with the victims and thus accountability for destructive acts toward others.[38]

The theory of the unconscious is a complex one that will not be fully explored here. It is "that part of the mind or psyche containing information that has never been conscious, or that was once conscious but is no longer."[39] In identifying the unconscious, Freud made important contributions to our understanding, namely that large parts of our experience are outside of conscious awareness and cannot be easily retrieved, and that these unconscious experiences have major influence on thought and behavior.[40] In process thought, consciousness is a result of intense contrast between relationships within the subjectivity of an individual and is dependent on the causal efficacy of the entire relational web.[41] An individual moment of consciousness rides on a sea of unconscious reality that determines its being. These several theories of the unconscious all assume that knowledge of one's unconscious reality is both important and difficult. That is, we must acknowledge that our experience is based on whole realms of reality of which we have only dim awareness, and that living in this reality requires sensitivity, patience, and courage. In addition, experience requires that we trust ourselves to a reality about which we know only a small part. In every moment of consciousness, there is a small degree of freedom to choose what will become based on the causal efficacy from the past. Although the margin of freedom is slight in any moment, its potential impact over a lifetime is significant. We are what we have been given by the past, and what we have decided from moment to moment about the present and future. The long-term trajectory of our accumulated pattern of decisions constitutes our intentionality, even though we have only marginal awareness of our full experience at any particular moment. We construct our identity in accord with our interests and values.

Accepting that evil requires the active agency of individuals becomes especially important in situations of racial and sexual violence. As the stories in previous chapters have demonstrated, interpersonal violence does not happen because someone is "out of control" or "out of my mind." Violence is a choice that an individual makes to engage in particular behaviors for specific reasons and to ignore (through denial and dissociation) values or consequences that call that behavior into question. Slaveholders assumed they had a right to sexually exploit the men, women, and children who were slaves. Child molesters decide to sexually exploit children in vulnerable situations and to manipulate and confuse other adults about what they are doing. White citizens decide to sue for rights to a job because they believe affirmative action puts them at a disadvantage. Evil occurs when people decide to participate in behaviors that are destructive to the bodies and spirits of others.

However, evil also usually requires the silent collusion of many others not directly responsible. Such collusion is a form of unconscious and conscious personal intentionality at two levels. First, evil does not just spring into existence out of nothing (*creatio ex nihilo*), but is carefully constructed over a long period of time. The construction of evil systems requires the cooperation of many people in many ways through countless decisions to ignore the possible consequences for those who are vulnerable. Second, evil does not endure unless many people decide to continue their participation. For example, the Women's Rights Convention of 1848 challenged

United States society to give women the right to vote and other rights such as custody of children, owning property, education, and jobs. Yet not until 1920 did women win the right to vote, and other forms of equality remain to be won. The movement for women's equality has been long and difficult because of the actions of many to delay and prevent such changes. I believe that whenever we find a situation of genuine evil, it has been constructed through the conscious and unconscious actions and intentions of individuals who were directly and indirectly involved.

To see evil's existence in our daily lives, the Christian community needs a language more adequate for describing it. Whenever we see genuine evil, we must ask, What have I done to contribute to this evil, and how will I have to change in order not perpetuate it? This does not mean that all people are equally responsible for every situation of evil, but it does point to the importance of self-critical awareness in all situations.

Social Evil

Evil is organized by economic forces, institutions, and ideologies but mystified by illusions of necessity and truth.

When I discovered how personal actions and intentions led to evil, I felt the impulse to change my theology and locate all evil within individuals. For example, in my early work with child molesters, I began to see that abusive fathers were often able to spin webs of pathological motives, behaviors, and lies with such insidious creativity that the partner and the children in the family did not understand what was happening. In a majority of cases, the deceptions were so clever that the mothers did not even know that sexual abuse was occurring, and the children were effectively silenced. I was tempted to locate the total responsibility for these evil family systems in the perpetrators, and there is a certain truth to that perception. Some of my colleagues in the field of family violence believe that human nature is a sufficient explanation for evil, and they feel no need to look for social explanations for what happens.

However, the issue that has challenged an individualist view is the silence of church and society about certain kinds of violence. When people of high social status experience violence, we seem to have no confusion about their need for protection, prevention, and healing. We don't blame the victim for provoking the violence. However, violence against certain vulnerable populations (children, women, persons of color, gays and lesbians, persons with disabilities) is often accepted as "the way things are." The attitude seems to be that some children will be beaten and that this is a risk of family life, or that poor persons will experience more violent crime and this is the price of a democratic society.

I continue to be troubled by the response of the church to certain situations of violence. How does one understand the many cases in which a violated child disclosed abuse to an adult at church and was told that this could not be happening, that her father was a good man and that she should not speak of it again? Time after time, pastors, deacons, elders, Sunday school teachers, and other church leaders refuse to listen to the pain of children who are victims of sexual or physical violence. An example of this reality is the story told by Karen Doudt in my book *The Abuse of Power*. Karen was a victim of incest by her father beginning in preschool and continuing until early adolescence. During this time, she gave many clues to family members, teachers, doctors, and others. But they refused to hear the pain of a little girl who came from such a good home.[42] Such powerful stories have led me to conclude that somehow ideas and social practices about gender, race, class, family, and sexuality must be included in any definition of evil. Social analysis must include the economic forces, institutional forms, and ideas and ideologies of modern life.[43] Social analysis can be done in at least three ways: by economic forces, institutional forms, or ideologies.

Economic Forces. "Economic forces" refers to modes of production, the material bases of everyday life, the division of labor by class, gender and race, and the macroeconomic structures that emerge from national and global economies.[44] The situation of Black women in the United States clearly shows the convergence of race, gender, and class in economic stratification.

> In 1985, 50 percent of Black families headed by women were below the official poverty line (U.S. Department of Commerce, 1986). The situation was more extreme for young African-American women. In 1986, 86 percent of families headed by Black women between the ages of 15 and 24 lived below the poverty line.[45]

In 1989, 25% of all children under age six were poor, most of whom were European American children.[46] Such high poverty rates correlate with limited access to resources such as health care, education, and employment opportunities. In previous chapters, we examined how economic systems were formed and maintained, and how the need for cheap and expendable labor supported slavery and the exploitation of women and children. Understanding how social evil visits the most vulnerable members of society requires a complex and detailed economic analysis that is missing from much of the church's awareness. One way to detect the presence of evil is to ask who benefits from current economic systems.

Social Institutions. "Social institutions" refers to mediating structures closely related to the daily life of the people, namely families, educational endeavors, local and regional political processes, voluntary organizations, and social interactions at work. Social institutions influence individual behavior through implicit and explicit rules, roles, and values enforced by laws, customs, and rituals. For example, although individuals express shared understandings of the various family forms, legislatures and courts regularly define the forms. The current debate about whether single mothers and gay and lesbian couples can be considered Christian families hides the crisis of the family as an institution. We know that there is no correlation between the structure of a family and the quality of life in a family. No family system ensures that children will be loved. Some research even shows that the nuclear family is the most dangerous place for children because the unchecked power of parents too often results in physical and sexual abuse. The real issue of "family values" is how to provide the resources, education, and accountability for multiple models of family so that children are safe and nurtured. Those who attack single-parent families refuse to consider the discrimination and isolation that many of these families experience in a society of racial and gender violence. One way to detect the presence of evil is to ask who benefits from marginalizing all but nuclear families headed by heterosexual couples. Analyzing the institutional arrangements of everyday life helps us understand the organization of systematic evil.[47]

Ideologies. According to David Tracy, "ideologies" refers to the "unconscious but systematically functioning attitudes, values, and beliefs produced by and in the material conditions of all uses of language, all analyses of truth, and all claims to knowledge."[48] Ideologies are the big ideas, the "elephantine" concepts[49] mostly out of our awareness that provide a horizon of meaning and value within which the people of a culture and society live their lives. In the United States, race continues to serve as a reigning mythology that maintains "the values of the dominant society as the norm by which all else will be measured."[50] The debate about race and intelligence triggered by Charles Murray and Richard Herrenstein's *The Bell Curve* (1994)[51] demonstrates racist ideology at work. Murray and Herrenstein, having reviewed empirical studies on intelligence and culture, have concluded that intelligence is primarily heredity, that it is stable over the human life cycle, and that average scores are consistent within racial groups. They further assert that success in society correlates directly with I.Q. test scores, and they draw certain political conclusions, namely that remedial education and economic programs make little difference for people with low intelligence. "As the authors see it, social pathologies like poverty, welfare dependency, illegitimacy and crime are all strongly related to low IQ. . . . and they criticize liberal attempts to use government subsidies to move people out of poverty. Most of these not-so-smart people, they imply, will *never* become middle class."[52] Murray and Herrenstein have been strongly criticized for statistical and methodological errors by scholars.[53] However, as we have seen in Part One of this book, the power of this position depends on a historically constructed ideology of African American inferiority, which has been used to support racial violence since the eighteenth century. Racial and gender evil depend on ideologies.

The following definitions of racism and patriarchy show how evil is organized at a social level and how economic forces, institutional forms, and ideologies all play their part. The definition of the matrix of domination discussed in chapter 6 is an example of social evil. The authors from The Cornwall Collective go on to say:

> Racism takes personal, institutional, and cultural forms and operates at intentional and unintentional, overt and covert levels. Thus the elimination of racism requires a continual reexamination of our cultural assumptions, institutional policies, and personal attitudes.[54]

Cornel West identifies some of the issues that must be examined if we are to understand the history of slavery and racism: "the objective demands of the prevailing mode of production, the political interests of the slaveholding class, the psychological needs of the dominant white racial group."[55] In addition, evil has been created over many centuries and is therefore embedded in the words, grammar, and assumptions of language systems. Racism must also be understood as

> the way in which the very structure of modern discourse at its inception produced forms of rationality, scientificity, and objectivity as well as aesthetic and cultural ideals which require the constitution of the idea of white supremacy. . . . This requirement follows from a logic endemic to the very structure of modern discourse. This logic is manifest in the way in which the controlling metaphors, notions, and categories of modern discourse produce and prohibit, develop and delimit, specific conceptions of truth and knowledge, beauty and character, so that certain ideas are rendered incomprehensible and unintelligible.[56]

Adrienne Rich defines patriarchy in a similar way:

> Patriarchy is the power of the fathers: a familial-social, ideological, political system in which men—by force, direct pressure, or through ritual, tradition, law, and language, customs, etiquette, education, and the division of labor, determine what part women shall or shall not play, and in which the

female is everywhere subsumed under the male. . . . The power of the fathers has been difficult to grasp because it permeates everything, even the language in which we try to describe it. It is diffuse and concrete, symbolic and literal; universal, and expressed with local variations which obscure its universality. . . . [W]hatever my status or situation, my derived economic class, or my sexual preference, I live under the power of the fathers, and I have access only to so much of privilege or influence as the patriarchy is willing to accede to me, and only for so long as I will pay the price for male approval.[57]

These definitions—through a complex social analysis that is psychological, economic, political, cultural, linguistic, and religious—challenge the dominant views designed to make current power arrangements seem natural and legitimate. However, United States scientific and educational communities have coopted these theories of analysis, thus supporting the web of evil. Economics, institutions, and ideologies serve the interests of the ruling classes, with distortions about race and gender built into their methods and theories. So the pressing question is, How can we engage in social analysis so that it is liberating and empowering for the victims and survivors of evil?

Social analysis adequate for discerning evil does not correspond to any discipline or area of study. Such analysis requires attention to issues of power, accountability, resistance, and empowerment. Patricia Hill Collins has suggested giving authority to African American women's experiences when engaging in critical social analysis. I will adapt some of her key ideas to illustrate a method of social analysis of evil.[58]

1. *Giving hermeneutical privilege to the concrete experiences of the victims of evil.* Patricia Hill Collins argues for the validity of giving hermeneutical privilege to the concrete experiences of African American women in the United States because this group faces a "complex nexus of relationships [including] biological classification, the social constructions of race and gender as categories of analysis, the material conditions accompanying these changing social constructions, and Black women's consciousness about these themes."[59] The intense suffering and resilient hope of Black women deserves privilege because it gives important clues to analyzing the nature of evil and the resistance that evil requires. Black women have hermeneutical privilege in this book because we are exploring the root causes and cures of racial and sexual violence.

What is required if we give hermeneutical privilege to African American women? Collins suggests that such a starting point requires accountability to three groups that often conflict with one another. (1) "Black feminist thought must be validated by ordinary African-American women.

. . . To be credible in the eyes of this group, scholars must be personal advocates for their material, be accountable for the consequences of their work, have lived or experienced their material in some fashion, and be willing to engage in dialogues about their findings with ordinary, everyday people." (2) "Black feminist thought also must be accepted by the community of Black women scholars." (3) "Afrocentric feminist thought within academia must be prepared to confront Eurocentric masculinist political and epistemological requirements."[60]

I do not claim that my work is a project of Black feminist thought, but I do intend to work in solidarity with and in accountability to African American women. This section raises the serious question of what solidarity and accountability mean for a member of the White male elite. Solidarity and accountability call me to be willing to give priority to Black feminist narrative and analysis, to be willing to be self-critical about my own social location and my economic and sexual interests in this and other topics, and to be willing to submit my work to communities of African American women for accountability. These steps do not ensure that my work will be free of racist and sexist distortion, but they do commit me to a methodological principle of giving hermeneutic privilege to those who suffer violence rather than to those who perpetuate and benefit from it.

2. *Thematizing resistance to evil as a source of knowledge and analysis.* Evil cannot be studied directly because its reality is mystified by illusions of necessity and legitimate power. The dominant society has worked to create an illusion of necessity for its institutional, economic, and political arrangements, and has constructed ideologies of race and gender to hide the evil within. Therefore, thematizing resistance is an indirect way of studying the existence of evil. As Patricia Hill Collins states,

> because Black women have had to struggle against white male interpretations of the world in order to express a self-defined standpoint, Black feminist thought can best be viewed as subjugated knowledge. The suppression of Black women's efforts for self-definition in traditional sites of knowledge production has led African-American women to use alternative sites such as music, literature, daily conversations, and everyday behavior as important locations for articulating the core themes of a Black feminist consciousness. . . . Like other subordinate groups, African American women have not only developed a distinctive Black women's standpoint, but have done so by using alternative ways of producing and validating knowledge.[61]

Describing and studying resistance is a method for discerning the presence and power of evil.

3. *Analyzing the matrix of domination: race, gender and class as interlocking systems of oppression*. Social analysis of evil cannot be done with an objective wish to understand how a society is organized. Evil is not a morally neutral category that can be studied within the normal academic and scientific disciplines. As an organized, destructive force that tries to mask itself as legitimate, its unmasking requires an analysis of the matrix of domination. Domination—belief in the right of "mastery or supremacy [of some] over another or others"[62]—is based on the "either/or dichotomous thinking of Eurocentric, masculinist thought, . . . a belief in the notions of superior and inferior . . . and the ideological ground that they share, which is a belief in domination [itself]."[63]

Both racial and gender forms of domination must be studied as structures or systems designed to destroy and control people. But these two interlocking structures are only part of the evil system we are trying to understand and defeat.

> The significance of seeing race, class, and gender as interlocking systems of oppression is that such an approach fosters a paradigmatic shift of thinking exclusively about other oppressions, such as age, sexual orientation, religion, and ethnicity. Race, class and gender represent the three systems of oppression that most heavily affect African-American women. But these systems and the economic, political and ideological conditions that support them may not be the most fundamental oppressions, and they certainly affect many more groups than Black women. Other people of color, Jews, the poor, white women, and gays and lesbians have all had similar ideological justifications offered for their subordination. All categories of humans labeled Others have been equated to one another, to animals, and to nature.[64]

4. *Actualizing a politics of empowerment*. Finally, social analysis requires a political commitment to empowerment of dominated groups. In some historical situations, this empowerment serves the purposes of survival, because survival is the most that the systems of evil will allow.[65] In other historical situations, this empowerment is for the purposes of revolution or radical social change in power structures. As Patricia Hill Collins shows in the following paragraph, survival and revolution are internally related, and both provide the focus of any analysis of evil.

> To Sara Brooks survival is a form of resistance, and her struggles to provide for the survival of her children represent the foundation for a powerful Black women's activist tradition. Historically African Americans' resistance to racial oppression could not have occurred without an accompanying struggle for group survival. Sara Brooks's contributions in caring for her

children and in rejecting the controlling images of herself as the objectified Other represent the unacknowledged yet essential actions taken by countless Black women to ensure this group survival. Without this key part of Black women's activism, struggles to transform American educational, economic, and political institutions could not have been sustained.[66]

We can only judge any social analysis by whether it serves to empower the dominated group for survival and/or revolution and social change.

In summary, evil is an organized social system of economic forces, institutional forms, and ideologies that seeks dominance and destruction of the bodies and spirits of those who are dominated. Since every aspect of society—political, economic, cultural, and linguistic—perpetuates evil, theories and methods of analysis employed by institutions and systems have been coopted to serve the interests of one group over all others. Evil can be unmasked through solidarity with and accountability to communities of resistance. From giving privilege to resistance communities, thematizing resistance, analyzing dominance, and actualizing "the politics of empowerment" will come insight and strategies for resisting evil and constructing alternative realities.

Religious Evil

Evil is sanctioned by religion and theology, but masked by abstract claims to virtue, love, and justice.

We have discussed how evil is personal, that is, how it is an expression of the personal intentionality of individuals. We have discussed how evil is social, that is, how it organizes itself into institutional and ideological forms. We have now come to the discussion of religious evil.

In the popular imagination, religion and evil are antipathies; that is, religion is the antidote for evil, and evil is the opposite of religion. We want to believe that at some level every person believes in God and wants to do good, and that every society, inspired by a vision of transcendent good, is committed to justice. On the contrary, evil often has roots in religious beliefs and practices as well as in personal and social structures.

The word "evil" is itself a religious concept; that is, its definition requires reference to a religious worldview of good and evil.[67] In Christianity, evil is sometimes defined as organized opposition to God's love and power as revealed in Jesus Christ; or as the spiritual power that is against the reign of God on earth, as in "the evil empire"; or the evil of the military-industrial complex. Therefore, evil cannot exist apart from religion, for it must be understood in relation to fundamental religious premises about the way God created the world.

To justify their existence, evil systems usually appeal to religious claims of virtue, love, and justice. For example, slaveholders proclaimed that God created Africans as an inferior species or type of human being meant for subordination to White people in the European-American economic and plantation system. Many Christian churches today claim that women are inferior and that equality with men in the family and in the church violates God's natural and sacred laws. Every violent empire has made a religious argument for its destiny and dominance over other nations and peoples. In the United States, many citizens believe that they are God's chosen people, chosen to bring democracy and freedom to the world. Even Nazi Germany appealed to its ultimate right to dominate the world, to create a superior Aryan race, and to practice a final solution to the problem of inferior races. Most evil systems hope to be understood as religious systems doing God's will.[68]

Religious systems, often by their own testimony, contain evil within themselves. The Westminster Confession (1647) of the Presbyterian Church (U.S.A.) states, "The purest churches under heaven are subject both to mixture and error; and some have so degenerated as to become apparently no churches of Christ. Nevertheless, there shall be always a Church on earth to worship God according to his [sic] will."[69] Many other churches believe, similarly, that God is always leading God's people in ways they do not understand, and that inner resistance to God's will is a constant danger, thus creating the potential and reality of evil within the church. Many religious worship services include confession of individual and corporate sin before God. Jewish, Islamic, and other religions have committed themselves to self-criticism and self-correction. Every faith, however, has the problem of how to identify particular evil in its midst and face its destructive power.

How do we discern the presence of religious evil in our midst, especially when religious evil masks itself by appealing to abstract claims to virtue, love, and justice? We must develop critical tools for exposing the religious doctrines that we have used to justify slavery. We must challenge the church's theology when its so-called pro-family attitudes and policies increase violence toward women and children. We must engage the whole church in a critical discussion of how our theology puts children, women, and lesbians and gaymen in jeopardy of rape and violence.

Religious evil is a difficult topic, because we people of faith depend on religious systems to protect us from evil. We fear we might lack an adequate defense against internal and external evil. Because of the trust of people in religion, it thus becomes a favorite hiding place for evil, because it is the last place most of us are inclined to look. In other words, religious evil is the hardest to disclose because we turn to religious institutions, theologies, and practices for safety from evil. In later chapters, we will look at ways in which religion is both a form of evil and a resource for resisting it. But first, let us define religious evil.

Religious evil occurs whenever the theology and/or practices of religious groups are destructive to bodies and spirits.

In 1711, Anglican Bishop William Fleetwood of the Society for the Propagation of the Gospel in Foreign Parts (S.P.G.) argued in favor of baptism for African slaves in this way:

> [Masters] are neither prohibited by the Laws of God, nor those of the Land, from keeping Christian slaves; their slaves are no more at Liberty after they are Baptized, than they were before. . . . The Liberty of Christianity is entirely spiritual.[70]

This passage, along with examples from Part One, demonstrates the manner in which Christian theology and practice were used to support the evil of slavery.

Rosemary Radford Ruether comments on recent statements by the Roman Catholic Church on the ordination of women.

> In recent Vatican and Roman Catholic episcopal statements, Christology is used as the keystone of the argument against women's ordination. It is said that women, by their very nature, cannot represent Christ. Therefore, they cannot be priests, since priests "represent" Christ. This argument has been echoed in other high church statements.[71]

The spiritual hierarchy of women and men within the church corresponds with the political and economic inequality of women and men within society. Some churches are unwilling to face the way in which a theology of inequality leads to vulnerability of women and children to violence.

Although religious faith and practice has been used to perpetuate evil, true faith is our only protection against it. African American scholars have been doing significant work in exploring ways in which the life, death, and resurrection of Jesus can bring liberty and salvation to all people. The corresponding task of Euro-American Christians is to examine the assumptions that have allowed Euro-American theology to contribute to racial oppression in the past and in our own time. Feminist scholars have been reconstructing Christology to support gender justice. The corresponding task of male Christians is to support efforts to root out male dominance at every level of church life. In chapter 7 we explore this dimension in more detail.

In this chapter, we have explored a rather complex definition of evil as a basis for understanding racial and sexual violence. Destructive to bodies and spirits, evil takes shape within personal, social, and religious systems. We have examined some of the critical theories and methodologies necessary for understanding and evaluating the history and structure of evil. In the following chapter, we will explore how religion functions as a structure of evil and a resource for resistance to evil.

CHAPTER EIGHT

RE-IMAGINING JESUS' RESISTANCE TO EVIL

For centuries, the name of Jesus has been a source of faith and courage for some communities of resistance. In this chapter I will focus on how faith in Jesus Christ empowers these communities to unmask racial and gender evil.

In the eighteenth and nineteenth centuries, large numbers of Black women and men and White women converted to Jesus, finding him to be a faithful friend and powerful authority figure in the midst of their suffering. Although some of this piety was doubtless a form of internalized oppression, as Elizabeth Cady Stanton believed,[1] faith in Jesus also supported the resistance of Black women and men to slavery and White women to subordination. Jacquelyn Grant presents one such dramatic witness from an unknown slave woman:

> "Come to we, dear Massa Jesus. De sun, he hot too much, de road am dat long and boggy (sandy) and we ain't got no buggy for send and fetch Ooner [you]. But Massa, you 'member how you walked dat hard walk up Calvary and ain't weary but tink about we all dat way. We know you ain't weary for to come to we. We pick out de torns, de prickles, de brier, de backslidin' and de quarrel and de sin out of you path so dey shan't hurt Ooner [your] pierce feet no more."[2]

Through identification of their own suffering with Jesus' suffering, Christian Black women created a religious and moral commentary on the evil and violence of slavery. Jesus provided a positive religious figure for Black resistance movements.

An 1858 "revival anthology" describes the religious piety of a Christian White woman.

A mother with several children was left a widow. Feeling her responsibility as a parent, she gave diligence to train her household for Christ. That her instructions might be blessed and her children converted, she was unceasing in her supplications at the throne of mercy. She would arise at midnight, and in the chamber where her little ones were sleeping, would kneel and pray for them with wrestling importunity.[3]

In this story, the mother's awareness of the dangers of single parenting fueled her piety.

Unfortunately, the name of Jesus also has been used for many centuries to support racial and gender oppression. Harriet Jacobs reported her experience of oppression by ordained White male ministers who were brought into her community as agents of social exploitation to preach Jesus:

When the Rev. Mr. Pike came, there were some twenty persons present. The reverend gentleman knelt in prayer, then seated himself, and requested all present, who could read, to open their books, while he gave out the portions he wished them to repeat or respond to. His text was, "Servants, be obedient to them that are your masters, according to the flesh, with fear and trembling, in singleness of your heart, as unto Christ."[4]

This is an example of the name of Jesus Christ being misused to support racial oppression.

During the nineteenth century, White women who were called by Jesus Christ to preach the gospel during the Second Great Awakening (ca. 1840) faced severe opposition from the church. Phoebe Palmer, one of the famous women preachers in mid-century revivalism, wrote:

Suppose one of the brethren who had received the baptism of fire on the day of Pentecost, now numbered among those who were scattered everywhere preaching the word, had met a female disciple who had also received the same endowment of power. He finds her proclaiming Jesus to an astonished company of male and female listeners. And now imagine he interferes and withstands her testimony by questioning whether women have a right to testify of Christ before a mixed assembly. Would not such an interference look worse than unmanly? And were her testimony, through this interference, restrained, or rendered less effectual, would it not, in the eye of the Head of the Church, involve guilt?[5]

In communities in which revivals were common, the church prohibited large numbers of women reborn into Christ from preaching the gospel. Even though some preached anyway, the granting of ordination and license to preach was unusual, and opposition to women preachers was strong in all the major denominations. The church's leadership maintained that Jesus had called only men to be the representatives of God the Father, and that Paul had preached subordination of women in the name of Jesus. In a culture in which women lacked basic human rights—such as the right to own property, control their own bodies, have custody of children, vote, and be educated—their exclusion from the ministry of Jesus Christ cemented their position as subordinate to the power and violence of men.

ISSUES OF CHRISTOLOGY IN THE COMMUNITIES OF RESISTANCE

Having cited examples of the witness to Jesus that empowered resistance to the evils of racism and patriarchy among African American women and White women, I turn now to some of the works of contemporary womanist and feminist theologians on the issue of Christology. What confessions about faith in Jesus have been liberating and comforting for African American women and White women? How has Christology been misused by evil systems to promote violence and oppression in the past and now? Discussing these questions will enable us to construct in chapter 9 suggestions about how images of Jesus Christ can continue the work of resistance and liberation from evil.

In discussing forms of Christology, I am aware of the dangers of fostering antisemitism. As Judith Plaskow warns, idealization of Jesus often projects negative issues onto Judaism, as if all responsibility for evil can be traced to the time before Jesus and to communities that are not Christian. In my attempt to locate the tensions of race and gender within the various Christologies themselves, I acknowledge the validity of Plaskow's critique, which discloses a danger for all Christian theologians.[6]

Questions and Confessions from Womanist Theologians

Womanist theology is Black feminist thought.[7] For *Kelly Brown Douglas*, womanist theology "begins with the Black woman's story of struggle."

> This portrayal of Christ reflects at least two aspects of that story: the multidimensionality of Black women's oppression and their determined efforts to survive and be free from that oppression. Specifically, a womanist portrayal of Christ confronts Black women's struggles within the wider society as well as within the Black community. It also affirms Black women's steadfast faith that God supports them in their fight for survival and freedom.

Such an understanding of Christ emerges as womanist theology engages a social-political analysis of wholeness and a religio-cultural analysis.[8]

Kelly Brown Douglas begins her quest for a womanist Christology by remembering her grandmother's confession of faith.

> Reflecting back on my grandmother's faith, I now realize that she must have trusted that the Christ she prayed to had a special appreciation of her condition. This was a Christ who seemingly identified with a poor Black woman in her day-to-day struggle just to make it. Mama was certain that this Christ cared about the trials and tribulations of an ordinary Black woman. Christ empowered her to get through each day with dignity.[9]

Contemplating her grandmother's faith caused Douglas to wonder about the history of religious evil in support of slavery and racism. How could faith in Jesus have provided such comfort and strength for her grandmother and for so many other Black women over the course of almost four centuries, yet also be used to justify the violence and cruelty of racism? She concludes that White theologians historically relied on a "White Christ," that is, a portrait of Jesus with European characteristics and attitudes, to serve the interests of the ruling classes and their oppressive practices. A complex theology about individual salvation and life after death spiritualized this Christ, making him irrelevant to the issues of everyday survival and to the liberation of oppressed people. This process of spiritualization served to mystify the evils of slavery in three ways: (1) by justifying the slave trade and slavery; (2) by using baptism of African Americans as a way to stabilize slavery; and (3) by making Christianity compatible with the extreme cruelty of slavery.[10]

First, to justify the slave trade and slavery, White theologians, such as Samuel D. How, emphasized the civilizing influence of faith in Jesus. "The condition of slaves is far better than that of the Africans from whom they have been brought. Instead of debased savages, they are, to a considerable extent, civilized, enlightened and christianized."[11] Douglas shows that identifying Jesus with White, European civilization made the slave trade and slavery appear benevolent to those who already believed in White supremacy. However, this maneuver required that the violence of what was actually happening not be closely examined. Such a spiritualized religion amounted to a form of dissociation from the historical life of Jesus and from any awareness of social oppression. This approach absolved the slaveholders of any guilt for their evil role in the social system, since belief in Jesus was only related to one's soul and life in the hereafter.

Second, the use of the baptism of African Americans as a way of stabilizing slavery required severing any ties between baptism and the biblical tradition of prophetic justice. Given the Protestant emphasis on Jesus as a social prophet, many slaveholders feared that baptizing African Americans would make slavery unstable. "An Anglican minister in Virginia explained, 'as for baptizing Indians and Negroes, several of the people disapprove of it, because they say it often makes them proud, and not so good servants.' "[12] Theologians faced the problem of how to reverse the usual meaning of baptism so that it signified submission to authority rather than freedom and equality.

> Evangelists were able to spiritualize the themes of Christian freedom and equality. They essentially reasoned that what Jesus did in human history was disconnected from the salvation that he offered. Subsequently, the salvation that he offered was unrelated to what took place in human history. Jesus' salvation had nothing to do with historical freedom. The slaves could be Christian without being freed.[13]

As a result, White evangelists of the Great Awakening (ca. 1740) preached a White Jesus to the slaves. Confessions such as the following were used at many baptismal events for African Americans:

> You declare in the presence of God and before this Congregation that you do not ask for the Holy Baptism out of any design to free yourself from the Duty and Obedience you owe to your Master while you live, but merely for the good of your Soul and to partake of the Graces and Blessings promised to the Members of the Church of Jesus Christ.[14]

As Douglas comments, "This Christ allowed for White enslavers to be Christians, and for Black Christians to be slaves."[15]

Third, making Christianity compatible with the extreme cruelty of slavery was an ongoing problem, especially as the abolitionist movement began to distribute stories about the terror of everyday life for African Americans under slavery. Frederick Douglass said:

> Were I to be again reduced to the chains of slavery, next to the enslavement, I should regard being the slave of a religious master the greatest calamity that could befall me. For of all slaveholders with whom I have ever met, religious slaveholders are the worst. I have ever found them the meanest and basest, more cruel and cowardly, of all others.[16]

How could slaveholders engage in such cruelty and yet still be Christians? Kelly Brown Douglas replies: "The answer to the above questions is the White Christ. . . . Enslavers are free to be as cruel as they want toward a slave, while at the same time being assured salvation. The religion of the White Christ places few demands on persons concerning how they should live their life in relation to others."[17] Theologians chose to explain away the tension between Jesus' love and compassion and the violence that slavery perpetrated on African Americans.

Kelly Brown Douglas shows how the spiritualized White Christ, who functioned as an object of faith and piety, was problematic in relation to ongoing issues of racial and gender oppression. She affirms the development of the Black Christ in the theology of Deotis Roberts and James Cone, because this development identifies Jesus with the Black liberation struggles and rejects the White Christ. However, Douglas criticizes this symbol because it ignores "the Black woman's story of struggle,"[18] and imagines what the symbol of Christ would be if Jesus were re-symbolized as an African American woman:

> Seeing Christ in the faces of [Black women] . . . suggests several things. First, it says that the Black Christ is present in the Black community wherever people are engaged in a struggle for that community's "wholeness." Second, it challenges Black people to participate in activities that advance the unity and freedom of their community. It allows them to know that Christ is with them and in them anytime they promote life and wholeness for Black men and women. Third, to portray Christ in the face of Black heroines and heroes signals that it was not who Jesus was, particularly as a male, that made him Christ, but what he did.[19]

This "spirituality of resistance"[20] provides a constructive alternative to the White, male Jesus. Douglas avoids a biological essentialism by saying that "Christ is a Black women . . . when Black women are acting to establish life and wholeness for the Black community."[21] Because it moves beyond the White Christ of the slaveholders, and beyond the male Christ of the male-dominant church, a Christ-symbol based on the experiences of Black women represents a move toward wholeness. The corresponding task of European American Christians is to ask whether the Christ we worship can meet the same criteria.

Jacquelyn Grant bases her reflections on the witness of Black women such as Sojourner Truth, an active leader of the Women's Rights and Abolition movements of the nineteenth century.

> "When I preaches, I has jest one text to preach from, an' I always preaches from this one. My text is, 'When I found Jesus!' " In this sermon Sojourner Truth recounts the events and struggles of her life from the time her parents

were brought from Africa and sold "up an' down, an' hither an' yon . . ." to
the time when she met Jesus within the context of her struggles for dignity
of Black people and women.[22]

How could faith in Jesus empower Sojourner Truth to survive and witness
in Jesus' name, and yet also justify those who oppressed her and other
Black women?

Grant raises up the issue of servanthood as a misinterpretation of Jesus in
a society with a history of slavery and racism. Given the brutal history of
"domestic service," which was a euphemism for slavery and later a form of
economically enforced servitude for many Black women, why has *servanthood*
become such a precious symbol of faithfulness to Jesus in the White
churches? Grant suggests that the theme of servanthood has been misused as
a tool of oppression against women, especially African American women.
One example is this short catechism, which was taught to slaves:

> Q: Who made you?
> A: God made me.
> Q: Why did God make you?
> A: To serve my earthly master.[23]

For several hundred years, servanthood was the primary image Christian theologians preached to African Americans in their attempt to justify
slavery. Following Jesus meant accepting one's servitude in a white society.
The White women's rights movement of the nineteenth century made this
same critical connection as a way of challenging their subordinate status
in church and society. "[W]hite women were challenging the fact that
they were relegated to the level of 'servants of men.' They were incensed
because they were being treated as second-class citizens in the larger society, and second-class Christians in the church."[24] If servanthood has
been a symbol of economic exploitation for many African American
women and White women, why has it been accepted as a positive symbol
for the whole church? Grant questions whether servanthood is not still
being used to deny women equal roles in leadership in church and society.
Thus she challenges one of the favorite doctrines of many Christian
churches in the United States.

Letty Russell, a European American feminist, has tried to rescue the
concept of servanthood from these difficulties. She argues that servanthood is useful exactly because it points to a form of mutual leadership that
is central to the life and gospel of Jesus Christ. The phrase "Jesus is Lord"
is a direct challenge to the hierarchical, authoritarian forms of leadership

in most churches, because Jesus taught that leadership is exercised through servanthood.[25]

But Grant remains unconvinced that servanthood should be retained as a primary symbol of Jesus for two reasons. First, social analysis shows that African American women have always made up large percentages of domestic servants. Although they were only 5% of the population in 1920, African American women made up 40% of domestic servants, 73% of laundresses, and high percentages of workers in other low-wage positions.[26] Second, the site of such work is often in the homes and small businesses of White families, and African American women are often supervised by White women. "In this context, generally, white women proved to be as oppressive as white men. Because domestic work was completely privatized, Black women suffered at the whims and wills of white women."[27] This means that the socioeconomic experiences of Black and White women are very different, even though they share some structures of subordination to men.

Thus Grant challenges whether servanthood can be a liberating image for African American women today, and whether it should be used by a White church with a long history of oppressing African American people.

> Service and oppression of Blacks went hand in hand. Therefore, to speak of service as empowerment, without concrete means or plans for economic, social, and political revolution that in fact lead to empowerment, is simply another form of "overspiritualization." It does not eliminate real pain and suffering, it merely spiritualizes the reality itself.[28]

What is the meaning of this split in consciousness, in which those who are not oppressed use a symbol of oppression to speak of faith in Jesus? Grant suggests that such ignorance of context shows at least a willingness to overlook the connection between servanthood as a symbol and the real servants in United States society. But perhaps it is more, she writes. Perhaps the symbol maintains the structures of evil in a church in which some are expected to be servants (Black women, White women), and others use the word but exercise dominance and control (White men, Black men). She concludes that the use of the servanthood image is not inadvertent but a form of collusion with the larger society and a way of sanctioning the evil power arrangements between men and women and between Blacks and Whites.

> The sin of servanthood is the sin of humanity that results from the sociopolitical interests of proponents of the status quo and their attempts to undergird their intended goal through psychological conditioning that comes

partially with the institutionalization of oppressive language, even theological language.[29]

When evil is blatant, we can often see it and resist its power. But evil is more difficult to see when it is hidden in oppressive language. The symbol of servanthood is precious for many Christians who believe that Jesus came not to be served but to serve, and that the faithful ought to express this love by serving one another. But, for others, servanthood means living in crushing poverty, with violence, sexual abuse, and economic exploitation. White men have controlled the development of theology and the church's practices through the power of church bureaucracies, colleges and seminaries, research and publishing, and ecumenical and parachurch agencies. The marketing of the theological image of servanthood comes from the leadership of White men. How is it that those with virtually no experience of actual servanthood have chosen this symbol as central to Christian theology? The response of White theologians is that servanthood reminds White men to exercise their leadership in a spirit of service and love rather than as tyrants. This rationalization is weakened when men do not confront one another about their abuses of power, especially against women and children. As Grant suggests, there is another hidden, unconscious intention behind this symbol.

> Those who are in control of the dominant culture are in control of the language, and consequently, men have produced language that is advantageous to men and disadvantageous to women. . . . Oppressors, for example, always have the advantage of determining who the real "servants" are. Even with institutional hierarchies that claim to be servants (be they church or government related), it is often difficult to determine which is more important, being served or serving.[30]

Whatever the conscious intentions of White men, the symbol of servanthood hides the fact that White men control the theology, institutions, and practices of the church, and that servanthood is not the way power is actually exercised. The symbol of servanthood hides the fact that White women are servants in the White church and are employed primarily in low-paying service industries, and that Black women are servants in the Black church and are frequently employed as domestic servants and in other service jobs. The symbol of servanthood is *spiritualized* and disconnected from the socioeconomic realities of life.

Grant suggests that the term servanthood should be dropped from the theological vocabulary because it is used for evil purposes, and that other terms should be found to symbolize mutuality and nonhierarchical styles of leadership and community. She feels the church should stop misusing the image of servanthood as the primary image of faithfulness to Jesus Christ, and instead use the equally biblical image of discipleship.

> Women have been invited to become disciples. In the historical records, women were left out of the inner circle of the disciples. Therefore, women must be empowered to become disciples. The language of discipleship for women provides the possibility of breaking down traditional stereotypical exclusivistic understandings of discipleship. Overcoming the sin of servant-hood can prepare us for the deliverance that comes through discipleship.[31]

Grant believes that discipleship as a symbol of faith in Jesus would lead to more equality between women and men, Blacks and Whites, in the church and in society.

By recounting examples of the ongoing violence in the lives of many Black women today—the rape and beating of Black women by White men who go unpunished, battering by husbands and partners, sexual harass-ment at work, subordinate positions in churches and everywhere—*Delores Williams* lifts up the will to survive of many Black women.

> Faith has taught me to see the miraculous in everyday life: . . . Ordinary black women doing what they always do: holding the family and church together; working for the white folks or teaching school; enduring what-ever they must so their children can reach for the stars; keeping hope alive in the family and community when money is scarce and white folks get mean and ugly.[32]

Using the perspective that many Black women survive through faith in Jesus, Williams looks at the story of Hagar and of Jesus' crucifixion as they have been interpreted by theologians. She surmises that both events have been misinterpreted in order to promote submission and obedience by op-pressed peoples. Hagar was forced to play a surrogate role for Abraham and Sarah by bearing a child, and when that surrogate role was no longer necessary, she was cast with her child into the desert to die. In spite of this injustice, Abraham has become a symbol of the meaning of faithfulness to God. In some theories of the atonement, Jesus was forced to assume a sur-rogate role for sinful humanity by dying a criminal's death on a cross, and his crucifixion is promoted as a model of faith. Williams raises the ques-tion of whether these stories implicitly sanctify surrogacy, whereby op-pressed people suffer for the privileges of those in power. In an observation somewhat similar to Grant's argument, Williams asks what it means when the White church holds up surrogacy as a positive virtue, but overlooks the fact that Black women have been forced to serve as surrogate mothers, housekeepers, and nannies for centuries.

> Coerced surrogacy . . . was a condition in which people and systems . . . forced black women to function in roles that ordinarily would have been filled by someone else. For example, black female slaves were forced to substitute for the slave-owner's wife in nurturing roles involving white children. Black women were forced to take the place of men in work roles that, according to the larger society's understanding of male and female roles, belonged to men. . . . More than in the areas of nurturance and field labor, coerced surrogacy in the area of sexuality was threatening to slave women's self-esteem and sense of self-worth. This is the area in which slave women were forced to stand in place of white women and provide sexual pleasure for white male slave owners.[33]

Williams challenges this misuse of the surrogacy role of Jesus without regard for the actual coerced surrogacy experienced by African American women. She suggests using in its place the images of resistance and survival—values that are also part of the story of Jesus' life and death.

> Salvation [for Black women] does not depend upon any form of surrogacy made sacred by traditional and orthodox understandings of Jesus' life and death. Rather their salvation is assured by Jesus' life of resistance and by the survival strategies he used to help people survive the death of identity caused by their exchange of inherited cultural meanings for a new identity shaped by the gospel ethics and world view. . . . The resurrection does not depend upon the cross for life, for the cross only represents historical evil trying to defeat good.[34]

Overemphasis on Jesus as a surrogate figure actually reinforces the social practice of enforced surrogacy of Black women. Therefore, the image of Jesus as one who resists evil and promotes survival and liberation is more faithful to the religious witness of Black women.

Questions and Confessions from Feminist Theologians

Joanne Carlson Brown writes about the fact that much modern theology is based on the suffering God, who died on the cross to reveal the sacrificial nature of love. Partly owing to the witness of survivors of sexual and domestic violence, feminist theologians have become interested in the theological theme of suffering. Perpetrators have often told their victims that they should not complain of their abuse because their suffering is like that of Jesus and they will be rewarded in the future. Pastors have instructed battered women to return to their violent partners because their suffering is holy. Brown rejects this misuse of the suffering of Christ.

> Is it any wonder that there is so much abuse in modern society when the predominant image or theology of the culture is of "divine child abuse"—God the Father demanding and carrying out the suffering and death of his own son? . . . Resurrection means that death is overcome in those precise instances when human beings choose life, refusing the threat of death. Jesus climbed out of the grave in the Garden of Gethsemene when he refused to abandon his commitment to the truth even though his enemies threatened him with death. On Good Friday, the Resurrected One was Crucified.[35]

Brown suggests that we must replace the emphasis on righteous suffering with a commitment to truth and justice. It is not Jesus' suffering that is redemptive, but his commitment to truth and justice, which could not be shaken even by torture and crucifixion. Pastors should not counsel victims of sexual and domestic violence to accept their unjust suffering, but should stand in solidarity with these victims, even if by doing so they will be misunderstood and vilified by those committed to male dominance.

Rita Nakashima Brock, too, bases her reflections on the witness of survivors of violence. Taught not only that they must obey patriarchal authority, especially when it is enforced by violence, women and children must also be innocent of any hatred or anger about their oppression. Drawing on her Asian and Asian American heritage, Brock urges resistance to this misuse of the submission of Jesus to his father.

> [Asian] writers depict innocence as something we must outgrow, or else we risk remaining superfluous and disempowered, which is the designated state of women and children. Innocence may be appropriate to babies, but innocence in adults is dangerous. Innocence is not a survival skill. It neither nurtures and empowers life nor passes it on. Cunning, quick wits, a tolerance for ambiguity, skills at manipulation, a creative imagination, sound moral reflection, and an active sense of agency emerge with the rejection of innocence.[36]

Thus Brock challenges some of the central values in the nineteenth-century "Cult of True Womanhood," which encouraged women to exhibit "piety, purity, submission and domesticity."[37] She explicitly emphasizes willfulness and resistance as characteristic of the life of Jesus, and suggests that women ought to imitate the prophetic and rebellious Jesus rather than the obedient, submissive one.

> Doctrines about the sinless purity of Jesus and the image of him as an innocent lamb taken obediently to slaughter reinforce the idea that victims ought to be

innocent and virtuous or else pain and suffering are deserved, even though the gospels tend to depict a more ambiguous and politically savvy Jesus.[38]

Brock says that romanticizing submission, obedience, and innocence, especially with regard to oppressed groups, is a misuse of Christology for the benefit of those who control economic and political power. Willfulness and rebellion are much more appropriate images for oppressed groups, and these values are equally biblical and Christological.

Ellen Wondra begins her exploration of Christology and women's experience by recounting a story Rosemary Radford Ruether heard when she and Susan Brooks Thistlethwaite taught a class on violence against women. Ruether writes,

> One woman in the class recounted her experience of being raped in a woods. During the rape she became convinced that she would be killed and resigned herself to her impending death. When the rapist finally fled and she found herself still alive, she experienced a vision of Christ as a crucified woman. This vision filled her with relief and healing, because she knew that "I would not have to explain to a male God that I had been raped. God knew what it was like to be a woman who had been raped."[39]

This story portrays Jesus' identification with women who experience violence and thus rejects the violent treatment of women perpetrated by patriarchal Christianity. The exclusive symbolic use of the male Christ has corresponded to the oppression of women. As Jacquelyn Grant states: "The only thing a male savior can do is what the male savior, Jesus, has done, and that is to legitimize the oppression of women through the perpetuation of the 'myth of sin and salvation.' . . . Women must [instead] look for the New Being."[40]

Wondra reclaims Jesus as a religious resistor to evil and as a symbol that can empower women's resistance today.

> Jesus' life, then, manifests and proclaims the actuality and possibility of authentic humanity that engages the conditions of human existence and actively and effectively resists their dehumanizing elements at individual and socio-systemic levels.[41]

RACE AND GENDER AS ASPECTS OF HERMENEUTICAL METHOD

Hermeneutics is the study of theories of interpretation of the Bible and the religious traditions. It is crucial that I discuss hermeneutics because of conflict between Christian groups over the authority of the scriptures, and because of the sensitivity about open discussion of symbols such as Jesus Christ. Obviously, persons and communities interpret Jesus differently, and often feel threatened when these differences are examined.

In the previous section, I briefly reviewed the approaches of six womanist and feminist theologians in their reflections about Christology. This overview suggests several hermeneutical principles that must guide our continued conversations.

First, all of these theologians give hermeneutical privilege to the witness of African American women and White women who have resisted racial and gender evil. Their resistance discloses the presence of religious evil by appealing to a Jesus who is *other* than that of White male theologians. Black women who speak for those who have been oppressed by slavery and racism deserve privileged voice because they know evil in their bodies and spirits, and they represent the spirits of all Black women who have resisted religious evil, sometimes unto death. Women who have suffered physical, sexual, and other forms of patriarchal violence deserve privileged voice because they represent the spirits of all women whose lives have been jeopardized by male violence. The principle for our theological reflection is that White male theologians must give hermeneutical privilege to African American women, White women, and women of other cultures whose religious experiences have been ignored in the formulations of Christology. Beginning to construct a Christology that can transform the power of European American men of the dominant class is a task we will address in chapter 9.

Second, all the theologians discussed in this section are profoundly suspicious and critical of the Christology inherited from centuries of White male theology. They all believe Jesus has been constructed White and male in order to justify the dominance of White men as a social class, resulting in an overemphasis on servanthood, surrogacy, suffering, obedience, and innocence. The hermeneutical principle here is that we must deconstruct the Christ-symbol of inherited theology so that it will no longer be used for oppression.

Third, all these theologians suggest alternative images of Jesus that empower the oppressed and create safe spaces for survival, liberation, and abundant life. Images such as the following create new possibilities for religious faith and practice: the Black Christ, Christ as a Black woman, Christ as a crucified woman, discipleship, rebellion, ambiguity, political shrewdness, a spirituality of resistance, Sophia, Goddess. Reconstructing the Christ symbol by all oppressed people is a crucial hermeneutical task needed so that God's beloved community may continue.

A Hermeneutics of Suspicion and Confession

In terms of hermeneutical method, I start with the premise that human beings do not have access to a pure Jesus undistorted by history. Although attempts to recover "the historical Jesus" can be helpful because they show that the first-century peasant bears little relationship to the debates about Christ throughout history,[42] the results of this research do little to resolve the conflicts between contemporary religious groups. Continually reappropriated by the principalities and powers of empires, the historical Jesus reveals no original truth that can easily settle debates among Christians today. Even conservative religious creeds teach that the scriptures must be "rightly explained" (2 Tim. 2:15, NRSV) and interpreted by the Holy Spirit.[43] Historical research is crucial because it forces the church to uncover the layers of distortion starting in the oral traditions and continuing through every version of the Bible and its interpretations.[44] Searching for the truth is a crucial aspect of deconstructing any lies about Jesus. But we must be *suspicious* of the attempts of Christian groups to misuse the symbol of Jesus for their own privilege and power.

My hermeneutical method is also based on my *confession* that Jesus is a spirit that continues to empower those who resist evil. The love and power of Jesus lives in the people's struggles for survival and freedom in the face of massive evil and injustice. Church leaders are called to become attuned to Jesus' spirit in the scriptures, and bring voice to the resistance to evil. Jesus lived and died and was resurrected in the past, and Jesus lives, dies, and is resurrected every day when violence against the vulnerable is resisted. Learning to see Jesus in the present is a way of remaining faithful to the Jesus the Bible proclaims as fellow-sufferer.

In practice, the hermeneutics of suspicion and confession work together to define the method for Christology. We must be suspicious of every individual and group who calls on the name of Jesus in such a way that their claims to power create systems of domination and evil. "Not everyone who calls me 'Lord, Lord' will enter the kingdom of Heaven, but only those who do the will of [God]" (Matt. 7:21). But we must also be willing to hear the confessions of those for whom Jesus has been a liberating and empowering figure of religious piety. Finding a healthy balance between suspicion and confession is a challenging task.

Clarice Martin, Black Womanist New Testament scholar, describes this tension when she distinguishes between a hermeneutics of truth and a hermeneutics of effects.

"[H]ermeneutics" is not simply a cognitive process wherein one seeks to determine the "correct meaning" of a passage or text. Neither are questions of penultimate truth and universality solely determinative of meaning. Also of essential importance in the interpretive task are such matters as the nature of the interpreter's goals, the effects of a given interpretation on a community of people who have an interest in the text being interpreted, and questions of cultural value, social relevance, and ethics.[45]

Martin continues by quoting from *The Responsibility of Hermeneutics*: "What is at stake in hermeneutics is not only the 'truth' of one's interpretation, but also the effects interpretation and interpretive strategies have on the ways in which human beings shape their goals and their actions."[46] This form of hermeneutics involves a rhythm or dynamic interplay between biblical texts from the canon and the lived faith and experience of communities of resistance. An interpreter cannot understand Jesus by studying the Bible in isolation, but must also be immersed in a community of resistance that lives out faith in Jesus today. Without participation in resistance today, one cannot comprehend the spirit of Jesus' resistance in the past. The truth of Jesus in scripture is revealed in the ongoing resistance in the name of Jesus.

Riggins Earl, Jr., Black male theologian, provides additional perspective on hermeneutical method for the study of Christology. For several centuries, slaves were denied the right to literacy and religious leaders of their own, and were dependent for their knowledge of the scriptures and Christian theology on preachers hired by the slaveholders. As we saw earlier, Harriet Jacobs observed that the slaveholder's purpose for providing religious worship and instruction was "to give the slaves enough of religious instruction to keep them from murdering their masters."[47] This systematic distortion of the Christian message resulted in the proclamation of an idolatrous Jesus to African Americans.

Earl deconstructs the slaveholders' method of distortion and calls it a "hermeneutical circle of double negativity."[48] The Christian masters were faced with a profound dilemma, namely, "Can we teach slaves to think of themselves as being absolutely worthless before God without being guilty of thinking of ourselves more highly than we ought before God?"[49] In other words, how could the White masters distort the Christian message of freedom and justice in service to the brutality and violence of slavery without being accountable for their violence against the gospel of Jesus Christ? Their solution was to teach that slaves's bodies and souls were evil because their skin was black, thus excluding those with White skin from the same judgments. White supremacy became the justification for violence against people of color.

> To teach slaves that they were "black of body" and "blacker of soul" was to teach them the theory of double self-negation. . . . This truth is illustrated by the following prayer lines a white missionary preacher composed for plantation masters to teacher their slaves: "O Thou great God, the Maker of all creatures, I, a poor black sinner, black in body and still blacker in sin." . . . Requiring slaves to ritualize their own inferiority in these prayer lines, masters were affirming their belief that white skin made them superior in the sight of God. Such spurious interpretation contributed to whites' false sense of divinely ordained preeminence over those of African origin.[50]

Using assumptions of White supremacy, White preachers could interpret their oppression of African Americans as benevolent and paternalistic—"for their own good." Earl clearly demonstrates how the social, political, economic, and religious dominance of the White slaveholders created the motives and the means to distort the gospel of Jesus Christ in support of White supremacy. His hermeneutics of suspicion gives profound insight into the racism of theology during slavery. The slaveholders interpreted the gospel of Jesus to maintain and increase their dominance over others. Earl's work suggests the following poignant question:

> If white ministers' objective of their conversion language was to dehumanize slaves, how did slaves reconstruct a humanized view of themselves? How did they deduce from the misconstrued conversion language of the plantation divines a liberation notion of themselves?[51]

The miracle of God's action in history is that Jesus' spirit has lived on in spite of the evil of those who are intent on dominating through religious power. Communities of resistance, such as the slave communities, have confessed that Jesus as friend and co-sufferer has provided nurture and liberation. How could the slave community in resistance confess such a Jesus in the midst of such profound evil?

> Slaves believed that God had transformed them into new beings with a radically different mission in the world—a mission that required them to live counter to plantation values. . . . This twofold perspective of new being and purpose gave the slaves a sense of divine worth in a world that negated their self-worth.[52]

Through trusting their own religious experience of Jesus' presence and rejecting the lies that created their captivity, converted slaves resisted evil and confessed the love and power of God in Jesus Christ. In the process, they found a precious interior spiritual space of freedom from domination, a sanctuary from evil. Through confession of Jesus as they understood him, they were able to reject the White, evil Jesus falsely created by the masters. They became appropriately suspicious of evil when it was personal in the attitudes and behaviors of masters, when it was social in the institution of slavery, and when it was religious in the false Jesus preached to them by evil ministers. As Earl recounts, with Jesus as friend and guide, slaves incorporated secular music, autobiographies, and Br'er Rabbit stories into their resistance.

White feminist theologians discuss another version of these hermeneutical principles. Ellen Wondra struggles with how, given the profound effects of patriarchy throughout all of written history, the truth of the scriptures and Jesus can be adequately understood and lived. Even the canons of scripture are the result of attempts to exclude women from their rightful place as disciples of Jesus.[53] How could Jesus, the ultimate symbol of God's love and justice, be misused throughout history to exclude and jeopardize women, thus exposing them to violence? Is the problem with the limitations of the various interpreters of Jesus, or has the symbolic content of Jesus Christ itself been distorted by patriarchy? According to Mary Daly,

> Defenders of [a] method [of reconstruction] argue that the symbol "can be used oppressively" or that it "has been used oppressively" but insist that it need not function in this way. This kind of defense is understandable but it leaves a basic question unanswered: if the symbol *can* be "used" that way and in fact has a long history of being "used" that way, isn't this an indication of some inherent deficiency in the symbol itself?[54]

Wondra believes that patriarchal misuse of theological symbols such as Jesus do point to an inherent sexism in theology that must be addressed.

> The challenge issued by feminist critics to Christology is apparently finally comprehensive. Not only are the core and indispensable symbols explicitly male to the exclusion of women, the character of the beings portrayed in these symbols is drawn from patriarchy, with the exaltation of individualism, idealism, and static perfection. The equation of this patriarchal ideal with divinity not only excluded the female from the Godhead; it sanctifies patriarchal maleness, with massively destructive historical effect. This is devastating also for understanding what it means to be human, for salvation is attained through the acceptance of passive victimization and coerced self-sacrifice, precisely what patriarchy demands of women who are defined

as less than fully human. There is, that is, no element of Christology that is left untouched.[55]

Therefore, Jesus cannot be understood solely through a hermeneutics of truth that focuses on whether contemporary theological symbols and ideas correspond with some aspect of the scriptures. Such a method avoids a hermeneutics of suspicion of the social location, motives, and methods of historical and contemporary interpreters. Without a full deconstruction of the personal, economic, and political motives of the communities of interpretation, the "truth" of the scriptures about Jesus can become a tool of domination and evil. However, when women from communities of resistance who are struggling for survival and liberation study the scriptures in search of Jesus, the patriarchal distortions in the scriptures are disclosed and the liberated text becomes a focus for acts of resistance. In brief, interpretations of Jesus must be evaluated within the context of organized resistance to patriarchy so that the historical oppression of women is not reproduced in the present.

Wondra also engages in a hermeneutics of confession by listening to the faith of women. Apart from the debate about the possibility of a feminist Christology and the judgment by some "that Christian feminism is impossible"[56] come the actual religious experiences of women—epiphanies and encounters with God that provide the basis of new theological reflection about Jesus Christ.

> Feminist religious thought is struggling to articulate a new kind of religious experience out of the life experience of women who have broken through at least some of the mediation imposed by patriarchal religious traditions. In so doing, some of these women have encountered an ultimate which is other than themselves, something indicative of the whole. They have encountered something they find meaningful, gracious, trustworthy, and profoundly true, something which stands with them against their subjugation and for their transformation.[57]

Women's religious experiences become confessions that provide the dynamic interplay between a hermeneutics of truth and confession. In resisting patriarchy and experiencing God as supportive and liberating, some women seek to know the truth of the scriptures and to understand their faith in relationships with Jesus.

> White feminist Christologies . . . rely on an interpretation of who Jesus is, emphasizing Jesus' egalitarian relations with others, his identification with the lowest of the low (many of whom are women), his renunciation of any

form of domination, his new understanding of service as mutual empower-ment, and his trust in God. White feminist Christologies also view his death as a consequence of a life of mutuality and justice in a historical situ-ation characterized by systems of domination, and they cast his resurrec-tion as the vindication by God of such a life.[58]

Wondra's confession of faith in the context of other critical tools creates the balance needed for a full hermeneutical method.

This review of womanist and feminist theologians challenges our inher-ited beliefs about Jesus. How can members of the dominant social class in the United States respond to this challenge? A constructive theological proposal follows in the next chapter.

CHAPTER ◆ NINE

JESUS AS RELIGIOUS RESISTER

The resistance communities we have studied claim that Jesus Christ empowers them to resist racial and gender evil. In spite of the established churches' abuse and misuse of Jesus Christ as a religious symbol, resistance communities draw on a liberated and critical consciousness to reject lies about Jesus and to find in Jesus a friend who empowers them for liberation. Even after centuries of evil appropriation of Jesus by the power elites, Jesus continues to function as a symbol of resistance and revolution. These resistance communities trust in Jesus rather than those who have power and resources. The issue for this chapter is whether Jesus can also be, for White males, a figure of liberation from the false consciousness that protects our power and privilege and hides our pain and suffering.

Ellen Wondra suggests that, in disclosing the relationship between God and humanity, Christology functions in two ways: manifestation and proclamation. In *manifestation*, Jesus Christ provides a firm foundation for faith and practice. Jesus is " 'the decisive re-presentation' of God and of the authentic character of human existence."[1] This is similar to a hermeneutics of confession that trusts personal and corporate experiences with Jesus. In *proclamation*, Jesus Christ shatters all theology and religious experience. "Here, the sacred or divine is encountered as a power that shatters, defamiliarizes, or stands over against the human as the radically other which is nonetheless like the self."[2] This is similar to a hermeneutics of suspicion that suspects all authoritative theological interpretations and interpreters, including oneself. Through this distinction Wondra helps us understand resistance communities' faith in Jesus Christ as authentic manifestations and proclamations of the reality of human and divine life.

Jesus is the Christ because he is the manifestation of the transformation of humanity in the struggle to resist dehumanization, *and* he is the definitive re-presentation of the only God who saves. In the Christ, redemption of all existence is accomplished in principle, but it will be actualized only fully in the future. Thus, the incarnation of God in Jesus the Christ is simultaneously revelation of what has always been the case, vindication of this enduring if concealed and distorted reality, and promise and prophecy of its greater future fulfillment.[3]

Our research in this project brings us to two christological formulations. First, Jesus' resistance to evil is a *manifestation* that assures us that human resistance to evil can be trusted, because it is the image of God in humans. Faith in Jesus thematizes resistance as a manifestation of "the true relation between the divine and the human (and so the true nature of both divine and human)."[4] Jesus resisted the evil of his day, even to death on a cross, and thus raises to ontological status human resistance to evil. Second, the mystery of Jesus' life, death, and resurrection is a *proclamation* that God is a mystery beyond all human understanding. Faith in Jesus therefore thematizes the mystery of God's Otherness as a proclamation of the multiplicity and ambiguity of both God and humanity. We consider each of these christological statements in the following sections.

JESUS AS RELIGIOUS RESISTER

A christological statement: *Jesus' resistance to evil discloses that resistance to evil is a fundamental attribute of God and humans.*
Wondra says:

For Christians, the resistance of both humanity and divinity to domination is decisively manifest and recognized in Jesus the Christ. In Christ, Christians find the dialectic movement from domination through resistance to transformation both vindicated in history and connected directly with the existence of God. Taken as a unity, Jesus Christ's life of active and transformative identification with the marginalized, his consequent death, and the vindication of his life and death manifested in the resurrection together reveal the possibilities of similar life for other persons, and vindicates its historical actualities.[5]

Jesus' spirit has not been fully destroyed by historical evil, because resistance to evil is a fundamental characteristic of God, and because Jesus' spirit lives on through those who resist evil. Thus, resistance to evil is not just a human response to life's difficulties, but is a fundamental attribute of divine and human life.

> Resistance to dehumanization thus discloses and develops previously un-recognized aspects of human being in history, and generates hope for further transformation, not only for the resisting victims, but also for those who remember them. Through resistance, thought and practice that are ruptured by the effects of domination are mended. Thus, resistance and reflection on it reconstitute human being as such, even in the midst of massive unjust suffering. Further, as resistance mends and motivates the human capacity to engage the very conditions of existence, resistance reveals anew the connection of human being to ongoing history and the transcendence toward which humanity strives. Resistance, then, is one of the elements that constitutes human being itself.[6]

While many stories about Jesus disclose resistance as a part of God's creation of humanity, the single event on which the Christian faith hinges is his death and resurrection. In an event that would be a failure by most human standards, God's commitment to resistance was most fully disclosed.

> The meaning of Jesus' life is confirmed in his death and vindicated in his resurrection. Jesus' own suffering and death are the outcome of a just life lived in resistance to an unjust world. . . . Jesus remained faithful to the marginalized in whose company he lived and taught, and to his prophetic and iconoclastic vision of God's reign. In suffering an ignominious and agonizing death, Jesus maintained his solidarity with the suffering and with victims of domination.[7]

This is how much Jesus loved the victims of oppression—that he loved them enough to die in solidarity with them.

For many Black and White citizens in the United States Martin Luther King, Jr., symbolizes faithfulness to Jesus by staying the course and fighting for justice to the end. Even though his life was in danger, even though in his final sermon in Memphis he told how he foresaw the end of his life, King remained faithful to his cause and maintained his resistance to evil.

Malcolm X became a christological symbol for many African Americans because "he loved us enough to die for us."[8] Malcolm X's courage to speak truth to power continues to be a symbol of the resistance of the oppressed to evil.

In Nicaragua, Augusto Sandino is also such a symbol. After many years of resisting a corrupt government from camps in the mountains, he trusted the promises of the government, laid down his arms to come for negotia-

tions and peace, and was assassinated. A full generation later, his followers, who called themselves Sandinistas, resisted a corrupt government for
many years, during which many of them were assassinated. The Sandinistas led a popular insurrection, after which they were elected to the government. Inspired by Sandino, many Nicaraguans hold fast to the love and
commitment to justice required for real justice to come.

In identifying King, Malcolm X, and Sandino as christological figures
for some people, I identify Jesus' resistance as a model of what is most
basically human as a basic God-created human characteristic.

> For Christians, then, Jesus is the Christ in that he is the decisive re-presen-
> tation of authentic humanity and the personification in history of the
> divine self. . . . Through Jesus the Christ, Christians recognize their own
> authentic existence in relation to God, and so are encouraged to see them-
> selves and others as continuously re-created in the form of the Christ.[9]

Jesus as religious resister reveals authentic humanity in the face of massive dehumanizing evils such as slavery, racism, and patriarchy. We recognize the holiness of the communities of resistance because they are
contemporary forms of Jesus' ongoing resistance to evil. In spite of centuries of distortion and betrayal, some communities of resistance find a
friend and co-sufferer in Jesus. He is the icon that defines the centrality
and limits of human resistance to evil.

JESUS' DISCLOSURE OF THE MULTIPLICITY
AND AMBIGUITY OF GOD AND HUMANS

A christological statement: *Jesus' relational love and power reveal the mystery of
God's Otherness and proclaim that multiplicity and ambiguity are fundamental attributes of divine and human life.*

Multiplicity is the existence of an Otherness that cannot be reduced to
unity and familiarity. God's love is irreducibly Other in human experience
and cannot be contained in any unity constructed by human systems. By
analogy, God has created human love as irreducibly Other, and it cannot
be reduced to a familiar unity.

Ambiguity is the existence of an Other morality that cannot be co-opted
by those in power, that stands against all systems of power that attempt to
oppress others. God's love and power are ambiguous in human experience
and cannot be contained in any human understanding of good and evil. As
creations of God, human love and power are ambiguous and cannot be
exhausted by appeals to any definitions of good and evil.

The ability to accept the love and power of God and self as multiple and ambiguous creates the possibility for resistance to evil.

Jesus reveals God to be fully relational and willing to risk relationships for the sake of love. Several conceptions of God—King, Lord, Father, Creator—have had historical primacy, but none of these terms fully captures the radical relationality of God as revealed in Jesus Christ. God in Christ was fully immersed in human historical existence; God was in Christ every step of his journey, even in his death upon the cross. Therefore, there is no human experience that is beyond the experience of God, including experiences of evil and death. God did not escape into heaven during the crucifixion, but hung on the cross with the full suffering of a human being. Therefore, God is crucified again whenever a child is raped or a woman murdered.

Jesus' life from beginning to end, as it is recorded in the Christian gospel, testifies to the existence of God's Otherness that cannot be reduced to familiarity by any principle of unity, and moral ambiguity that cannot be exhausted by appeals to any ethical system. The virgin birth, the baptism by John, the healing miracles, the parables, the crucifixion, and the amazing resurrection—all were familiar religious symbols in the world of the first century, and all testify to an Otherness and ambiguity that cannot be contained or controlled by those in power. People in the first century attributed the power of much of their experience to spirits and magic. However, the writers of the New Testament witness to the fact that Jesus was more than just another religious zealot or magician: He combined religion and subversive activity. He brought together the religious beliefs in mystery and Otherness and spoke "subversive speech [on behalf of] unknown others of uncertain morality."[10]

Jesus as a figure of mystery, especially evident in the crucifixion and resurrection, inspired the disciples to continue being a threat to established order, not only in Palestine but throughout the Roman Empire. By advocating an Otherness not included in the definitions of accepted human behavior, Jesus acted in "morally ambiguous" ways that violated the rules and procedures governing the ethics of the time. Jesus himself was other and ambiguous in the society of his time, and the movement he started continues to explode the categories set up by those who try to control his spirit.

Through the centuries, power elites have been trying to control the power of Jesus' spirit, mostly by coopting Jesus' images and language to oppress the poor. But, as we have seen in our study, Jesus' spirit regularly overcomes these distortions, exploding the categories of the powerful and empowering the poor to become subjects of history. We live in a time when resistance communities are challenging the very definitions of unity and morality imposed on them. I believe that Jesus' followers, and all who resist evil, reveal the mysterious Otherness that is fundamental to divine life.

African American Women

African American women have embodied multiplicity and ambiguity in the face of racial and gender evil. Slavery, racism, and patriarchy have combined to try to destroy the humanity of Black women. Christian theology in the nineteenth century instructed Black women who followed Jesus to be content as servants of White slaveholders, even if they were beaten and raped. Their inferiority was described as the will of God, and their proper place, they were told, was to serve as surrogates and slaves to their superiors. In effect, the one God of creation was defined as their righteous oppressor, and physical and sexual abuse was falsely defined as consistent with Christian, biblical ethics. Christian theology and natural law interpreted by White male theologians and enforced by the United States constitution labeled Black women nonpersons with no moral claims on justice and righteousness.

Against massive evil and violence, many Black women turned to Jesus. We have heard stories from Harriet Jacobs, Ida B. Wells, Sojourner Truth, and others whose names have been lost. What was their witness? That the definitions of unity and morality that created their oppression and its violence were evil. They witnessed that God was a spirit who could not be contained by the definitions of the powerful. They witnessed that God's morality differed from the morality written into the laws. They witnessed with their bodies and spirits that God's ways were not the ways of "men" who had the power to control official thoughts and actions. I believe God blessed the resistance of Black women and honored the wounds on their bodies and spirits. Through this community of resistance, God revealed Godself as multiple and ambiguous.

European American Women

European American women have embodied multiplicity and ambiguity in the face of gender and class evil. Patriarchy and classism in the United States have combined to oppress women and deny them the resources they need for full participation in families, church, and society. Although some women have been able to participate in the some of the privileges of wealth that come from social class, most have been trapped in poor and working-class families and in jobs that abuse their bodies and spirits. In addition, the subordination of women to men has been a primary cause of captivity, physical and sexual violence, and murder of women. Because women have had no legal protection against fathers, husbands, brothers, and other men, they often suffered and continue to suffer horrific violence. Our social categories—single women, poor women, working women, women forced into prostitution, domestic servants, and many others—leave women vulnerable. When the women's rights movement, in spite of its middle-class and racial bias, described the plight of women as analogous to slavery, they were not totally incorrect. Although United States slavery must always be understood as a category of systematic evil with no parallel in history, it is important to remember that vulnerable women frequently suffer exploitation and violence and must be counted among those who experience dehumanizing evil.

Against such massive evil and violence, many White women have turned to Jesus to support their resistance. And Jesus has supported their determination to survive. Elizabeth Cady Stanton, Susan B. Anthony, Phoebe Palmer, the Women's Christian Temperance Union, and hundreds of female revival preachers boldly spoke out. The resistance of many women in the name of Jesus questioned the definitions of gender and the official morality of the sexes. Women demanded the right to work, the right to vote, the right to preach as ordained ministers, the right to divorce alcoholic husbands, the right to own property and protect their children. In the name of Jesus, they resisted the unity and ethics of the social construction of gender. In this way, they were arguing for multiplicity and ambiguity. They were arguing that even though they were defined as Other, they had a right to be included in the definition of what was normatively human, and as moral agents they had a right to help decide what was right and wrong. Thus they presented their claims that God was Other than *men* defined God to be, and that the ambiguity of their moral lives deserved to be included in what was considered official morality.

We find moral ambiguity in the ongoing claim of women to control decisions about whether to bear children. Some versions of the dominant morality defines this claim, whether exercised through birth control or abortion, as equivalent to murder. Although some think they can easily define morality by equating abortion with murder, the right to choose whether or not to become a mother is a morally ambiguous decision. Yet women in large numbers claim this ambiguous morality as a right they intend to exercise, whether legal or not. The resistance of women to patriarchy and classism discloses the spirit of God, even though their claims cannot be included in the usual ways theology and ethics are defined, and even though no official doctrine of God or Christology can offer a firm foundation for these claims.

The multiple and ambiguous witness of resistance communities cri-
tiques White male theology. Furthermore, this witness has implications
for the way in which theology is constructed.

European American Men

Disclosure of multiplicity and ambiguity as fundamental characteristics of
the divine and human life point to major problems in traditional White
male theology in the United States; for instance, the emphasis on the
unity and perfection of God and Jesus. Just as God must be a unity and
must be perfect, so Jesus must be "one with the Father" and "without sin."
I am not arguing here that unity and perfection have not served useful
historical functions at various times in history. That would require a much
more extensive argument than I am prepared to make. What I am claiming
is that doctrines of the unity and perfection of God and Jesus have provided the occasion for the misuse of Christian theology to support slavery,
racism, and patriarchy in United States church and society. Although I
acknowledge a drive for unity and perfection in the godhead that is part
of theological reflection, here I argue that a drive for multiplicity and
ambiguity must also be a part of theological reflection. The fact that multiplicity and ambiguity are so often excluded, in spite of biblical warrant
in the theologies of creation and redemption, furnishes evidence for my
point. I want to ask how unity and perfection have been used for evil
purposes, and whether multiplicity and ambiguity have their place as
theological constructs worthy of our reflection and consideration. If multiplicity and ambiguity do become more widely accepted as characteristics of God and humanity, we will need to be alert to their misuse and
abuse by systems of evil. In any fully developed Christology, unity/
multiplicity and perfection/ambiguity probably belong together in dia-
lectical tension. For the sake of this discussion, given the dominance of
unity and perfection language, we need to consider the contribution of
multiplicity and ambiguity to the construction of a more fully developed
Christology. We need to ask why White male theology has been so pre-
occupied with unity and perfection in Christology. I believe the answer is
that these two ideas function very well to rationalize and justify power
arrangements that benefit the social class of those producing theology.

GOD AND CHRIST AS ONE AND MULTIPLE

If God is a unity who speaks with one voice concerning the human situation, and if Jesus Christ is the full and complete revelation of God's will

for humans, then those who control the content of this revelation can speak confidently about normative revelation. If those who speak with other voices can be marginalized or excluded from the conversation, it is easier for theologians to reach consensus on what God is saying through Jesus. To the extent that multiplicity can be eliminated through the exercise of power, the unity of God's revelation to humans can be more easily attained.

The context of power arrangements thus influences the content of God's unified voice to humans. Theologians who best serve the interests of those in power will be given the right to speak for God's unified revelation. This process of self-selection becomes a powerful motive for theologians who best protect their own class privilege by providing theological justification for the interests of the ruling class. When one examines the economic interests that fund theological schools and theologians in the United States, it is not hard to imagine why theologians would speak with unity in ways that support certain economic and political interests. For example, why did so many prominent Christian theologians in the nineteenth century provide proof of God's tolerance for slavery? Why were the arguments against slavery so easily marginalized?

The conflict between the Quakers and the Anglican Society for the Propagation of the Gospel provides part of the answer. The Quakers held to the principle that slavery was wrong and abolished it by 1800 within the Society of Friends. As a result, the Quakers remained a small, isolated minority voice in United States history. In contrast, the Anglican Society for the Propagation of the Gospel compromised its original position and provided theological justification for the compatibility of slavery and the baptism of African Americans. As a result, the Anglican Church flourished in the southern states, with money and prestige from the slaveholding classes supporting the mission of the Anglican Church. The result is the continued prominence of the Episcopal Church in the United States today.[11] This example shows how the interests of theologians who spoke for the unified voice of God and the economic and political interests of the slaveholders coincided and created a foundation for slavery in the United States.

Meanwhile, the voices of Quakers, and, much more tragically, the voices of African American Christians were silenced so that God's unity could be preserved. Anyone who challenged the unity of God's revelation was harshly treated. Theologians defined *orthodoxy*, so that any opposing beliefs became heresy or *heterodoxy*. Using our current knowledge, we see that *heterodoxy* represented the interests of the oppressed, and *orthodoxy* represented the interests of those in power. Thus, *orthodoxy* or the unified voice of God was used for violence and evil of slavery.

Likewise, the unity of God has been a tool of oppression against the interests of women. How did men come to identify themselves as a social class with such strong interests that they were willing to oppress all women for the sake of their own privilege? This question is especially interesting because the contemporary backlash criticizes feminism for promoting a divisive class consciousness among women. The idea that God's voice is male, and that the gender of Jesus and the disciples is theologically significant, continues to be powerful. The effectiveness of the arguments about the gender of God partly depends on the assumption that God must speak in one voice, and that this one voice must be consistent with the perception of how God's voice has spoken in the past. The fact that Jesus called God "Father" is used as an argument that God must forever be consistent with this one event. God can show no signs of disunity or of difference. Surely, then, God intends that humans forever understand *him* as *Father*, and that any Other address must be an offense to God *himself*. The unity of God has been used as a tool of oppression to privilege the voices of men at the expense of women whose voices are discounted. Keeping women divided and disempowered is a strategy of many male-dominant Christian groups.

Apparently, even though men themselves exist within several economic classes, they identify themselves with shared class interests in contrast to women. Although not all men can be wealthy and control society, all have the privilege of exercising power over women. The poorest man has the right to abuse women as long as he stays within his social class. Some of the most severe criminal penalties are reserved for the men of the poor and working classes who act out their violence on women who *belong* to men of the higher social classes.

Because male theologians too have traditionally benefited from a theology of male dominance, they have been willing to provide its theological justification. As we saw in chapter 4, when Augustus Hopkins Strong opposed women's suffrage in 1878, he provided theological support for northern liberals in their battle against southern conservatives. The successful division of the progressive movements along racial and gender lines served the interests of the ruling classes, and, in the compromise of 1877, White men of North and South reached an agreement that enabled them to share the power at the expense of both Blacks and women. Male dominance and White supremacy came together to benefit White men in power, and theologians made a significant contribution by providing a male-dominant theology. According to theologians such as Augustus Strong, God spoke in a unified White male voice, and the voices of resistance from White women and African American women and men were

marginalized, and their oppression was enforced by violence that was ignored by the same theologians.

In this section, I have argued that the assumptions about the unity of
God facilitated the existence and maintenance of evil systems such as slavery, racism and patriarchy. If God can speak in only one voice, then the
voices that differ from those in power can be repressed and declared he-
retical heterodoxy. The abusive label of heterodoxy can be used to destroy the economic and political claims of communities of resistance who
know another Jesus.

GOD AND CHRIST AS PERFECT AND AMBIGUOUS

If official theologians understand God as perfectly good, and if Jesus
became human without sinning, then the myth of perfection can be used
as a justification for abuse of power. The perfection of God and Jesus lead
to an ethic of purity. For example, the public perceives politics as a "dirty
business" and believes that those who engage in politics cannot avoid
"getting their hands dirty." But power gives one the ability to hide this
impurity, and when power is massive enough, individuals and groups can
claim perfect goodness for whatever they choose. In the early days of
slavery, little thought was given to whether or not it was moral, because it
was just an extension of many other dehumanizing realities of life in the
seventeenth century. Indentured servants had few rights and were treated
badly, regardless of their ethnic background. Some early proponents of
slavery believed that although it was not a good thing, the harsh life of
colonizing a new continent made it a necessary evil. But as slavery increased and become more identified as a racialized institution, it required
a more complex justification. Theologians then went to work to define
slavery as a positive good rather than as a necessary evil. They drew on
images of Africa as a continent of savages and heathens who were unci-
lized and unchristian, and argued that bringing the Africans into daily
contact with hard-working, upright White Christians improved both races.
White slaveholders could have help with the difficult task of harnessing
the energy of the frontier, and Africans could improve their condition by
adopting European, Christian values and attitudes. Thus the argument was
made that what initially looked like an evil exploitation of a vulnerable
group of people was actually a good that spread Christian values throughout the peoples of the world. Later, this argument became a problem,
when slaveholders argued that African inferiority was ordained by God,
which limited the extent to which Christian values could benefit Africans.
Their *natural* inferiority made them fit for slavery, but not for freedom and

citizenship under the Bible and the Constitution. Finally, in the antebellum period, the stereotype of the "happy slave" emerged to show that slavery was actually beneficial for Africans, and that they became unhappy and symptomatic if they were given too much freedom. Their *natural* place was servitude under the close supervision of their wise, Christian masters and mistresses.

The process of redefining evil as a positive good relates to the theology of divine perfection. If God is perfect, and if Jesus could not sin, the followers of Jesus are called to be perfect as well. This drive for perfection has often taken the form of constructing theological justifications for existing power arrangements, rather than providing a prophetic challenge based on historical principles of goodness. Thus, slaveholders created special privileges for theologians who were willing to tackle the difficult problems presented by the resistance communities. When Nat Turner led the 1831 rebellion, official theologians argued that the implicit social critique of slavery was only an illusion. This rebellion, theologians concurred, showed that when Africans were educated and exposed to Christian ideas, they could not tolerate such complexity and freedom, and reverted to a previous African savagery. Such savages could only understand greater control and supervision enforced by violence and death. Theologians willing to argue that literacy and Christianity were of limited value in ensuring obedient slaves were given prominence.

In like manner, the oppression of White women was enforced by appeals to images of perfection. The marks of "piety, purity, submissiveness and domesticity"[12] that characterized the "cult of true womanhood", were drawn largely from the Bible, especially from images of Jesus. Women were instructed to be especially religious, since that was their nature, and since they were too weak to cope with the harsh world men had to endure. The romantic ideas of Jesus as a meek, mild, nonresistant teacher were especially useful as a model for religious women. Thus the followers of Jesus, who were largely women, were encouraged to be like Jesus—to teach the children, to care for the sick, to feed the hungry, to visit those who were unfortunate, to make the home a safe place for men to return to. In regard to their sexuality, women were encouraged to remain pure, to deny any sexual desires of their own, and to patiently tolerate the sexual needs of their husbands. Women were instructed to endure their suffering as Jesus had done, and to be obedient to their fathers and husbands, as Jesus had been obedient to God. This double standard allowed men to use whatever means they chose for "making it" in the hostile world, and allowed them then to return to the sanctuary of the home where they could relax and have their needs met. Outside the home, as everyone knew, the Christian values of love, forgiveness, and submissiveness would never work. Fortunately, God had created men with the toughness they needed to survive, as long as they could come home to a faithful and submissive wife whose primary concern was her husband's welfare.

Thus the purity of Jesus was applied directly to women. Women were expected to guard their purity with their lives, since any hint of stain or disobedience threatened the future of society.[13] If women became impure, how would Christianity preserve its gentler values of faith, hope, and charity? Someday the hostile world would be conquered and every place would become like the Christian home. Women, therefore, because they were most like Jesus, became the repositories of Christian virtue.

Negative images also controlled the behavior of women. One image that enforced the "cult of true womanhood" was its opposite: the loose woman, the prostitute, the Jezebel. The fallen woman, who, like Eve, tempted men to sin and betray their identification with the Father God provided the foil that defined the meaning of religious purity. Preachers railed against the woman who had fallen from the graces of God and who threatened the very foundation of society.

Cast outside the protection of the family, women were vulnerable to the violence of men. In contrast to Dr. Norcom's wife, who guarded the virtue of the home, Harriet Jacobs was sexualized by Dr. Norcom. In the White religious imagination of pure and impure women, the sexualized Black woman functioned to reinforce the purity of the Jesus ethic. The pure women were wives and mothers whose virtue was to be guarded. The power of the image of the pure White woman served effectively after the Civil War to rationalize false rape charges and lynchings of Black men. The impure women—Black, single, and promiscuous—had no protection against violence and rape, but the existence of this ideology was crucial for the definition of the pure White woman who was threatened by the imagined lust of Black men. The ethic of purity, selectively applied to women depending on their race and class, served to maintain the subordination of all women to men.

Such subordination of women, enforced by the Jesus ethic of purity, served the economic and political interests of White men on several different levels. First, the subordination of women limited positions of power to half of the population and thus created less competition. No matter how able or strong a woman was, she could always be put in her place by appeals to gender. Men who felt competition from women had a ready-made ideology to protect their interests when they felt threatened.

Second, the subordination of women provided a form of negotiation and compromise in the competition for power between men. Any serious competition for dominance ran the risk of causing an escalation of violence and destruction. However, the subordination of women provided a medium of exchange and negotiation. Since women were vulnerable to male control, men could exchange them as part of the struggle for dominance. The man with control of more women could share his wife, daughters, concubines, and servants with other men in exchange for their cooperation with his power arrangements. Even the men at the bottom of the power pyramid could be given access to the most "worthless" women in exchange for cooperation and peaceful coexistence. Within this system of exchange, a pure woman was always worth more than an impure woman. The myth of the man who gives away his "virgin daughter" to his potential enemy shows the effectiveness of this exchange (Gen. 19:1–11; Judges 19:11–30).[14]

Third, the subordination of women created a surplus pool of exploitable labor for the needs of capitalism. When the factories in the northeast opened, they employed women and children, some of them immigrants and some from farms and villages, who worked to help the family survive hardship and illness. These women and children could be exploited by the factory owners because they provided cheap, dependable labor, and also because they sent their wages home to increase the wealth of the male heads of families. When the economic cycle turned downward, they could be sent home without any sense of responsibility for their welfare. Such an expendable labor force was crucial during the early stages of United States industrialization. Likewise, when the subordination of these women was compounded by racial oppression or oppression because of immigrant status, workers had even less protection and could be exploited in multiple ways. For such groups, economic exploitation, poverty, and physical and sexual abuse all came together to create massive oppression and dehumanization. Thus the social category of the impure woman whose virtue needed no protection served handily to reinforce White male dominance, with its ethic of purity.

A NEW IMAGE OF JESUS

In the preceding two sections, I showed several ways in which Christology has provided inspiration for African American and White women in communities of resistance, and several ways in which Christology has been misused by White men in systems of oppression. Multiplicity and ambiguity are implicit and explicit themes of African American and White women's resistance as they have challenged official definitions of the unity and purity of Jesus. In situations of massive oppression and evil, women have called on multiple and ambiguous images of Jesus for survival and resistance, and Jesus' spirit has supported their resistance because Jesus himself was a religious resister of evil.

My question for this section is whether drawing on the latent biblical tradition that points to the multiplicity and ambiguity of Jesus can loosen the stranglehold of racial and gender oppression in our contemporary situation. What would it mean to say that there is more than one Jesus, that there are many Jesuses in the contemporary church, and that, in fact, God is creating more Jesuses every day as new resistance communities find their religious voices and confess their knowledge of God? What would it mean to say that Jesus is morally ambiguous, not only because of the limitations of human morality, but because God is creating ever-new forms of morality and ambiguity as a necessary aspect of creativity itself?[15]

Multiplicity and ambiguity are major themes in contemporary philosophy, theology, and in critical theories in literature and other social and physical sciences. For example, some chaos theories suggest that human ideas of unity, integration, and perfection may misinterpret the creative urge of the physical world, and that chaos may be as much a principle of the universe as order. We will not review these arguments, except to acknowledge our indebtedness to this larger context of ideas that have influenced this project from its beginning.[16]

At first it seems frightening and unorthodox to suggest that Jesus may be multiple and ambiguous, not only as a symbol of humanity but also as a manifestation of God. We know that human beings are fragmented and morally ambiguous—this is what classical theological formulations mean by finitude and original sin. There is no way humans can escape the limits of historical and corporeal existence, and it is only by the grace of God that we can live, knowing that the God of the universe, who is *not* subject to this same fragmentation and ambiguity, loves and cares for us and has power to accomplish God's purposes. In moving toward a relational God, one involved in history and in all dynamic processes, most theologians are willing to make some adjustments in the traditional impassibility of God. At least in relation to human freedom, God must be limited in some kinds of power. Why would God create human freedom, and then make this freedom an illusion? God must have a kind of power that is limited by the ontological right of humans to make decisions that are opposed to the will of God. Otherwise, a relational God is logically impossible, and our religious experience of a God who respects mutual covenants of trust and faithfulness is a lie. In response to this postmodern crisis, some theologians are reverting to classical definitions of sovereignty and omnipotence, but most theologians and many believers are willing to curtail the doctrine of impassible power in favor of a relational God.[17]

More difficult for most theologians and believers is the set of ideas I am proposing, namely that God, as revealed in Jesus Christ, may be multiple and ambiguous in some fundamental way. Most Christians are attached to two ideas: that God speaks in one voice if we can only hear it, and that God is perfect in love. How could we live in a world of evil and destructiveness if we could not hold on to the idea of God's unity and perfection?

My research into racial and gender violence has forced me to question these assumptions of faith and theology for two reasons: first, unity and perfection have been used to promote racial and gender evil; second, the witnesses from African American and European American women in communities of resistance raise the themes of multiplicity and ambiguity. This has led me to wonder whether the attachment to Jesus' unity and perfection is not motivated by fear of the new thing God is doing in history through resistance communities, and by a nostalgia for a past theological security that never existed in the first place. I have been moved by the attempts of Jacquelyn Grant, Delores Williams, and Kelly Brown Douglas to reexamine such doctrines as servanthood, atonement, and the gender and race of Jesus for evidence of racism and sexism. Likewise, I have been moved by the attempts of Joanne Carlson Brown, Rita Nakashima Brock, and Ellen Wondra to reexamine such doctrines as suffering, obedience, innocence, and resistance to evil. Each of these theologians challenges my faith and forces me to take seriously insights into the nature of Jesus that have never before been a part of my experience. In themselves, these claims are multiple and ambiguous because they force me to confront thoughts and feelings about Jesus that I did not have before, and which threaten to open me to a future I cannot predict or control.

Beyond my own encounter with multiplicity and ambiguity in my religious experience, I am led to wonder, as a believer and a theologian, about Jesus as a manifestation and proclamation of God. It is striking to me that Jesus has taken so many forms in the religious imaginations of some women in communities of resistance. It is amazing that White male theologians, with orthodox, unified, and perfect Christologies, have been the most supportive of racial and gender oppression. I am led to wonder how ideas really matter, since the most heterodox are more faithful to the spirit of Jesus as I have experienced it, and the most orthodox are more susceptible to evil influence. I believe in Jesus, but can I really face the fact his multiplicity and ambiguity is a further revelation of God in my life and in history? What would it look like if I tried?

A CHRISTOLOGY TO INSPIRE WORSHIP

I believe the task of White men at this time in United States history is to engage in a process of decentering power arrangements.[18] For God's history to move without increasing the incidence of violence, White men must be willing to be vulnerable and accountable to the power of others, which, in the case of this book, means especially the power of those who resist racial and gender evil. I believe God is creating a new world in which White male power *per se* must radically change its function in church and society. This means that we must relinquish our power positions in order to live within a world of relationality and mutuality with other persons and groups. God has chosen to empower those who are Other to me, so that I might enjoy qualities of relationships that have been impossible before.

As a result, for me and for many others, Jesus will be Other and ambiguous. I have the option of rejecting this vision of the future, and holding on to my ideas of Jesus' unity and perfection with an assumption that Jesus today is the same as he was when I was first converted. I can defend my claims that I know Jesus in a special way and have the right to interpret his life and teachings as I like. The risk I take, however, is that I am rejecting the living Jesus in favor of an idol I have constructed to protect my social and religious power and privilege.

For me as a White person, Jesus as Other and ambiguous is found in the witness of African American Christians. Because I have been raised in a racist society with a long history of racial oppression, identification with the moral and religious claims of the African American community is frightening. Yet I believe that one of the manifestations of God to me, as Martin Luther King, Jr., believed, is that God has elected African American Christians as a special revelation of God's truth and justice at this time in history. This religious insight stands in direct contrast to the religious and secular appropriation of African American music and culture, which denies the witness about economic and political oppression. Many fundamentalist preachers have modeled their evangelistic style after the tradition of Black preaching, yet appeal to racist stereotypes in the content of their messages. Believing that Jesus is being revealed through the African American churches means accepting responsibility for the historic and contemporary injustice in the United States that keeps two-thirds of the Black community in economic subordination, and half of Black children in poverty. Yet, it also acknowledges that racism and paternalism prevent the White church, of which I am a part, from seeing today's Jesus. Few projects of mutual accountability between Black and White churches have actually created powerful symbols of social and personal transformation.

The insight that Jesus appears to me in the form of African American women also opens me to the possibility that Jesus can appear in the form of women from other oppressed groups. My experiences in Nicaragua confirm this possibility and the moral claims of such Christian women against the United States churches are profound.

Believing that Jesus is Other and ambiguous is to give up on my ability to know and do the will of God as long as my doing and knowing depends on my experience as a White person. As long as I have confidence that I understand God's will for my life based solely on my own experience, I am worshipping a White idol of perfection that is an extension of my own prejudices. Jesus is not who I have always thought Jesus was. God is raising up Other images of Jesus that are transforming the world. These images of Jesus can decenter me from my ethnocentrism in a radical way and leave me without the culture I have depended on for my identity. Trusting in the God of Others will be my greatest test of faith.

For me as a male person, Jesus as Other and ambiguous is found in the witness of women, gaymen, and lesbians. I find it frightening to think of God as female because I have been socialized to identify being female with being dominated and abused. I find it frightening to think that gender itself is a socially constructed fiction, and that the otherness and ambiguity of Jesus might be revealed through genders that do not fit my categories of male and female. The gay and lesbian communities have been experimenting with such possibilities for more than a century,[19] and their claims are just now being re-presented in church and society. The church's panic about a world of multiplicity of sexualities and genders is palpable. For me, the question is whether Jesus can be a religious figure for worship as a woman, gayman, or lesbian.

For many, the questions of gender raise basic fears that drive them back to the unity and perfection of God. Nostalgia for a God who created two and only two genders, man and woman in a dominant and subordinate hierarchy, is a deep assumption that cannot easily be challenged. But I believe this is what God is asking me to do. My attachment to certain definitions of gender are idols that must be smashed in order to experience my own liberation. For me, God is necessarily multiple and ambiguous because I cannot comprehend the majesty and creativity of such a God. I must trust that the multiplicity and ambiguity of my life is the revelation of God, and to follow Jesus means to trust in God.

These deeply personal reflections have led me to conclude that Jesus Christ has revealed multiplicity and ambiguity as foundational attributes of God. Jesus, a member of the lower class in Palestine, participated in a resistance movement against the economic, political, and religious domination of his time. His spirit has lived on in the long history of resistance against evil, even when his name has been misused to sanction the violence of empires and individuals. In the contemporary United States, Jesus is known through the resistance of African American women and men to slavery and racism, and through the resistance of women to patriarchy. For me, as a White male Christian, this revelation of Jesus decenters me from the tradition I have most identified with, namely the dominant White male power structure. If God is no longer working through the domination system, then my discipleship to Jesus Christ takes me away from my cherished identifications, to a new land where I don't know the people, the genders, the cultures, the language, the customs. Can I trust in the living God in this new place? Or will I flee back to the security of the idols I have created? I believe in God, and I want to follow Jesus. I will worship the God of multiplicity and ambiguity, with the help of my friend and co-sufferer, Jesus.

In the next chapter we will briefly examine what this christological statement might mean in terms of Christian praxis.

POSTSCRIPT

PRACTICING GOODNESS

During one of my trips to Nicaragua, a group of North Americans and Europeans were discussing the difficulty of living a relational life in a world in which so much evil exists. One person said he avoids feeling overwhelmed by such moral dilemmas by concentrating on the issues most immediate to himself—his own integrity and his relationships with friends. He tries to wrestle some mutual satisfaction and pleasure from life.

"What about practicing goodness?" another person asked. He went on to say that a basic need of everyone is to practice goodness so that we know our life is not just for ourselves and a few friends, but also for the good of the world. That simple phrase—practicing goodness—can be a form of faithfulness to the multiple, ambiguous life that comes when we follow Jesus.

What does it mean for persons of the dominant cultures to practice goodness in the world of racial and gender evil? I suggest six responses:

1. *Develop a spirituality of resistance.*[1] People from the dominant cultures must join the struggles of the resistance communities to avoid hopelessness. To develop a spirituality of resistance, we must immerse ourselves in the stories and lives of Others. In the midst of suffering, those who have resisted evil and survived have found that God's love is stronger than the power of evil. Some have lived to tell about their experiences, of their suffering and their hope. The more we hear, read, and meditate on such stories, the more they shape our identities. We need to remember, however, that most victims of evil do not survive, and we must mourn those losses.

A spirituality of resistance requires conversion of the inner imagination so that identity is located in the history of resistance to evil rather than in oppressive structures. Disidentifying with established power is a soul-wrenching experience for those of us who have been formed by the dominant culture, for we are forced to face our complicity and open ourselves to the massive suffering whose existence we have denied. However, we can be empowered as we join in the grief of Jesus over the ongoing crucifixion of the children of God.

During this stage, we need a place to share our fears about what is happening. We may experience rejection from others whom we have counted on in the past, but we may also find new co-travelers anxious to talk about their own fears. We can provide mutual support for one another.

2. *Live in solidarity with resistance communities.* As persons of the dominant culture experience a transformation of imagination, we can discover a new identity, one in solidarity with victims and survivors. We can become engaged in communities of resistance, emotionally bonding in interpersonal relationships. A friend said to me about a good-hearted person who had worked in Nicaragua for five years: "She has no Nicaraguan friends." This means that in all her charity work to help the poor of Central America, she had not bonded with a single person from the group she has been trying to help. Practicing goodness requires nurturing relationships with persons whose lives are in jeopardy because of their social class and their resistance activities.

Solidarity with communities of resistance requires action. Sometimes using words in speeches, articles, and books can be forms of action. But most of the time actions require working with our hands, experiencing rejection, sharing deprivation, going hungry, putting our bodies in danger, fearing assault or murder. Communities of resistance always exist in a web of violence and danger; therefore, living in solidarity brings us face-to-face with violence and fear.

3. *Take moral and material inventory.* As members of the dominant culture, we may imagine that we care about the poor and oppressed, but most of us are hard pressed to identify specific moral or material resources we have shared. Nurturing relationships with communities of resistance does little good unless we are willing to be accountable to them and unless we take an inventory of how we organize our lives. In doing an inventory of my life and work, I recently discovered that all my forms of accountability to resistance groups were psychological and voluntary, while all my forms of accountability to the dominant institutions of society were material and mandatory.[2]

Taking an inventory requires help, because we hide our privileges and resources from ourselves. More aware of the resources we lack than those we have, we tend to devalue what we have in order to maintain our innocence and limit responsibility for our power. The best help for taking a moral and material inventory usually comes from those in the resistance who lack the same privileges and resources.

4. *Confront the abuser within*. Central to accepting responsibility for power is boldly facing attitudes and actions for which we are individually responsible—times we have asserted patriarchal privilege at the expense of individual women; times we have willfully overlooked our own racism even when we could see its consequences for persons of color; times when our sexual desires have objectified and abused persons who were temporarily dependent on our nurture and love. For these individual actions, we must confess our sins and repent of our evil deeds.

But confession and repentance are not enough in a world in which violence damages the spirits and wounds the bodies of those oppressed by racial and gender evil. By building relationships with communities of resistance, we begin mending the relational web wherever it can be repaired and working to reestablish justice and trustworthiness.

5. *Confront persons of power*. We must be willing to use the power we have to confront those who abuse their power. Confrontation involves speaking truth to power, defecting in place, and taking the consequences.

When we stand in solidarity alongside communities of resistance, we join them in speaking truth to power. Thus, as members of the dominant class, we contribute to the strengthening of coalitions who are presenting the moral claims of the oppressed and who are working for social justice.

We defect in place when we act against our narrow class interests for the sake of justice for all people. Scripture mandates defection from the principalities and powers of this world, but we see too few examples of its practice. In fact, defectors often become scapegoats as the systems of power work to reestablish their hegemony.

If we speak truth to power or defect in place, we must be willing to take the consequences. Taking the consequences requires that we persevere during times of testing and failure of our commitments. Confronting the powerful nearly always results in making enemies. Enemies are those who have the will to destroy us, and are waiting for the opportunity.[3]

6. *Negotiate with institutions*. When the credibility and survival of many institutions is on the line, what does it mean to be an institutional leader concerned about evil? As institutions shrink in size and influence, we need to ask who will benefit from these changes. Survival can never be an adequate goal for those with institutional power, because the question must always be asked—survival for whom? Who will benefit from any change, whether an institution is expanding or shrinking? It is possible for an institution to decrease in size without losing its commitment to multiple groups with different needs. But in order for this to occur, leaders need to overcome their institutional fears and work self-consciously toward goals of justice and love for all people. Change therefore needs to be made through careful compromises and bold initiatives. How do we

relate to institutions that have betrayed their function as healing and liberating communities? As support for justice work dwindles, we must find alternative communities where we can maintain our commitments to our basic values.

During a lecture by Ernesto Cardenal, author of *The Gospel in Solentiname*—one of the texts that defines the meaning of Latin American liberation theology[4]—someone in the audience asked, "What kind of change are you really asking for?" He answered by telling about the Bishops' Conference in Pueblo, Mexico (1979), that created and popularized the term "liberation theology." Representatives of grass-roots movements of priests and poor people all over Latin America came to the Bishops' Conference to promote the idea of fundamental economic and political change. After long debate, the bishops passed some of the proposals, but they rejected the word chosen by the people, "revolution," and chose instead "liberation." The effect of this change, according to Cardenal, was to spiritualize the theology of the Base Christian Communities and to deemphasize their socioeconomic analysis. That one change eclipsed the revolutionary character of theology as a resource for addressing massive poverty and dehumanization. As a result, liberation theology has become a popular middle-class term in the United States, without the full implications of social justice for the oppressed.

In the United States, we do not have a good word for the kind of change that is needed. Given the analysis resulting from our study, the imperatives of the Gospel, and our solidarity with communities of resistance, we share their vision of the future: a time when European and North American male power is no longer dominant in the world; a time when the world's resources are equally shared; a time when violence in service of oppression is no longer the tool of governments; a time when wealth and opportunity are redistributed. For this vision to become reality current systems of power and wealth must change.

For middle-class North Americans who benefit in so many ways from the current system, such changes seem frightening. But unless we understand and work in solidarity with the communities of resistance here and around the world, we will never be able to face the needs of the world at this time in history. Disidentifying with our known world, the one we feel comfortable with, and forming a new identity based on multiplicity and ambiguity is a hard task.

The multiple and ambiguous Jesus calls us to follow him. Which Jesus will we follow? Which of the moral codes attributed to him will we live out? We are called to live courageously with the uncertainty and confusion of these questions. Long live God's Revolution.

NOTES

Introduction: Deliver Us from Evil

1. I have adapted this definition from the following sources: Patricia Hill Collins, *Black Feminist Thought: Knowledge, Consciousness, and the Politics of Empowerment* (New York: Routledge, 1990), 92–93; Audre Lorde, *Sister Outsider* (Freedom, Calif.: The Crossing Press, 1984), 42.

2. Gerda Lerner, *The Emergence of Feminist Consciousness* (New York: Oxford University Press, 1993).

3. For a definition of power, see James Newton Poling, *The Abuse of Power: A Theological Problem* (Nashville: Abingdon, 1991), 23–33.

4. For other definitions of practical theology see Poling, *The Abuse of Power*, 186–91; James Poling and Donald Miller, *Foundations for a Practical Theology of Ministry* (Nashville: Abingdon, 1985), 62–99.

5. I especially thank Evelyn Kirkley and Donald Matthews.

6. I give special thanks to Toinette Eugene, Emilie Townes, Donald Matthews, Gilbert Bond, Marie Fortune, Evelyn Kirkley, Ellen Wondra, and Nancy Poling, who read all or part of my manuscript and gave me critical feedback.

7. My special thanks to Brenda Consuelo Ruiz, who gave me critical feedback on my manuscript; to the faculty of Seminario Teologico Bautista; and the staff at Asociacion Evangelica de Asesoramiento Familiar in Managua, Nicaragua.

Chapter 1. Race, Gender, and White Supremacy

1. Henry Louis Gates, *The Classic Slave Narratives* (New York: Penguin, 1987), 361.

2. Ibid., 367.

3. Ibid.

4. Ibid., 369.

5. Ibid., 371.

6. Ibid., 385.

7. See Hazel Carby, *Reconstructing Womanhood: The Emergence of the Afro-American Woman Novelist* (New York: Oxford University Press, 1987). "She thought that in his fury Dr. Flint would sell her to her newly acquired lover and that it would be easier in the future to obtain her freedom from her lover than from her master. Linda's reasoning was shown to

be motivated by consideration not only for her own welfare but also for improving the chances for survival for any children she might bear. From her experience she knew that Dr. Flint sold his offspring from slave women and hoped that if her children were fathered by Sands he could buy them and secure their future" (58).

8. Gates, *The Classic Slave Narratives*, 385.

9. Ibid.

10. "Linda Brent's decision as a slave, to survive through an act that resulted in her loss of virtue, placed her outside of parameters of the conventional heroine. . . . Jacobs's narrative was unique in its subversion of a major narrative code of sentimental fiction: death, as preferable to loss of purity, was replaced by "Death is better than slavery.' " Carby, *Reconstructing Womanhood*, 58.

11. Gates, *The Classic Slave Narratives*, 386.

12. Ibid., 387–88.

13. Ibid., 403.

14. Ibid.

15. Ibid., 404.

16. Harriet A. Jacobs, *Incidents in the Life of a Slave Girl Written by Herself*, Jean Fagan Yellin, editor (Cambridge, Mass.: Harvard University Press, 1987). See also Gates, *The Classic Slave Narratives*.

17. Shawn Copeland, "Wading through Many Sorrows," in Emilie M. Townes, editor, *A Troubling in My Soul: Womanist Perspectives on Evil and Suffering* (Maryknoll, N.Y.: Orbis, 1993), 111.

18. "This narrator tells a double tale, dramatizing the triumph of her efforts to prevent her master from raping her, to arrange for her children's rescue from him to hide, to escape, and finally to achieve freedom; and simultaneously presenting her failure to adhere to sexual standards in which she believed." Jacobs, *Incidents in the Life of a Slave Girl*, xiv.

19. Gates, *The Classic Slave Narratives*, 391.

20. Ibid., 345.

21. Copeland, "Wading through Many Sorrows," in Townes, 121.

22. Gates, *The Classic Slave Narratives*, 371.

23. Patricia Hill Collins, *Black Feminist Thought: Knowledge, Consciousness, and the Politics of Empowerment* (New York: Routledge, 1990), 93.

24. The term "matrix of domination" is from Collins, *Black Feminist Thought*, 225. The rest of the definition is adapted from The Cornwall Collective, *Your Daughters Shall Prophesy* (New York: Pilgrim, 1980), 39.

25. Gates, *The Classic Slave Narratives*, 371.

26. Ibid., 403.

27. Ibid., 368.

28. Yellin has validated the historical accuracy of Harriet Jacob's story. Jacobs, *Incidents in the Life of a Slave Girl*, 224, 265.

29. Ronald Takaki, *Iron Cages: Race and Culture in Nineteenth Century America* (New York: Oxford University Press, 1990), 14, attributed to Benjamin Franklin, *Observations Concerning the Increase of Mankind* (1751).

30. Winthrop Jordan, *White over Black: American Attitudes toward the Negro: 1550–1812* (New York: W. W. Norton and Co., 1968), 317.

31. John Hope Franklin and Alfred A. Moss, Jr., *From Slavery to Freedom: A History of Negro Americans* (New York: Knopf, 1988), 488.

32. Jordan, *White over Black*, 431.

33. Ibid., 433–34.

34. Ibid., 433.
35. Ibid., 481.
36. Takaki, *Iron Cages*, 44.
37. Jordan, *White over Black*, 436–37.
38. Ibid., 439.
39. Ibid., 458.
40. Ibid., 458–59.
41. Ibid., 466.
42. Takaki, *Iron Cages*, 51. Other historians object more strongly to the charges and the scandal it produced. "It is impossible to believe that Jefferson abandoned his love for Maria Cosway to force his affections on even the most beautiful adolescent slave girl, just as it is beyond belief that Jefferson would pay the blackmail demanded fifteen years later by a hireling political scrivener to keep the affair out of print." Willard Sterne Randall, *Thomas Jefferson: A Life* (New York: Henry Holt, 1993), 477.
43. Takaki, *Iron Cages*, 54–55.
44. Ibid., 24.
45. James Newton Poling, *The Abuse of Power: A Theological Problem* (Nashville: Abingdon, 1991), 75–91.
46. Takaki, *Iron Cages*, 27.
47. Jordan, *White over Black*, 423.
48. Ibid., 424.
49. Takaki, *Iron Cages*, 30.
50. Ibid., 30–31.
51. Ibid., 16.
52. Ibid., 31–32.
53. Jordan, *White over Black*, 578–79.

Chapter 2. Women and Male Dominance

1. Sigmund Freud, *Dora: An Analysis of a Case of Hysteria* (New York: Collier Books, 1963), 41.
2. Ibid., 42.
3. Ibid.
4. Ibid., 50.
5. Ibid., 42.
6. Ibid., 51.
7. Ibid., 44.
8. Ibid.
9. "A glance back at her history will remind us that her family had exposed her to multiple sexual *infidelity*, while all concerned—father and mother, Mr. K. and Mrs. K.—tried to compensate for all their pervading *perfidy* by making Dora their *confidante*, each burdening her (not without her perverse provocation, to be sure) with half-truths that were clearly unmanageable for an adolescent." Erik Erikson, in Charles Bernheimer and Claire Kahane, editors, *In Dora's Case: Freud, Hysteria, Feminism* (New York: Columbia University Press, 1985), 51–52.
10. For a good discussion of how patriarchy turns a woman's "no" into a "yes," see Marie Fortune, *Do No Harm: Sexual Ethics for the Rest of Us* (New York: Continuum, 1995).

11. Freud, *Dora*, 76, 75. This view of Freud's is an infamous example of the hidden influence of psychoanalytic theory on United States society. This clever statement denies the possibility of consent in a patriarchal society. If there is no such thing as an unconscious "no," then how does a woman withhold consent from an abusive sexual assault?

12. "It is possible for a man to talk to girls and women upon sexual matters of every kind without doing them harm and without bringing suspicion upon himself." Ibid., 65.

13. Ibid., 81.

14. Ibid., 88.

15. Ibid.

16. In fairness, we must acknowledge that this case study may be Freud's earliest reference to transference. Thus he does not have the advantage of the later research and development of this idea. "He was, in fact, just beginning to learn about this therapeutic phenomenon, and the present passage is the first really important one about it to have been written." Steven Marcus, "Freud and Dora: Story, History, Case History," in Bernheimer and Kahane, *In Dora's Case*, 89.

17. Freud, *Dora*, 114.

18. Ibid., 129.

19. Ibid., 131.

20. Ibid., 132.

21. Ibid., 140.

22. Ibid., 142.

23. Ibid., 143.

24. Ibid., 144.

25. Ibid., 7.

26. "Dora is thus no longer read as merely a case history or a fragment of an analysis of hysteria but as an urtext in the history of woman, a fragment of an increasingly heightened critical debate about the meaning of sexual difference and its effects on the representations of feminine desire." Claire Kahane, in Bernheimer and Kahane, *In Dora's Case*, 31.

27. Ibid., 130.

28. Ibid., 47, 76, 88, 126.

29. Ibid., 126.

30. The term "matrix of domination" is appropriated from Patricia Hill Collins, *Black Feminist Thought: Knowledge, Consciousness, and the Politics of Empowerment* (New York: Routledge, 1990), 225. The rest of the definition is appropriated from The Cornwall Collective, *Your Daughters Shall Prophesy* (New York: Pilgrim Press, 1980), 39.

31. Freud, *Dora*, 53.

32. Ibid., 22.

33. Ibid., 44.

34. Hazel Carby, *Reconstructing Womanhood: The Emergence of the Afro-American Novelist* (New York: Oxford University Press, 1987), 23.

35. Felix Deutsch, in Bernheimer and Kahane, *In Dora's Case*, 35–43.

36. Toril Moi, "Representation of Patriarchy: Sexuality and Epistemology in Freud's *Dora*," in Bernheimer and Kahane, *In Dora's Case*, 182.

37. Maria Ramas, "Freud's Dora, Dora's Hysteria," in Bernheimer and Kahane, *In Dora's Case*, 150. "See Juliet Mitchell, *Psychoanalysis and Feminism* (New York: Pantheon, 1974). Mitchell's important contribution to feminist theory was her insight that classical psychoanalysis, which has as one objective the study of formation of gender identity and sexuality in patriarchal culture, is a useful tool for feminism. The critical task is to separate those

aspects of the theory that are ideological from those that are insightful and useful—if incomplete." Note 2, 177.

38. David R. Blumenthal, *Facing the Abusing God: A Theology of Protest* (Louisville, Ky: Westminster John Knox Press, 1993), 12–13.

39. Jacquelyn Rose, "Dora: Fragment of an Analysis," 130, and Moi, "Representation of Patriarchy," 184, in Bernheimer and Kahane, *In Dora's Case.*

40. Maria Ramas, "Freud's Dora, Dora's Hysteria," in Bernheimer and Kahane, *In Dora's Case,* 150. See Mark Kanzer and Jules Glenn, eds., *Freud and His Patients* (New York: Aronson, 1980; essays by Glenn, Scharfman, Langs, Kanzer, and Bernstein); Samuel Slipp, "Interpersonal Factors in Hysteria: Freud's Seduction Theory and the Case of Dora," *Journal of the American Academy of Psychoanalysis* 5 (1977); Jean Laplanche, "Panel on 'Hysteria Today,'" *International Journal of Psycho-Analysis* 55 (1974); Hyman Muslin and Merton Gill, "Transference in the Dora Case," *Journal of the American Psychoanalytic Association* 26 (1978).

41. Philip Rieff, Introduction, in Freud, *Dora,* 17.

42. Maria Ramas, "Freud's Dora, Dora's Hysteria," in Bernheimer and Kahane, *In Dora's Case,* 151–52.

43. Ibid., 161.

44. Ibid., 162.

45. Ibid., 165.

46. Freud, *Dora,* 88.

47. Ibid., 92.

48. Ibid., 96.

49. Ibid., 113.

50. Ibid., 140–41.

51. Ibid., 35.

52. Ibid., 107.

53. Ibid., 121.

54. Ibid., 125.

55. Ibid., 130.

56. Ibid., 126.

57. For discussion about the importance of Freud in the intellectual debates within the United States, see Ann Douglas, *Terrible Honesty* (New York: Farrar, Straus, Giroux, 1995).

58. Ibid., 43.

59. Ibid., 140.

60. Ibid., 121.

61. Maria Ramas, "Freud's Dora, Dora's Hysteria," in Bernheimer and Kahane, *In Dora's Case,* 156.

62. Ibid., 157.

63. Judith Lewis Herman, *Trauma and Recovery* (New York: HarperCollins), 1992.

64. Maria Ramas, "Freud's Dora, Dora's Hysteria," in Bernheimer and Kahane, *In Dora's Case,* 173–74.

65. Jane Gallop, "Keys to Dora," ibid., 216.

66. Moi, "Representation of Patriarchy," ibid., 191, 194.

67. Ibid., 195.

68. Gallop, "Keys to Dora," in Bernheimer and Kahane, *In Dora's Case,* 217.

69. Freud, *Dora,* 114.

70. Ibid., 120.

71. Ibid., 130.

Chapter 3. The Revolution Betrayed

1. The historical analysis we make in this project is frequently from the perspective of our own time and thus is not completely fair to people in that time. We have the advantage of hindsight and sets of ideas and critical tools that were not available to these leaders. The moral consequences of their ideas for oppressed peoples were profound, but they were caught in the limitations of their time, just as we are caught in the limitations of ours. One reason for historical analysis is to be able to see how persons, institutions, and ideas work together to construct certain realities that benefit some people over others. Our goal is to be able to improve our ability to see in our own time. It is easier to see racism at work in White men of 150 years ago than it is to see racism at work in our own lives and ideas. Throughout this book, I will be moving back and forth between historical and contemporary debates about race and gender in order to enhance our perception and judgment about justice in our time.

2. Winthrop Jordan, *White over Black: American Attitudes toward the Negro, 1550–1812* (New York: W. W. Norton, 1968), 44.

3. Ibid., 11–42.

4. Ibid., 44.

5. Ibid.

6 H. Shelton Smith, *In His Image, But . . . : Racism in Southern Religion, 1780–1910* (Durham, N.C.: Duke University Press, 1972), 6.

7. Ibid., 6–8.

8. Ibid., 12, 13.

9. Ibid., 14.

10. Riggins R. Earl, Jr., *Dark Symbols, Obscure Signs: God, Self, and Community in the Slave Mind* (Maryknoll, N.Y.: Orbis, 1993), 66.

11. Rosemary Radford Ruether and Rosemary Skinner Keller, editors, *Women and Religion in America, Volume 2: The Colonial and Revolutionary Periods* (New York: Harper & Row, 1983), 132.

12. Mary P. Ryan, *Womanhood in America: From Colonial Times to the Present*, 3d edition (New York: Franklin Watts, 1983), 69.

13. Gerder Lerner, *The Creation of Feminist Consciousness: From the Middle Ages to 1970* (New York: Oxford University Press, 1993), 158.

14. Mary Beth Norton and Carol Ruth Berkin, *Women of America: A History* (Boston: Houghton Mifflin, 1979).

15. Vern L. Bullough and Bonnie Bullough, *The Subordinate Sex: A History of Attitudes Toward Women* (Urbana, Ill.: University of Illinois Press, 1973), 296–97.

16. Nancy F. Cott, editor, *Roots of Bitterness: Documents of the Social History of American Women* (New York: E. P. Dutton, 1972), 78.

17. Ronald Takaki, *Iron Cages: Race and Culture in 19th Century America* (New York: Oxford University Press, 1990), 151.

18. Ibid., 152.

19. Angela Davis, *Women, Race, and Class* (New York: Vintage, 1983), 54–55.

20. Ibid., 32.

21. Takaki, *Iron Cages*, 76–77.

22. John Hope Franklin and Alfred A. Moss, Jr., *From Slavery to Freedom: A History of Negro Americans* (New York: Knopf, 1988), 488.

23. Ibid., 108.

24. Ibid., 116.

25. Takaki, *Iron Cages*, 77, 78, 79.

26. Ibid., 215.

27. Ibid., 125.

28. Jordan, *White over Black*, 375–76.

29. Takaki, *Iron Cages*, 121.

30. Jordan, *White over Black*, 434.

31. Davis, *Women, Race, and Class*, 22.

32. Ibid., 23.

33. Vincent Harding, *There Is a River: The Black Struggle for Freedom in America* (New York: Vintage, 1983), 86.

34. Ibid., 188.

35. Ibid., 179–94.

36. Jordan, *Black over White*, 404.

37. Ibid., 407.

38. Ibid., 406–14.

39. Henry Louis Gates, Jr., *The Classic Slave Narratives* (New York: Penguin Books, 1987).

40. Franklin and Moss, *From Slavery to Freedom*, 124. See also Albert J. Raboteau, *Slave Religion: The "Invisible Institution" in the Antebellum South* (Oxford: Oxford University Press, 1978), and Earl, *Dark Symbols, Obscure Signs*.

41. Earl, *Dark Symbols, Obscure Signs*, 160.

42. Lerner, *Feminist Consciousness*, 27–28.

43. Davis, *Women, Race, and Class*, 12.

44. Ibid., 5–6.

45. Ibid., 12.

46. Rosemary Radford Ruether and Rosemary Skinner Keller, editors, *Women and Religion in America, Volume 1: The Nineteenth Century* (New York: Harper & Row, 1981), 5.

47. Ibid., 9.

48. Davis, *Women, Race, and Class*, 39.

49. Ruether and Keller, *Women and Religion in America*, vol. 1, 313–14.

50. Ellen Carol DuBois, editor, *Elizabeth Cady Stanton and Susan B. Anthony: Correspondence, Writings, Speeches* (New York: Schocken Books, 1981), 31.

51. Jacquelyn Grant, *White Women's Christ and Black Women's Jesus: Feminist Christology and Womanist Response* (Atlanta: Scholars Press, 1989), 220.

52. Jordan, *Black over White*, 422–23.

53. Smith, *In His Image, But . . .*, 38–41. Quotation is from Leah Townsend, *South Carolina Baptists* (Florence, S.C., 1935), 281.

54. Ibid., 46.

55. Ibid., 48.

56. Ibid., 52.

57. Ibid., 53.

58. Ibid., 69, 74.

59. Jordan, *Black over White*, 491.

60. Marcus Garvey, *Marcus Garvey and the Vision of Africa*, John Henrik Clarke, editor (New York: Random House, 1974).

61. George M. Fredrickson, *The Black Image in the White Mind: The Debate on Afro-American Character and Destiny, 1817–1914* (Hanover, N.H.: Wesleyan University Press, 1971), 71.

62. Term of Smith's presidency, 1795–1812; ibid., 72.

63. Ibid.

64. Ibid., 73.

65. Ibid., 74–75. Here is explicit evidence that some nineteenth-century intellectuals believed that Jesus was ethnically white or Caucasian.

66. Ibid., 76.

67. Ibid., 80.

68. Ibid., 79.

69. Ibid.

70. Ibid., 91.

71. Ibid., 93.

72. Ibid.

73. Ibid., 92.

74. Ibid., 99.

75. 1854; ibid., 100.

76. Ibid., 101.

77. Thomas F. Gossett, editor, *Race: The History of an Idea in America* (New York: Schocken, 1965).

78. Fredrickson, *The Black Image in the White Mind*, 111.

79. Ibid., 113.

80. 1863; ibid., 115.

81. Ibid., 119.

82. Ibid., 127.

83. Takaki, *Iron Cages*, 125–26.

84. Ibid.

85. The Cornwall Collective, *Your Daughters Shall Prophesy* (New York: Pilgrim, 1980), 39.

86. Hazel V. Carby, *Reconstructing Womanhood: The Emergence of the Afro-American Woman Novelist* (New York: Oxford University Press, 1987), 23. For additional resources, see the books in the bibliography by Barbara Welter, Catherine Clinton, Barbara Epstein, and Eleanor Flexnor.

87. Patricia Hill Collins, *Black Feminist Thought: Knowledge, Consciousness, and the Politics of Empowerment* (New York: Routledge, 1990), 70.

88. Cheryl Gilkes, quoted in ibid., 70.

89. Carby, *Reconstructing Womanhood*, 25.

90. Collins, *Black Feminist Thought*, 71.

91. Ibid., 77.

92. Jordan, *White over Black*, 578–79.

Chapter 4. Emancipation for Whom?

1. Samuel Eliot Morison, *The Oxford History of the American People* (New York: Oxford University Press, 1965), 743.

2. Ibid., 747.

3. Ibid., 761.

4. Ibid.

5. Ibid., 762.

6. Ronald Takaki, *Iron Cages: Race and Culture in Nineteenth Century America* (New York: Oxford University Press, 1990), 197.

7. Ibid., 198.

8. W. E. B. Du Bois, *Black Reconstruction in America* (New York: Meridian Books, 1964), 698. Quoted in Angela Y. Davis, *Women, Race, and Class* (New York: Vintage, 1983), 89.

9. Ibid., 88.

10. Ibid., 90.

11. Ibid., 91.

12. Vincent Harding, *There Is a River: The Black Struggle for Freedom in America* (New York: Vintage, 1983), 298ff.

13. Davis, *Women, Race, and Class,* 100. Quote is from Frederick Douglass, *The Life and Times of Frederick Douglass* (New York: Collier, 1962), 79.

14. John Hope Franklin and Alfred A. Moss, Jr., *From Slavery to Freedom: A History of Negro Americans* (New York: Knopf, 1988), 238.

15. Evelyn Brooks Higginbotham, *Righteous Discontent: The Women's Movement in the Black Baptist Church, 1880–1920* (Cambridge, Mass.: Harvard University Press, 1993), 5.

16. Emilie M. Townes, *Womanist Justice, Womanist Hope* (Atlanta: Scholars Press, 1993), 8–9.

17. Ibid., 140.

18. Ibid., 143.

19. Ibid., 140.

20. Ibid., 140–41.

21. Ibid., 151.

22. Ibid., 147.

23. Ibid.

24. Hazel V. Carby, *Reconstructing Womanhood: The Emergence of the Afro-American Novelist* (New York: Oxford University Press, 1987), 116.

25. Higginbotham, *Righteous Discontent,* 5.

26. Ibid., 16.

27. Davis, 149–71.

28. Rosemary Radford Ruether and Rosemary Skinner Keller, *Women and Religion, Volume 1: The Nineteenth Century* (San Francisco: Harper & Row, 1981), 199.

29. George M. Fredrickson, *The Black Image in the White Mind: The Debate on Afro-American Character and Destiny, 1817–1914* (Hanover, N.H.: Wesleyan University Press, 1971), 145.

30. Ibid., 150–51.

31. Ibid., 153.

32. Ibid., 156.

33. Ibid., 239.

34. Ibid., 240.

35. Ibid.

36. Ibid., 245.

37. Ibid., 246.

38. Ibid., 255. For information about Darwin and racism, see Pat Shipman, *The Evolution of Racism: Human Differences and the Use and Abuse of Science* (New York: Simon & Schuster, 1994).

39. Fredrickson, *The Black Image in the White Mind,* 198.

40. Takaki, *Iron Cages,* 200.

41. Ibid., 201.

42. Townes, *Womanist Justice,* 132–33.

43. Fredrickson, *The Black Image in the White Mind,* 201.

44. Takaki, *Iron Cages,* 205.

45. Fredrickson, *The Black Image in the White Mind,* 217.

46. Takaki, *Iron Cages,* 213.

47. Ibid., 214.

48. W. E. B. Du Bois, *The Souls of Black Folk* (New York: Vintage, 1990 [1903]), 43.

49. Fredrickson, *The Black Image in the White Mind*, 207.

50. Ibid., 259.

51. Ibid., 259–62.

52. Ibid., 266.

53. Ibid., 267.

54. Ibid., 280.

55. Ibid., 281.

56. Patricia Hill Collins, *Black Feminist Thought: Knowledge, Consciousness, and the Politics of Empowerment* (New York: Routledge, 1990), 177.

57. H. Shelton Smith, *In His Image . . . But: Racism in Southern Religion, 1780–1910* (Durham, N.C.: Duke University Press, 1972), 227, 229, 237.

58. Ibid., 229.

59. Ibid., 258.

60. Ibid., 261.

61. Ibid., 264–65.

62. Ibid., 265.

63. Townes, *Womanist Justice*, 134–35.

64. Fredrickson, *The Black Image in the White Mind*, 302–3.

65. Ibid., 304.

66. Higginbotham, *Righteous Discontent*, 5.

67. Nancy F. Cott, editor, *Roots of Bitterness: Documents of the Social History of American Women* (New York: E. P. Dutton, 1972), 14.

68. Ibid., 15.

69. Ruether and Keller, *Women and Religion*, vol. 1, 223.

70. Ibid.

71. Ibid., 224.

72. Ibid., 224–25.

73. Augustus Hopkins Strong, *Philosophy and Religion* (New York: A. C. Armstrong, 1888), 401.

74. Ibid., 408–9.

75. Barbara Hilkert Andolsen, *Daughters of Jefferson, Daughters of Bootblacks* (Macon, Ga.: Mercer University Press, 1986), 26–27.

76. A good summary of the issues and debates between Black and White women can be found in Andolsen, *Daughters of Jefferson, Daughters of Bootblacks*. See also Susan Thistlethwaite, *Sex, Race, and God: Christian Feminism in Black and White* (New York: Crossroad, 1989).

77. Carby, *Reconstructing Womanhood*, 114–15.

78. Davis, *Women, Race, and Class*, 81.

79. Josiah Strong, *Our Country: Its Possible Future and Its Present Crisis* (New York: Baker and Taylor, 1885, 1891), 222, 223, 224, 227.

Chapter 5. Contemporary Resistance and Betrayal

1. The term "backlash" was popularized by Susan Faludi, *Backlash: The Undeclared War against American Women* (New York: Crown, 1991). For some of the best commentary on the backlash against racial justice, see books by bell hooks, Cornel West, and Michael Dyson.

2. See James H. Cone, *Black Theology and Black Power* (New York: Seabury, 1969). For astute descriptions of the development of Black theology, see Peter J. Paris, *Black Religious Leaders: Conflict in Unity* (Louisville, Ky.: Westminster John Knox, 1991); Robert Michael Franklin, *Liberating Visions: Human Fulfillment and Social Justice in African-American Thought* (Minneapolis: Fortress Press, 1990); Walter Fluker, *They Looked for a City: A Comparative Analysis of the Ideal of Community in the Thought of Howard Thurman and Martin Luther King, Jr.* (New York: University Press of America, 1989).

3. The poverty rate for African American children generally runs about twice the White rate in terms of percentage, although much less in terms of numbers. Children's Defense Fund, *The State of America's Children Yearbook, 1994* (Washington, D.C.: Children's Defense Fund, 1994), 73.

4. James H. Evans, Jr., *We Have Been Believers: An African-American Systematic Theology* (Minneapolis: Fortress Press, 1992), 4–5; Gayraud S. Wilmore and James H. Cone, editors, *Black Theology: A Documentary History, Volume 1: 1966–1979* (Maryknoll, N.Y.: Orbis, 1979); James H. Cone and Gayraud S. Wilmore, editors, *Black Theology: A Documentary History, Volume 2: 1980–1992* (Maryknoll, N.Y.: Orbis, 1993).

5. Children's Defense Fund, *The State of America's Children Yearbook, 1994*, 78–79.

6. George M. Fredrickson, *The Black Image in the White Mind: The Debate on Afro-American Character and Destiny* (Hanover, N.H.: Wesleyan University Press, 1971).

7. Cornel West, *Race Matters* (Boston: Beacon, 1993), 84.

8. For a sensitive discussion of social scientific issues of violence and race, see Robert L. Hampton, *Violence in the Black Family: Correlates and Consequences* (Lexington, Mass.: Lexington Books, 1987).

9. Robert S. Michaelson and Wade Clark Roof list three theological characteristics of the historical liberal movement. (1) An openness to new truth and a suspicion of established authorities: "Understood theologically, we mean by liberal Protestantism a view that has stressed freedom, liberation from earthly authoritarianism, closed systems, in the name of the ultimate authority whose way is dynamically disclosed in and through the Bible" (pp. 3–4). (2) A concern about social evil: Most liberal theology assumes that social evil endangers the fulfillment of God's creation: "Puritan Protestants, so important to American beginnings, sought to build biblical commonwealths in the new world. . . . But a fundamental split occurred within American Protestantism in the late nineteenth century between those who continued to seek to shape the society of which they were a part—to build the kingdom of God on earth, as some put it—and those who understood the Christian call to entail escape from this corrupt world into the kingdom that is not of this world. The social concern that motivated the former and that provided the impetus for the Social Gospel movement became another of the distinctive marks of liberal Protestantism" (p. 5). (3) A commitment to incarnational relationships: Liberal theology assumes that Christian faith is lived out in the real world of personal and social relationships. "God's ultimate and most intimate expression to humankind came (and comes) in the form of a human person: the word made flesh. . . . These convictions have led liberal Protestants in the past to stress the immanence of God, to be optimistic about the prospect of humankind, and to join with the power of God in improving themselves and the world . . . " (p. 4). (*Liberal Protestantism: Realities and Possibilities* [New York: Pilgrim, 1986])

10. For a spirited discussion of the decline of liberal churches, see Wade Clark Roof and William McKinney, editors, *American Mainline Religion: Its Changing Shape and Future* (New Brunswick, N.J.: Rutgers University Press, 1987); also Robert Wuthnow, *The Struggle for America's Soul* (Grand Rapids: Eerdmans, 1989).

11. Cone and Wilmore, editors, *Black Theology: A Documentary History, Volume 2: 1980–1992,* 69.

12. Rebecca S. Chopp and Mark Lewis Taylor, editors, *Reconstructing Christian Theology* (Minneapolis: Fortress Press, 1994), 88–89.

13. For a thorough discussion of women's poverty as an issue of public policy for the churches, see Pamela Couture, *Blessed Are the Poor: Women's Poverty, Family Policy, and Practical Theology* (Nashville: Abingdon, 1991).

14. Ibid., 2.

15. Ibid., 94.

16. See Janet Fishburn, *Confronting the Idolatry of Family: A New Vision for the Household of God* (Nashville: Abingdon, 1991).

17. Carter Heyward, *Our Passion for Justice: Images of Power, Sexuality, and Liberation* (New York: Pilgrim, 1984), 11.

18. Katie G. Cannon, *Black Womanist Ethics* (Atlanta: Scholars Press, 1989). See also Jacquelyn Grant, *White Women's Christ and Black Women's Jesus: Feminist Christology and Womanist Response* (Atlanta: Scholars Press, 1989); Emilie Townes, *Womanist Justice, Womanist Hope* (Atlanta: Scholars Press, 1993); Kelly Brown Douglas, *The Black Christ* (Maryknoll, N.Y.: Orbis, 1994); Delores Williams, *Sisters in the Wilderness: The Challenge of Womanist God-Talk* (Maryknoll, N.Y.: Orbis, 1993).

19. Jacquelyn Grant, *White Women's Christ, Black Women's Jesus,* 202.

20. Patricia Hill Collins, *Black Feminist Thought* (New York: Routledge, 1990), 67–78.

21. See Grant, *White Woman's Christ, Black Woman's Jesus.* See also Susan Thisthlethwaite, *Sex, Race and God: Christian Feminism in Black and White* (New York: Crossroad, 1989), and Barbara H. Andolsen, *Daughters of Jefferson, Daughters of Bootblacks: Racism and American Feminism* (Macon, Ga.: Mercer University Press, 1986).

22. Delores Williams, in Emilie Townes, editor, *A Troubling in My Soul: Womanist Perspectives on Evil and Suffering* (Maryknoll, N.Y.: Orbis, 1993), 149.

23. For this topic, I am especially dependent on the sociological analysis of Angela Y. Davis, *Women, Race, and Class* (New York: Vintage, 1983); Angela Y. Davis, *Women, Culture, Politics* (New York: Vintage, 1990).

24. For a contemporary analysis of this phenomenon, see David Remnick, "Lost in Space," an article on Congressperson Newt Gingrich, *The New Yorker* (Dec. 5, 1994), 79–86.

25. Daniel P. Moynihan, *The Negro Family: The Case for National Action* (Washington, D.C.: United States Department of Labor, 1965); reprinted in Lee Rainwater and William L. Yancey, *The Moynihan Report and the Politics of Controversy* (Cambridge, Mass.: M.I.T. Press, 1967).

26. E. Franklin Frazier, *The Negro Family in the United States* (Chicago: University of Chicago Press, 1966). See 102–13, 245–55, 359–68.

27. Davis, *Women, Race, and Class,* 13.

28. Ibid.

29. For an analysis of the socioeconomic realities affecting the black community, see Cornel West, *Keeping Faith* (New York: Routledge, 1993), 251–70.

30. For research that challenges this view of the black family, see Herbert Gutman, *The Black Family in Slavery and Freedom: 1750–1925* (New York: Vintage, 1976), and Andrew Billingsley, *Climbing Jacob's Ladder: The Enduring Legacy of African-American Families* (New York: Simon & Schuster, 1992).

31. The new argument for Black inferiority can be seen in Charles Murray and Charles Herrenstein, *The Bell Curve: Intelligence and Class Structure in American Life* (New York: Free Press, 1994). See chapter 7 for further discussion.

32. Davis, *Women, Culture, Politics*, 81.

33. Ibid., 77.

34. Ibid.

35. Winthrop Jordan, *White over Black: American Attitudes toward the Negro, 1550–1812* (New York: W. W. Norton, 1968), 439.

36. For sensitive discussion of these issues, see Marian Wright Edelman, *Families in Peril: An Agenda for Social Change* (Cambridge, Mass.: Harvard University Press, 1987). See also Davis, *Women, Culture, Politics*, 73–90; Betty Carter and Monica McGoldrick, *The Changing Family Life Cycle* (New York: Gardner, 1988); and Pamela D. Couture, *Blessed Are the Poor: Women's Poverty, Family Policy, and Practical Theology* (Nashville: Abingdon, 1991).

37. Richard Cohen, editorial, *Democrat and Chronicle*, Rochester, New York, November 2, 1994.

38. Hester Eisenstein, *Contemporary Feminist Thought* (Boston: G. K. Hall, 1983), 36.

39. Ibid., 38.

40. See Peter Rutter, *Sex in the Forbidden Zone: When Men in Power—Therapists, Doctors, Clergy, Teachers, and Others—Betray Women's Trust* (Los Angeles: Jeremy Tarcher, 1989).

41. Marie Fortune, *Is Nothing Sacred? The Story of a Pastor, the Women He Sexually Abused, and the Congregation He Nearly Destroyed* (San Francisco: HarperSanFrancisco, 1989).

42. Ibid., 20.

43. Ibid., 24.

44. Ibid., 30.

45. Ibid., xiii.

46. Ibid., 50.

47. *The American Heritage Dictionary of the English Lanugage, Third Edition* (Boston: Houghton Mifflin Company, 1992), 1157.

48. For more discussion of these issues, see James N. Poling and Marie Fortune, *Sexual Abuse by Clergy: A Crisis for the Church* (Decatur, Ga.: Journal of Pastoral Care Publications, 1994).

49. For a good discussion of moral agency in relation to sexual abuse by clergy, see Marie Fortune's chapters in Poling and Fortune, *Sexual Abuse by Clergy: A Crisis for the Church*, 19–20.

Chapter 6. Understanding Resistance to Evil

1. I have adapted this definition from the following sources: Patricia Hill Collins, *Black Feminist Thought* (New York: Routledge, 1990), 92–93; Audre Lorde, *Sister Outsider* (Freedom, Calif.: Crossing Press, 1984), 42.

2. Cheryl Townsend Gilkes, quoted in Collins, *Black Feminist Thought*, 67. See Cheryl Townsend Gilkes, "From Slavery to Social Welfare: Racism and the Control of Black Women," in *Class, Race, and Sex: The Dynamics of Control*, Amy Swerdlow and Hanna Lessinger, editors (Boston: G. K. Hall, 1983), 294.

3. Ibid., 176.

4. Ellen Carol DuBois, editor, *Elizabeth Cady Stanton and Susan B. Anthony: Correspondence, Writings, Speeches* (New York: Schocken Books, 1981), 31.

5. Collins, *Black Feminist Thought*, 91. Quotations are from Lorde, *Sister Outsider*, 114.

6. Ellen Wondra, *Humanity Has Been a Holy Thing* (New York: University Press of America, 1994), 87. See also the essay "Resistance and Hope: The Question of Religion," by David Tracy, in *Plurality and Ambiguity: Hermeneutics, Religion, Hope* (San Francisco: Harper & Row, 1987), 82–114.

7. Collins, *Black Feminist Thought*, 141–42.

8. Ibid., 142.

9. I have adapted this definition from the following sources: Collins, *Black Feminist Thought*, 92–93, and Lorde, *Sister Outsider*, 42.

10. Collins, *Black Feminist Thought*, 92–93.

11. Ibid., 93. This quote from Pauli Murray, *Song in a Weary Throat* (New York: Harper & Row, 1987), 106.

12. Collins, *Black Feminist Thought*, 235–38.

13. Ibid., 92.

14. James Newton Poling, original poem, 1991.

15. Lorde, *Sister Outsider*, 42. The essay is titled, "The Transformation of Silence into Language and Action."

16. Ibid.

17. Shawn Copeland, in Emilie Townes, editor, *A Troubling in My Soul: Womanist Perspectives on Evil and Suffering* (Maryknoll, N.Y.: Orbis, 1993), 109–10, 123. The quotation is from William R. Jones, *Is God a White Racist? A Preamble to Black Theology* (Garden City, N.Y.: Anchor/Doubleday, 1973), 21–22.

18. The term "matrix of domination" is from Collins, *Black Feminist Thought*, 225. The rest of the definition is adapted from The Cornwall Collective, *Your Daughters Shall Prophesy*, 39.

19. Collins, *Black Feminist Thought*, 229–30.

20. Ibid.

Chapter 7. Defining Evil

1. Original definition, James N. Poling, 1995.

2. Reinhold Niebuhr, *Moral Man and Immoral Society* (New York: Scribner's, 1932).

3. In the bibliography, see the following authors on evil: Marjorie Suchocki, Edward Farley, David Ray Griffin, Emilie Townes, Nel Noddings, Stephen Davis, Walter Wink, Ted Peters, Scott Peck.

4. Ted Peters, *Sin: Radical Evil in Soul and Society* (Grand Rapids: Eerdmans, 1994), 9.

5. James Poling, *The Abuse of Power: A Theological Problem* (Nashville: Abingdon, 1991), 315.

6. David Ray Griffin, *God, Power, and Evil: A Process Theodicy* (Philadelphia: Westminster, 1976), 253. This volume has an excellent summary of the historical and contemporary theodicy debate.

7. For a good edited volume on theodicy, see Stephen T. Davis, editor, *Encountering Evil: Live Options in Theodicy* (Atlanta: John Knox Press, 1981). See also Edward Farley, *Good and Evil: Interpreting a Human Condition* (Minneapolis: Fortress Press, 1990); Marjorie Suchocki, *The Fall to Violence: Original Sin in Relational Theology* (New York: Continuum, 1994); Nel Noddings, *Women and Evil* (Berkeley, Calif.: University of California Press, 1989).

8. Alfred North Whitehead, *Process and Reality*, David Ray Griffin, editor (New York: Macmillan, 1978), 340.

9. Marie Fortune, *Sexual Violence: The Unmentionable Sin* (New York: Pilgrim, 1983), 196–97.

10. Scott Peck has stimulated a debate about the nature of personal and social evil. See *People of the Lie* (New York: Simon & Schuster, 1983). See also Ted Peters, *Sin*, 9.

11. Poling, *The Abuse of Power*, 27. Loving power is one of my terms for the good. I draw on two others scholars who make similar attempts at such definitions. Relational power is the term used by Bernard Loomer, "Two Conceptions of Power," *Criterion* 15, no. 1 (1976):

12. Erotic power is the term used by Rita Nakashima Brock. See *Journeys by Heart: A Christology of Erotic Power* (New York: Crossroad, 1988), 26, 37, 39.

12. Poling, "A Theological Integration of the Personal and Social in Pastoral Care and Counseling: A Process View" (Ph.D. diss., School of Theology, Claremont, California, 1980), 67, 79.

13. Ibid., 95, 97.

14. For a longer discussion, see Poling, *The Abuse of Power.*

15. Riggins Earl, Jr., *Dark Symbols, Obscure Signs: God, Self, and Community in the Slave Mind* (Maryknoll, N.Y.: Orbis, 1993), 16.

16. Paula M. Cooey, *Religious Imagination and the Body: A Feminist Analysis* (New York: Oxford University Press, 1994), 9, 10, 132.

17. Daniel Day Williams, *The Spirit and Forms of Love* (New York: Harper & Row, 1968), 3.

18. For further discussion of the body-spirit issue in theology, see James Nelson, *Body Theology* (Louisville, Ky.: Westminster John Knox, 1992), and Walter Wink, *Unmasking the Powers: The Invisible Forces That Determine Human Existence* (Minneapolis: Fortress, 1986).

19. Bernard F. Meland, *The Realities of Faith: The Revolution in Cultural Forms* (New York: Oxford University Press, 1962), 233.

20. Ellen Wondra, *Humanity Has Been a Holy Thing: Toward a Contemporary Feminist Christology* (New York: University Press of America, 1994), 73. Wondra is quoting from Teresa de Lauretis, *Alice Doesn't: Feminism, Semiotics, Cinema* (Bloomington, Ind.: Indiana University Press, 1984), 159, 182.

21. William Dean and Larry E. Axel, editors, *The Size of God: The Theology of Bernard Loomer in Context* (Macon, Ga.: Mercer University Press, 1987).

22. For understanding my use of the term "form," see Bernard E. Meland, *Fallible Forms and Symbols: Discourses on Method in a Theology of Culture* (Philadelphia: Fortress Press, 1976).

23. Griffin, *God, Power, and Evil*, 283.

24. Bernard E. Meland, *Faith and Culture* (Carbondale, Ill.: Southern Illinois University Press, 1953), 119.

25. Williams, *The Spirit and Forms of Love*, 3.

26. Suchocki, *The End of Evil.*

27. Dean and Axel, *The Size of God*, 46.

28. Meland, *Faith and Culture*, 147.

29. See Karl Barth, *Church Dogmatics: The Doctrine of Creation* (3/3) (Edinburgh: T & T Clark, 1960); Paul Tillich, *Systematic Theology*, vol. 1 (Chicago: University of Chicago Press, 1957).

30. Wink, *Unmasking the Powers*, 30–39.

31. Poling, "A Theological Integration," 95, 97.

32. For an analysis of multiple personal systems, see Urie Bronfenbrenner, *The Ecology of Human Development* (Cambridge, Mass.: Harvard University Press, 1979).

33. For this insight about the role of personal actions, I am especially indebted to the work of Raul Hilberg on the Holocaust. Richard L. Rubenstein and John K. Roth summarize Hil-

berg's views that apply to this point: "What a campaign of 'paper violence' required instead was a vast bureaucratic network, a web of offices to plan, interpret, implement, and enforce the required actions. The twisted road to Auschwitz was engineered neither by Hitler alone nor solely by his Nazi party. Its construction enlisted, in the words of Raul Hilberg, 'an ever larger number of agencies, party offices, business enterprises, and military commands. . . . The machinery of destruction was the organized community in one of its special roles.' " Richard L. Rubenstein and John K. Roth, *Approaches to Auschwitz: The Holocaust and Its Legacy* (Atlanta: John Knox, 1987), 111. See also Raul Hilberg, *The Destruction of the European Jews*, 3 vols., rev. ed. (New York: Holmes and Meier, 1985); Raul Hilberg, *Perpetrators, Victims, Bystanders: The Jewish Catastrophe, 1933–1945* (New York: HarperCollins, 1992).

34. James N. Poling and Donald E. Miller, *Foundations for a Practical Theology of Ministry* (Nashville: Abingdon, 1985), 81. See also Thomas Groome, *Christian Religious Education* (New York: Harper & Row, 1980), 170.

35. For a good discussion of the influence of postmodern and critical theories on theology, see Rebecca Chopp and Mark Lewis Taylor, editors, *Reconstructing Christian Theology* (Minneapolis: Fortress Press, 1994), especially chapter 1.

36. Otto Kernberg, *Severe Personality Disorders* (New Haven, Conn.: Yale University Press, 1984), 17.

37. Rodney Hunter, editor, *Dictionary of Pastoral Care and Counseling* (Nashville: Abingdon, 1990), 292.

38. See the works of Alice Miller, especially *For Your Own Good: Hidden Cruelty in Childrearing and the Roots of Violence* (New York: Farrar, Straus, Giroux, 1983).

39. Hunter, *Dictionary of Pastoral Care and Counseling*, 1290.

40. Ibid.

41. Whitehead, *Process and Reality*, 162.

42. Poling, *The Abuse of Power*, 35–48.

43. David Tracy, *Plurality and Ambiguity: Hermeneutics, Religion, Hope* (San Francisco: Harper & Row, 1987), 77.

44. Good examples of economic analysis by theologians include Herman E. Daly and John B. Cobb, Jr., *For the Common Good: Redirecting the Economy toward Community, the Environment, and a Sustainable Future* (Boston: Beacon, 1989); M. Douglas Meeks, *God the Economist: The Doctrine of God and Political Economy* (Minneapolis: Fortress, 1989); John B. Cobb, Jr., *Sustaining the Common Good: A Christian Perspective on the Global Economy* (Cleveland: Pilgrim, 1994).

45. Patricia Hill Collins, *Black Feminist Thought: Knowledge, Consciousness, and the Politics of Empowerment* (New York: Routledge, 1990), 64.

46. Children's Defense Fund, *The State of America's Children Yearbook, 1994* (Washington, D.C.: Children's Defense Fund), 73.

47. Often historians are the best interpreters of institutional life. See Evelyn Brooks Higginbotham, *Righteous Discontent: The Women's Movement in the Black Baptist Church, 1880–1920* (Cambridge, Mass.: Harvard University Press, 1993).

48. Tracy, *Plurality and Ambiguity*, 77. Tracy adds, in a footnote, "Those 'material' conditions need not include, of course, only economic realities, but also physical (e.g., climatic), biological, and demographic and social realities—as any full theory of a 'materialist dialectic' or, alternatively, a naturalistic pragmatism must allow and even demand. Dewey and Marx, on this reading, despite their otherwise vital differences, can both be read as attempting full . . . positions."

49. Bernard Loomer, "Elephantine Analysis" (unpublished paper, February, 1970). Loomer uses the old story about the world being held on the backs of several elephants,

each of which is unaware that it is standing on another elephant, and thus unconscious of its own standpoint.

50. The Cornwall Collective, *Your Daughters Shall Prophesy* (New York: Pilgrim, 1980), 39.

51. Charles Murray and Richard Herrenstein, *The Bell Curve: Intelligence and Class Structure in American Life* (New York: Free Press, 1994).

52. Tom Morganthau, "I.Q.: Is It Destiny?" *Newsweek.* (October 24, 1994), 54.

53. See Charles Lane, "The Tainted Sources of 'The Bell Curve,'" *New York Review of Books* 41, no. 20 (December 1, 1994): 14–19; Ellen K. Coughlin, "Class, IQ, and Heredity," *The Chronicle of Higher Education* (October 26, 1994), A12, A20.

54. The Cornwall Collective, *Your Daughters Shall Prophesy,* 39–49.

55. Cornel West, *Prophesy Deliverance! An Afro-American Revolutionary Christianity* (Philadelphia: Westminster, 1982), 47.

56. Ibid.

57. Adrienne Rich, *Of Woman Born,* Tenth Anniversary Edition (New York: W. W. Norton, 1986), 57–58.

58. Collins, *Black Feminist Thought,* 19–40.

59. Ibid., 21–22.

60. Ibid., 232.

61. Ibid., 202.

62. *The American Heritage Dictionary, Third Edition* (Boston: Houghton Mifflin, 1992), 550.

63. Collins, *Black Feminist Thought,* 225–26.

64. Ibid., 225.

65. Delores Williams, *Sisters in the Wilderness* (Maryknoll, N.Y.: Orbis, 1993).

66. Collins, *Black Feminist Thought,* 140.

67. Some might say religious *or* philosophical. However, until the Enlightenment invention of secularity, this was not a clear distinction, because all known philosophical systems were religious.

68. Nel Noddings extends this part of the argument to maintain that even the category of evil as defined by the western tradition may be a form of evil, especially since evil has often been equated with women, people of color, and Others who are different. "So far we have seen that evil became associated early with disobeying the father and his representatives. . . . Now it is time to look at evil from the perspective of women's experience, to adopt the standpoint of women." Noddings, *Women and Evil,* 90.

69. *The Constitution of the United Presbyterian Church in the United States of America: Part I: Book of Confessions* (Philadelphia: Office of the General Assembly, 1967), 6.129.5.

70. H. Shelton Smith, *In His Image, But . . .: Racism in Southern Religion, 1780–1910* (Durham, N.C.: Duke University Press, 1972), 9. See also Kelly Brown Douglas, *The Black Christ* (Maryknoll, N.Y.: Orbis, 1994), for commentary on the spiritualization of Christian theology during the debate on slavery.

71. Maryanne Stevens, editor, *Reconstructing the Christ Symbol: Essays in Feminist Christology* (New York: Paulist, 1993), 7. "This argument was repeated in the pastoral letter by Pope John Paul II, 'The Dignity and Vocation of Women,' sec. 26 (September 31, 1988)" (25).

Chapter 8. Re-imagining Jesus' Resistance to Evil

1. Ellen Carol DuBois, editor, *Elizabeth Cady Stanton and Susan B. Anthony: Correspondence, Writings, Speeches* (New York: Schocken, 1981), 184.

2. Jacquelyn Grant, *White Women's Christ and Black Women's Jesus: Feminist Christology and Womanist Response* (Atlanta: Scholars Press, 1989), 213. Quotation is from Harold A. Carter, *The Prayer Tradition of Black People* (Valley Forge, Pa.: Judson, 1976), 49.

3. Rosemary Radford Ruether and Rosemary Skinner Keller, *Women and Religion in America, Volume 1: The Nineteenth Century* (San Francisco: Harper & Row, 1981), 28.

4. Henry Louis Gates, Jr., *The Classic Slave Narratives* (New York: Penguin, 1987), 397.

5. Ruether and Keller, *Women and Religion in America*, vol. 1, 217.

6. See Judith Plaskow, "Christian Feminism and Anti-Judaism," *Cross Currents* (Fall 1978); and "Christian Feminist Anti-Judaism: Some New Considerations," *New Conversations* (Spring 1987), 20–25.

7. The term "womanist" was first coined by Alice Walker in *In Search of Our Mother's Gardens: Womanist Prose* (San Diego: Harcourt Brace Jovanovich, 1983), xi. One of its early uses was by the theologian Katie G. Cannon, *Black Womanist Ethics* (Atlanta: Scholars Press, 1988).

8. Kelly Brown Douglas, *The Black Christ* (Maryknoll, N.Y.: Orbis, 1994), 97.

9. Ibid., 2.

10. Ibid., 12.

11. Ibid., 13.

12. Winthrop Jordan, *White over Black: American Attitudes toward the Negro, 1550–1812* (Chapel Hill, N.C.: University of North Carolina Press, 1968), 182.

13. Douglas, *The Black Christ*, 15–16.

14. Ibid., 17.

15. Ibid.

16. Ibid., 18.

17. Ibid., 18–19.

18. Ibid., 97.

19. Ibid., 108.

20. Ibid., 105.

21. Ibid., 110.

22. Grant, *White Women's Christ, Black Women's Jesus*, 214.

23. Jacquelyn Grant, "Come to My Help, Lord, for I'm in Trouble: Womanist Jesus and the Mutual Struggle for Liberation," in Maryanne Stevens, editor, *Reconstructing the Christ Symbol: Essays in Feminist Christology* (New York: Paulist, 1993), 63.

24. Jacquelyn Grant, "The Sin of Servanthood," in Emilie M. Townes, editor, *A Troubling in My Soul: Womanist Perspectives on Evil and Suffering* (Maryknoll, N.Y.: Orbis, 1993), 200.

25. Grant, "The Sin of Servanthood," 201–4. See Letty M. Russell, *Growth in Partnership* (Philadelphia: Westminster, 1981).

26. Grant , "The Sin of Servanthood," 205.

27. Ibid.

28. Ibid., 209.

29. Ibid., 210.

30. Ibid., 210–11.

31. Ibid., 216.

32. Delores S. Williams, *Sisters in the Wilderness: The Challenge of Womanist God-Talk* (Maryknoll, N.Y.: Orbis, 1993), x.

33. Ibid., 60, 67.

34. Ibid., 164–65.

35. Joanne Carlson Brown and Carole R. Bohn, editors, *Christianity, Patriarchy, and Abuse: A Feminist Critique* (New York: Pilgrim, 1989), 26–28.

36. Rita Nakashima Brock, "Losing Your Innocence but Not Your Hope," in Stevens, editor, *Reconstructing the Christ Symbol*, 41.

37. Hazel Carby, *Reconstructing Womanhood: The Emergence of the Afro-American Novelist* (New York: Oxford, 1987), 23.

38. Brock, "Losing Your Innocence," in Stevens, editor, *Reconstructing the Christ Symbol*, 42.

39. Rosemary Radford Ruether, "The Future of Feminist Theology in the Academy," *Journal of the American Academy of Religion* 53, no. 4 (December 1985): 710–11, quoted in Ellen K. Wondra, *Humanity Has Been a Holy Thing: Toward a Contemporary Feminist Christology* (New York: University Press of America, 1994), 65.

40. Wondra, *Humanity Has Been a Holy Thing*, 132.

41. Ibid., 331.

42. William Herzog II, *Parables as Subversive Speech: Jesus as Pedagogue of the Oppressed* (Louisville, Ky.: Westminster John Knox, 1994); John Dominic Crossan, *Jesus: A Revolutionary Biography* (San Francisco: HarperSanFrancisco, 1994); Burton L. Mack, *The Lost Gospel: The Book of Q and Christian Origins* (San Francisco: HarperSanFrancisco, 1993).

43. "The Westminster Confession of Faith (1647)," 6.010, *The Book of Confessions* (Louisville, Ky.: Presbyterian Church U.S.A.).

44. Itumeleng T. Mosala, *Biblical Hermeneutics and Black Theology in South Africa* (Grand Rapids, Mich.: Eerdmans, 1989); Cain Hope Felder, editor, *Stony the Road We Trod: African American Biblical Interpretation* (Minneapolis: Fortress Press, 1991); Elisabeth Schüssler Fiorenza, *Bread Not Stone: The Challenge of Feminist Biblical Interpretation* (Boston: Beacon, 1984).

45. Clarice J. Martin, "Black Theodicy and Black Women's Spiritual Autobiography," in Emilie M. Townes, editor, *A Troubling in My Soul: Womanist Perspectives on Evil and Suffering* (Maryknoll, N.Y.: Orbis, 1993), 25.

46. Martin here quotes from Roger Lunden, Anthony Thistleton, and Clarence Walhout, *The Responsibility of Hermeneutics* (Grand Rapids: Eerdmans, 1985), x, xi.

47. Henry Louis Gates, *The Classic Slave Narratives* (New York: Penguin, 1987), 397.

48. Riggins R. Earl, Jr., *Dark Symbols, Obscure Signs: God, Self and Community in the Slave Mind* (Maryknoll, N.Y.: Orbis, 1993), 22.

49. Ibid.

50. Ibid.

51. Ibid., 46.

52. Ibid.

53. Elisabeth Schüssler Fiorenza, *Bread Not Stone.*

54. Wondra, *Humanity Has Been a Holy Thing*, 17, quoting Mary Daly, *Beyond God the Father* (Boston: Beacon, 1973), 72.

55. Wondra, *Humanity Has Been a Holy Thing*, 22–23.

56. Ibid., 61.

57. Ibid., 68.

58. Ibid., 133.

Chapter 9. Jesus as Religious Resister

1. Ellen K. Wondra, *Humanity Has Been a Holy Thing: Toward a Contemporary Feminist Christology* (New York: University Press of America, 1994), 96.

2. Ibid., 97.

3. Ibid., 326.

4. Ibid., 315.

5. Ibid., 330.

6. Ibid., 329.

7. Ibid., 333.

8. This phrase has been attributed to Ossie Davis, who spoke at the funeral of Malcolm X in 1965.

9. Wondra, *Humanity Has Been a Holy Thing*, 335.

10. William Herzog II, *Parables as Subversive Speech: Jesus as Pedagogue of the Oppressed* (Louisville, Ky.: Westminster John Knox, 1994).

11. H. Shelton Smith, *In His Image But . . .: Racism in Southern Religion* (Durham, N.C.: Duke University Press, 1972), 8–10, 23–73. Even today, members of the Episcopal Church in the United States are overrepresented among political and business leaders of the dominant elite.

12. Hazel Carby, *Reconstructing Womanhood: The Emergence of the Afro-American Novelist* (New York: Oxford University Press, 1987), 23.

13. See interpretation of the story of Maria Goretti, Roman Catholic saint, in Marie Fortune, *Sexual Violence: The Unmentionable Sin* (New York: Pilgrim, 1983), 64–65.

14. Claude Lévi-Strauss, *The Elementary Structures of Kinship* (Boston: Beacon, 1986).

15. I am dependent in this section for the insights of Bernard Loomer, my teacher. See William Dean and Larry Axel, *The Size of God: The Theology of Bernard Loomer in Context* (Macon, Ga.: Mercer University Press, 1987), 43–48. See also Poling, *The Abuse of Power: A Theological Problem* (Nashville: Abingdon, 1991), 110–18, 177–78.

16. David Tracy, *Plurality and Ambiguity: Hermeneutics, Religion, Hope* (San Francisco: Harper & Row, 1987); Rebecca Chopp and Mark Lewis Taylor, editors, *Reconstructing Christian Theology* (Minneapolis: Fortress Press, 1994).

17. David Ray Griffin, *God, Power, and Evil: A Process Theodicy* (Philadelphia: Westminster, 1976); Marjorie Suchocki, *The End of Evil* (Albany, N.Y.: State University of New York Press, 1988); Marjorie Suchocki, *The Fall to Violence: Original Sin in Relational Theology* (New York: Continuum, 1994).

18. Toinette M. Eugene, "On 'Difference' and the Dream of Pluralist Feminism" and "To Be of Use," *Journal of Feminist Studies in Religion* 8, no. 2 (Fall 1992): 91–98, 141–47.

19. Adrienne Rich, "Compulsory Heterosexuality and Lesbian Existence," in Elizabeth Abel and Amy Abel, editors, *The Signs Reader: Women, Gender, and Scholarship* (Chicago: University of Chicago Press, 1983), 139–68.

Postscript: Practicing Goodness

1. Kelly Brown Douglas, *The Black Christ* (Maryknoll, N.Y.: Orbis, 1994), 105.

2. James Poling, "Where I Live is How I Work," *Pastoral Psychology* 23, No. 3 (January 1995): 177–85.

3. See Psalms 18, 25, 41, and many others.

4. Ernesto Cardenal, *The Gospel in Solentiname* (3 vols.) (Maryknoll, N.Y.: Orbis, 1985).

BIBLIOGRAPHY

ABBOTT, Franklin, editor. *Men and Intimacy: Personal Accounts Exploring the Dilemmas of Modern Male Sexuality*. Freedom, Calif.: The Crossing Press, 1990.

_____. *New Men, New Minds: Breaking Male Tradition: How Today's Men are Changing the Traditional Rules of Masculinity*. Freedom, Calif.: The Crossing Press, 1987.

ALLPORT, Gordon. *The Nature of Prejudice*. Garden City, N.Y.: Doubleday, 1954.

ADAMS, Carol J., and Marie Fortune, editors. *Violence Against Women and Children: A Christian Theological Sourcebook*. New York: Continuum, 1995.

ANDERSON, Margaret, and Patricia Hill Collins. *Race, Class, and Gender: An Anthology*. Belmont, Calif.: Wadsworth, 1992.

ANDOLSEN, Barbara Hilkert. *Daughters of Jefferson, Daughters of Bootblacks: Racism and American Feminism*. Macon, Ga.: Mercer University Press, 1986.

ANDOLSEN, Barbara, Christine Gudorf, and Mary Pellauer, editors. *Women's Consciousness, Women's Conscience*. San Francisco: Harper & Row, 1985.

ANDREWS, William. *To Tell a Free Story: The First Century of Afro-American Autobiography, 1769–1865*. Urbana, Ill.: University of Illinois Press, 1986.

ASANTE, Molefi Kete. *Kemet, Afrocentricity, and Knowledge*. Trenton, N.J.: African World Press, 1990.

BAKER, Houston. *Blues, Ideology, and Afro-American Literature*. Chicago: University of Chicago Press, 1984.

BARKER-BENFIELD, G. J. *The Horrors of the Half-Known Life: Male Attitudes toward Women and Sexuality in Nineteenth Century America*. New York: Harper & Row, 1976.

BARSTOW, Anne Llewellyn. *Witchcraze: A New History of the European Witch Hunts*. San Francisco: HarperCollins, 1994.

BARTH, Karl, *Church Dogmatics: The Doctrine of Creation* (3/3). Edinburgh: T & T Clark, 1960.

BATSTONE, David, editor. *New Visions for the Americas: Religious Engagement and Social Transformation*. Minneapolis: Fortress Press, 1993.

BECKER, Ernest. *Escape from Evil*. New York: Macmillan, 1975.

BELL, Derrick. *Faces at the Bottom of the Well*. New York: Basic Books, 1992.

BERKHEIMER, Charles, and Claire Kahane, editors. *In Dora's Case: Freud, Hysteria, Feminism*. New York: Columbia University Press, 1985.

BILLINGSLEY, Andrew. *Climbing Jacob's Ladder: The Enduring Legacy of African-American Families*. New York: Simon & Schuster, 1992.

BLANCK, Ruben, and Gertrude Blanck. *Beyond Ego Psychology*. New York: Columbia University Press, 1986.

_____. *Ego Psychology: Theory and Practice*. New York: Columbia University Press, 1974.

_____. *Ego Psychology II*. New York: Columbia University Press, 1979.

BLUMENTHAL, David. *Facing the Abusing God: A Theology of Protest*. Louisville, Ky.: Westminster John Knox Press, 1993.

BLY, Robert. *Iron John: A Book about Men*. Boston: Addison-Wesley, 1991.

BOSWELL, John. *Christianity, Social Tolerance, and Homosexuality: Gay People in Western Europe from the Beginning of the Christian Era to the Fourteenth Century*. Chicago: University of Chicago Press, 1980.

BOTKIN, B. A. *Lay My Burden Down: A Folk History of Slavery*. Athens: Ga.: University of Georgia Press, 1989. Originally published by the University of Chicago Press, 1945.

BOYD-FRANKLIN, Nancy. *Black Families in Therapy: A Multisystems Approach*. New York: Guilford, 1989.

BRADLEY, David. *The Chaneysville Incident*. New York: Harper & Row, 1981.

BRAUDE, Ann. *Radical Spirits: Spiritualism and Women's Rights in Nineteenth-Century America*. Boston: Beacon, 1989.

BROCK, Rita Nakashima. *Journeys by Heart: A Christology of Erotic Power*. New York: Crossroad, 1988.

BRONFENBRENNER, Urie. *The Ecology of Human Development*. Cambridge, Mass.: Harvard University Press, 1979.

BROWN, Joanne Carlson, and Carole R. Bohn, editors. *Christianity, Patriarchy and Abuse: A Feminist Critique*. New York: Pilgrim, 1989.

BULLOUGH, Vern L. and Bonnie Bullough. *The Subordinate Sex: A History of Attitudes toward Women*. Urbana, Ill.: University of Illinois Press, 1973.

CALHOUN, Arthur W. *Social History of the American Family, Vol. 3, Since the Civil War*. Cleveland: Arthur Clark, 1919.

CAMPBELL, Bebe Moore. *Your Blues Ain't Like Mine*. New York: G. P. Putnam's Sons, 1992.

CANNON, Katie G. *Black Womanist Ethics*. Atlanta: Scholars Press, 1988.

CARBY, Hazel. *Reconstructing Womanhood: The Emergence of the Afro-American Novelist*. New York: Oxford University Press, 1987.

CARDENAL, Ernesto. *The Gospel in Solentiname*. 3 vols. Maryknoll, N.Y.: Orbis, 1985.

CARTER, Harold A. *The Prayer Tradition of Black People*. Valley Forge, Penn.: Judson, 1976.

CASTLE, Terry. *The Apparitional Lesbian: Female Homosexuality and Modern Culture*. New York: Columbia University Press, 1993.

CHILDREN'S Defense Fund. *The State of America's Children Yearbook, 1994*. Washington, D.C.: Children's Defense Fund, 1994.

CHODOROW, Nancy J. *Femininities, Masculinities, Sexualities: Freud and Beyond*. Lexington, Ky,: University Press of Kentucky, 1994.

_____. *The Reproduction of Mothering: Psychoanalysis and the Sociology of Gender*. Berkeley, Calif.: University of California Press, 1978.

CHOPP, Rebecca, and Mark Lewis Taylor, editors. *Reconstructing Christian Theology*. Minneapolis: Fortress Press, 1994.

CLEAGE, Pearl. *Mad at Miles: A Blackwoman's Guide to Truth*. Southfield, Mich.: The Cleage Group, 1990.

CLINTON, Catherine. *The Other Civil War: American Women in the Nineteenth Century*. New York: Hill & Wang, 1984.

COBB, John B. *Christ in a Pluralistic Age*. Philadelphia: Westminster, 1975.

_____. *Sustaining the Common Good: A Christian Perspective on the Global Economy*. Cleveland: Pilgrim, 1994.

COBB, John B., and David Ray Griffin. *Process Theology: An Introductory Exposition*. Philadelphia: Westminster, 1976.

COLLINS, Patricia Hill. *Black Feminist Thought: Knowledge, Consciousness, and the Politics of Empowerment*. New York: Routledge, 1990.

COLLINS, Sheila D. "The Familial Economy of God" (Document #8, Theology in the Americas, 475 Riverside Drive, Room 1268, New York, N.Y. 10027), 1979.

COMER, James P. *Maggie's American Dream: The Life and Times of a Black Family*. New York: Penguin, 1988.

COMSTOCK, Gary David. *Violence against Lesbians and Gay Men*. New York: Columbia University Press, 1991.

CONDE, Maryse. *I, Tituba, Black Witch of Salem*. Charlottesville, Va.: University Press of Virginia, 1992.

CONE, James H. *A Black Theology of Liberation*. Philadelphia: Lippincott, 1970.

_____. *Black Theology and Black Power*. New York: Seabury, 1969.

_____. *God of the Oppressed*. New York: Seabury, 1975.

_____. *Martin and Malcolm and America*. Maryknoll, N.Y.: Orbis, 1991.

_____. *The Spirituals and the Blues*. New York: Seabury, 1972.

CONE, James H., and Gayraud Wilmore, editors. *Black Theology: A Documentary History, Volume 2: 1980–1992*. Maryknoll, N.Y.: Orbis, 1993.

COOEY, Paula M. *Religious Imagination and the Body: A Feminist Analysis*. New York: Oxford University Press, 1994.

COOEY, Paula M, Sharon A. Farmer, and Mary Ellen Ross. *Embodied Love: Sensuality and Relationship as Feminist Values*. San Francisco: HarperSanFrancisco, 1987.

CORNWALL Collective, The. *Your Daughters Shall Prophesy*. New York: Pilgrim, 1980.

COTT, Nancy, editor. *Roots of Bitterness: Documents of the Social History of American Women*. New York: E. P. Dutton, 1986.

COUNTRYMAN, L. William. *Dirt, Greed, and Sex: Sexual Ethics in the New Testament and Their Implications for Today*. Philadelphia: Fortress Press, 1988.

COUTURE, Pamela D. *Blessed Are the Poor: Women's Poverty, Family Policy, and Practical Theology*. Nashville: Abingdon, 1991.

CROSSAN, John Dominic. *The Historical Jesus: The Life of a Mediterranean Jewish Peasant*. San Francisco: HarperSanFrancisco, 1991.

_____. *Jesus: A Revolutionary Biography*. San Francisco: HarperSanFrancisco, 1994.

DALY, Herman E., and John B. Cobb, Jr. *For the Common Good: Redirecting the Economy toward Community, the Environment, and a Sustainable Future*. Boston: Beacon, 1989.

DALY, Mary. *Beyond God the Father*. Boston: Beacon, 1973.

DAVIS, Angela Y. *Women, Culture, Politics*. New York: Random House, 1990.

_____. *Women, Race, and Class*. New York: Random House, 1983.

DAVIS, Stephen T., editor. *Encountering Evil: Live Options in Theodicy*. Atlanta: John Knox Press, 1981.

DEAN, William, and Larry E. Axel. *The Size of God: The Theology of Bernard Loomer in Context*. Macon, Ga.: Mercer University Press, 1987.

DECKER, Hannah S. *Freud, Dora, and Vienna: 1900*. New York: Free Press, 1991.

DIAGNOSTIC and Statistical Manual of Mental Disorders: Fourth Edition. Washington, D.C.: American Psychiatric Association, 1994.

DINNERSTEIN, Dorothy. *The Mermaid and the Minotaur: Sexual Arrangements and Human Malaise*. New York: Harper & Row, 1976.

DITTES, James. *The Male Predicament: On Being a Man Today*. San Francisco: Harper & Row, 1985.

DOEHRING, Carrie. *Internal Desecration: Traumatization and Representations of God*. New York: University Press of America, 1993.

DOUGLAS, Ann. *The Feminization of American Culture*. New York: Avon Books, 1978.

DOUGLAS, Kelly Brown. *The Black Christ*. Maryknoll, N.Y.: Orbis, 1994.

DOUGLASS, Frederick. *The Life and Times of Frederick Douglass*. London: Collier-Macmillan, 1962.

DuBOIS, Ellen Carol, editor. *Elizabeth Cady Stanton and Susan B. Anthony: Correspondence, Writings, Speeches*. New York: Schocken, 1981.

Du BOIS, W. E. B. *The Souls of Black Folk*. New York: Bantam, 1989 [1903].

DYSON, Michael Eric. *Reflecting Black: African-American Cultural Criticism*. Minneapolis: University of Minnesota Press, 1993.

EARL, Riggins R., Jr. *Dark Symbols, Obscure Signs: God, Self, and Community in the Slave Mind*. Maryknoll, N.Y.: Orbis, 1993.

EDELMAN, Marian Wright. *Families in Peril: An Agenda for Social Change.* Cambridge, Mass.: Harvard University Press, 1987.

EHRENREICH, Barbara, and Deirdre English. *For Her Own Good: 150 Years of the Experts' Advice to Women.* New York: Doubleday, 1978.

EILBERG-SCHWARTZ, Howard. *The Savage in Judaism: An Anthropology of Israelite Religion and Ancient Judaism.* Bloomington, Ind.: Indiana University Press, 1990.

EISENSTEIN, Hester. *Contemporary Feminist Thought.* Boston: G. K. Hall, 1983.

EPSTEIN, Barbara. *The Politics of Domesticity, Women Evangelism and Temperance in Nineteenth Century America.* Middletown, Conn.: Wesleyan University Press, 1981.

EUGENE, Toinette M. "Coming to Terms: Sisterhood for Black and White Feminists." *New Women/New Church* 4:6, 3–6.

_____. "On 'Difference' and the Dream of Pluralist Feminism" and "To Be of Use." *Journal of Feminist Studies in Religion* 8, No. 2 (Fall 1992): 91–98, 141–47.

_____. "Moral Values and Black Womanists," *Journal of Religious Thought* 44, no. 1 (Spring, 1988): 23–34.

_____. "Reflections of a Black Sistuh!" *Freeing the Spirit.*, 3, no. 2 (Summer 1974): 11–15.

EVANS, James H.. *Black Theology: A Critical Assessment and Annotated Bibliography.* New York: Greenwood Press, 1987.

_____. *We Have Been Believers: An African-American Systematic Theology.* Minneapolis: Fortress Press, 1992.

FALUDI, Susan. *Backlash: The Undeclared War against American Women.* New York: Crown, 1991.

FANON, Frantz. *The Wretched of the Earth: A Negro Psychoanalyst's Study of the Problems of Racism and Colonialism in the World Today.* New York: Grove, 1963.

FARLEY, Edward. *Good and Evil: Interpreting a Human Condition.* Minneapolis: Fortress Press, 1990.

FELDER, Cain Hope. *Troubling Biblical Waters: Race, Class, and Family.* Maryknoll, N.Y.: Orbis, 1989.

FELDER, Cain Hope, editor. *Stony the Road We Trod: African American Biblical Interpretation.* Minneapolis: Fortress Press, 1991.

FINE, Michelle, and Adrienne Asch. *Women with Disabilities: Essays in Psychology, Culture, and Politics.* Philadelphia: Temple University Press, 1988.

FIORENZA, Elisabeth Schüssler. *Bread Not Stone: The Challenge of Feminist Biblical Interpretation.* Boston: Beacon, 1984.

FIORENZA, Elisabeth Schüssler, and Mary Shawn Copeland, editors. *Violence against Women.* Concilium Series, vol. 1. Maryknoll, N.Y.: Orbis, 1994.

FISHBURN, Janet. *Confronting the Idolatry of Family: A New Vision for the Household of God.* Nashville: Abingdon, 1991.

FLEXNOR, Eleanor. *Century of Struggle: The Woman's Rights Movement in the United States.* 2d ed. Cambridge, Mass.: Harvard University Press, 1975.

FLUKER, Walter E. *They Looked for a City: A Comparative Analysis of the Ideal of Community in the Thought of Howard Thurman and Martin Luther King, Jr.* New York: University Press of America, 1989.

FOGLE, Robert William. *Time on the Cross: The Economics of American Negro Slavery.* Boston: Little-Brown, 1974.

FONER, Eric. *The New American History.* Philadelphia: Temple University Press, 1990.

_____. *A Short History of Reconstruction, 1863–1877.* New York: Harper & Row, 1990.

FORD, S. Dennis. *Sins of Omission: A Primer on Moral Indifference.* Minneapolis: Fortress Press, 1990.

FORTUNE, Marie. *Do No Harm: Sexual Ethics for the Rest of Us.* New York: Continuum, 1995.

_____. *Is Nothing Sacred? The Story of a Pastor, the Women He Sexually Abused, and the Congregation He Nearly Destroyed.* San Francisco: HarperSanFrancisco, 1989.

_____. *Sexual Violence: The Unmentionable Sin.* New York: Pilgrim, 1983.

FOUT, John C., and Maura Shaw Tantillo, editors. *American Sexual Politics: Sex, Gender, and Race Since the Civil War.* Chicago: University of Chicago Press, 1993.

FOX-GENOVESE, Elizabeth. *Within the Plantation Household: Black and White Women of the Old South.* Chapel Hill, N.C.: University of North Carolina Press, 1988.

FRAMPTON, E. Lorraine. *Night Colors.* D. Min. diss., Colgate Rochester Divinity School, Rochester, N.Y., May 1994.

FRANKENBURG, Ruth. *White Women, Race Matters: The Social Construction of Whiteness.* Minneapolis: University of Minnesota Press, 1993.

FRANKLIN, John Hope, and Alfred A. Moss, Jr. *From Slavery to Freedom: A History of Negro Americans.* New York: Knopf, 1988.

FRANKLIN, Robert Michael. *Liberating Visions: Human Fulfillment and Social Justice in African-American Thought.* Minneapolis: Fortress Press, 1990.

FRAZIER, E. Franklin. *The Negro Family in the United States.* Chicago: University of Chicago Press, 1966.

FREDRICKSON, George M. *The Arrogance of Race.* Middletown, Conn.: Wesleyan University Press, 1988.

_____. *The Black Image in the White Mind: The Debate on Afro-American Character and Destiny, 1817–1914.* Hanover, N.H.: Wesleyan University Press, 1971.

_____. *White Supremacy: American and South African History.* New York: Oxford University Press, 1981.

FREUD, Sigmund. *Dora: An Analysis of a Case of Hysteria.* New York: Collier Books, 1963.

GALLOP, Jane. "Feminism and Sexual Harassment," *Academe* (Sept.–Oct. 1994), 16–23.

_____. *Reading Lacan.* Ithaca, N.Y.: Cornell University Press, 1985.

_____. *The Seduction of the Daughter: Feminism and Psychoanalysis.* Ithaca, N.Y.: Cornell University Press, 1982.

GARNER, Shirley N., Claire Kahane, and Madelon Sprengnether, editors. *The (M)other Tongue: Essays in Feminist Psychoanalytic Interpretation.* Ithaca, N.Y.: Cornell University Press, 1985.

GARNETS, Linda, and Douglas Kimmel, editors. *Psychological Perspectives on Lesbian and Gay Male Experiences.* New York: Columbia University Press, 1993.

GARVEY, Marcus. *Marcus Garvey and the Vision of Africa.* John Henrik Clarke, editor. New York: Random House, 1974.

GATES, Henry Louis, Jr. *The Classic Slave Narratives.* New York: Penguin, 1987.

_____. *Colored People: A Memoir.* New York: Knopf, 1994.

_____. *Figures in Black: Words, Signs, and the Racial Self.* New York: Oxford University Press, 1987.

_____. *Loose Canons: Notes on the Culture Wars.* New York: Oxford University Press, 1992.

_____. *The Signifying Monkey.* New York: Oxford University Press, 1988.

GATES, Henry Louis, Jr., and Charles T. Davis, editors. *The Slave's Narratives.* New York: Oxford University Press, 1985.

GENOVESE, Eugene D. *Roll Jordan Roll: The World the Slaves Made.* New York: Pantheon, 1974.

GIDDINGS, Paula. *When and Where I Enter: The Impact of Black Women on Race and Sex in America.* New York: Bantam, 1984.

GILLIGAN, Carol. *In a Different Voice: Psychological Theory and Women's Development.* Cambridge, Mass.: Harvard University Press, 1982.

GILLIGAN, Carol, Janie Victoria Ward, and Jill McLean Taylor, with Betty Bardige. *Mapping the Moral Domain: A Contribution of Women's Thinking to Psychological Theory and Education.* Cambridge, Mass.: Harvard University Press, 1988.

GIRARD, René. *Violence and the Sacred.* Baltimore: Johns Hopkins University Press, 1979.

GLAZ, Maxine, and Jeanne Stevenson Moessner, editors. *Women in Travail and Transition: A New Pastoral Care.* Minneapolis: Fortress Press, 1991.

GOLDBERG, David Theo. *Anatomy of Racism.* Minneapolis: University of Minnesota Press, 1990.

GOLDENBERG, Naomi, R. *Returning Words to Flesh: Feminism, Psychoanalysis, and the Resurrection of the Body.* Boston: Beacon, 1990.

GOODRICH, Thelma Jean, editor. *Women and Power: Perspectives for Family Therapy.* New York: W. W. Norton, 1991.

GOSS, Robert. *Jesus Acted Up: A Gay and Lesbian Manifesto.* San Francisco: HarperSanFrancisco, 1993.

GOSSETT, Thomas F. *Race: The History of an Idea in America.* New York: Schocken, 1965.

GRANT, Jacquelyn. *White Women's Christ and Black Women's Jesus: Feminist Christology and Womanist Response.* Atlanta: Scholars Press, 1989.

GREENBERG, David F. *The Construction of Homosexuality*. Chicago: University of Chicago Press, 1988.

GREVEN, Philip J. *The Protestant Temperament: Patterns of Child-Rearing, Religious Experience and the Self in Early America*. New York: Knopf, 1977.

_____. *Spare the Child: The Religious Roots of Punishment and the Psychological Impact of Physical Abuse*. New York: Knopf, 1991.

GRIFFIN, David Ray. *God, Power, and Evil: A Process Theodicy*. Philadelphia: Westminster, 1976.

GROOME, Thomas. *Christian Religious Education*. New York: Harper & Row, 1980.

_____. *Sharing Faith: A Comprehensive Approach to Religious Education and Pastoral Ministry*. New York: HarperCollins, 1994.

GUDORF, Christine. *Body, Sex, and Pleasure*. Cleveland: Pilgrim Press, 1994.

_____. *Victimization: Examining Christian Complicity*. Philadelphia: Trinity Press International, 1992.

GUTMAN, Herbert. *The Black Family in Slavery and Freedom: 1750–1925*. New York: Vintage Books, 1976.

HALLER, John S., and Robin M. Haller. *The Physician and Sexuality in Victorian America*. Urbana, Ill.: University of Illinois Press, 1974.

HAMERTON-KELLY, Robert G. *The Gospel and the Sacred: Poetics of Violence in Mark*. Minneapolis: Fortress Press, 1994.

_____. *Sacred Violence: Paul's Hermeneutic of the Cross*. Minneapolis: Fortress Press, 1992.

HAMPTON, Robert L. *Violence in the Black Family: Correlates and Consequences*. Lexington, Mass.: Lexington Books, 1987.

HARDING, Vincent. *There Is a River: The Black Struggle for Freedom in America*. New York: Vintage, 1983.

HEGEN, Carolyn Holderread. *Sexual Abuse in Christian Homes and Churches*. Scottsdale, Penn.: Herald Press, 1993.

HELMS, Janet E. *Black and White Racial Identity: Theory, Research, and Practice*. New York: Greenwood Press, 1990.

_____. *A Race Is a Nice Thing To Have: A Guide to Being a White Person or Understanding White Persons in Your Life*. Topeka, Kan.: Content Communications, 1992.

HERMAN, Judith Lewis. *Father-Daughter Incest*. Cambridge, Mass.: Harvard University Press, 1981.

_____. *Trauma and Recovery*. New York: HarperCollins, 1992.

HERZOG, William II. *Parables as Subversive Speech: Jesus as Pedagogue of the Oppressed*. Louisville, Ky.: Westminster John Knox, 1994.

HEWITT, Nancy A. *Women's Activism and Social Change: Rochester, N.Y., 1822–1872*. Ithaca, N.Y.: Cornell University Press, 1984.

HEYWARD, Carter. *Our Passion for Justice: Images of Power, Sexuality, and Liberation*. New York: Pilgrim, 1984.

_____. *The Redemption of God: A Theology of Mutual Relation.* New York: University Press of America, 1982.

_____. *Speaking of Christ: A Lesbian Feminist Voice.* New York: Pilgrim, 1989.

_____. *Touching Our Strength: The Erotic as Power and the Love of God.* San Francisco: HarperSanFrancisco, 1989.

_____. *When Boundaries Betray Us: Beyond Illusions of What Is Ethical in Therapy and Life.* San Francisco: HarperSanFrancisco, 1993.

HIGGINBOTHAM, Evelyn Brooks. *Righteous Discontent: The Women's Movement in the Black Baptist Church, 1880–1920.* Cambridge, Mass.: Harvard University Press, 1993.

HILBERG, Raul. *The Destruction of the European Jews.* 3 vols., rev. ed. New York: Holmes and Meier, 1985.

_____. *Perpetrators, Victims, Bystanders: The Jewish Catastrophe, 1933–1945.* New York: HarperCollins, 1992.

HODGSON, Peter C. *God in History: Shapes of Freedom.* Nashville: Abingdon, 1989.

HOLLIES, Linda H., editor. *Womanistcare: How to Tend the Souls of Women.* Joliet, Ill.: Woman to Women Ministries, 1991.

HOOD, Robert E. *Must God Remain Greek? Afro Cultures and God-Talk.* Minneapolis: Fortress Press, 1990.

HOOKS, bell. *Ain't I a Woman: Black Women and Feminism.* Boston: South End Press, 1981.

_____. *Black Looks: Race and Representation.* Boston: South End Press, 1982.

_____. *Feminist Theory: From Margin to Center.* Boston: South End Press, 1984.

_____. *Sisters of the Yam.* Boston: South End Press, 1993.

_____. *Talking Back: Thinking Feminist, Thinking Black.* Boston: South End Press, 1989.

_____. *Yearning: Race, Gender, and Cultural Politics.* Boston: South End Press, 1990.

HOOKS, bell, and Cornel West. *Breaking Bread: Insurgent Black Intellectual Life.* Boston: South End Press, 1991.

HOPKINS, Dwight, and George Cummings. *Cut Loose Your Stammering Tongues: Black Theology and the Slave Narratives.* Maryknoll, N.Y.: Orbis, 1991.

HORNER, Althea. *Object Relations and the Developing Ego in Therapy.* New York: Aronson, 1984.

_____. *Psychoanalytic Object Relations Therapy.* Northvale, N.J.: Aronson, 1991.

HORSLEY, Richard A. *Jesus and the Spiral of Violence: Popular Jewish Resistance in Roman Palestine.* Minneapolis: Fortress Press, 1993.

HOUGH, Joseph. *Black Power and White Protestants: A Christian Response to the New Negro Pluralism.* New York: Oxford University Press, 1968.

HUNT, Mary. *Fierce Tenderness.* New York: Crossroad, 1991.

HUNTER, Rodney, editor. *Dictionary of Pastoral Care and Counseling.* Nashville: Abingdon Press, 1990.

IMBENS, Annie, and Ineke Jonker. *Christianity and Incest*. Minneapolis: Fortress Press, 1992.

ITZIN, Catherine. *Pornography: Women, Violence, and Civil Liberties: A Radical New View*. Oxford: Oxford University Press, 1992.

JACOBS, Harriet. *Incidents in the Life of a Slave Girl*. Jean Fagen Yellin, editor. Cambridge: Harvard University Press, 1987.

JAMES, Jay, and Ruth Farmer. *Spirit, Space, and Survival: African American Women in (White) Academe*. New York: Routledge, 1993.

JAMES, Stanlie M., and Abena Busia, editors. *Theorizing Black Feminists*. New York: Routledge, 1993.

JOHNSON, Elizabeth A. *She Who Is: The Mystery of God in Feminist Theological Discourse*. New York: Crossroad, 1993.

JONES, William R. *Is God a White Racist? A Preamble to Black Theology*. Garden City, N.Y.: Anchor/Doubleday, 1973.

JORDAN, Winthrop. *Tumult and Silence at Second Creek: An Inquiry Into a Civil War Slave Conspiracy*. Baton Rouge, La.: Louisiana State University Press, 1993.

_____. *White Man's Burden: Historical Origins of Racism in the U.S.* New York: Oxford University Press, 1974.

_____. *White over Black: American Attitudes toward the Negro, 1550–1812*. Chapel Hill, N.C.: University of North Carolina Press, 1968.

KANZER, Mark, and Jules Glenn, editors. *Freud and His Patients*. New York: Aronson, 1980.

KEEN, Sam. *Fire in the Belly: On Being a Man*. New York: Bantam, 1991.

KELLER, Catherine. *From a Broken Web: Separation, Sexism, and Self*. Boston: Beacon, 1986.

KELSEY, George. *Racism and the Christian Understanding of Man*. New York: Scribner's, 1985.

KELSEY, Morton. *Discernment: A Study in Ecstasy and Evil*. New York: Paulist, 1978.

KERNBERG, Otto. *Internal World and External Reality*. New York: Aronson, 1980.

_____. *Severe Personality Disorders*. New Haven, Conn.: Yale University Press, 1984.

KIM, C. W. Maggie, Susan St. Ville, and Susan Simonaitis. *Transfigurations: Theology and the French Feminists*. Minneapolis: Fortress Press, 1993.

KIMMEL, Michael S., and Michael A. Messner, editors. *Men's Lives*. New York: Macmillan, 1992.

KIPNIS, Aaron R. *Knights without Armor: A Practical Guide for Men in Quest of Masculine Soul*. Los Angeles: Jeremy P. Tarcher, 1991.

KOHUT, Heinz. *The Analysis of the Self*. New York: International University Press, 1971.

_____. *How Does Analysis Cure?* Chicago: University of Chicago Press, 1984.

_____. *The Restoration of the Self*. New York: International University Press, 1977.

_____. *Self Psychology and the Humanities*. New York: W. W. Norton, 1985.

KOVEL, Joel. *In Nicaragua*. London: Free Press, 1988.

_____. *White Racism*. New York: Columbia University Press, 1984.

LAKOFF, Robin. *Language and Woman's Place*. New York: Harper & Row, 1975.

LAKOFF, Robin, and James Coyne. *Father Knows Best: The Use and Abuse of Power in Freud's Case of Dora*. New York: Teacher's College Press, 1993.

LAURETIS, Teresa de. *Alice Doesn't: Feminism, Semiotics, Cinema*. Bloomington, Ind.: Indiana University Press, 1984.

LEBACQZ, Karen. *Professional Ethics: Power and Paradox*. Nashville: Abingdon, 1985.

LEBACQZ, Karen, and Ronald Barton. *Sex in the Parish*. Louisville. Ky.: Westminster John Knox, 1991.

LEE, Jarena. *The Life and Religious Experience of Jarena Lee*. Philadelphia: The Author, 1836.

LERNER, Gerda. *Black Women in White America: A Documentary History*. New York: Vintage, 1973.

_____. *The Creation of Feminist Consciousness: From the Middle Ages to 1870*. New York: Oxford University Press, 1993.

_____. *The Creation of Patriarchy*. New York: Oxford University Press, 1986.

_____. *The Female Experience*. New York: Oxford University Press, 1977.

LÉVI-STRAUSS, Claude. *The Elementary Structures of Kinship*. Boston: Beacon, 1986.

LINCOLN, C. Eric, and Lawrence H. Mamiya. *The Black Church in the African American Experience*. Durham, N.C.: Duke University Press, 1990.

LOOMER, Bernard. "Elephantine Analysis" (unpublished paper). 1978.

_____. "Two Conceptions of Power." *Criterion* 15, no. 11 (1976): 12–29.

LORDE, Audre. *A Burst of Light*. Ithaca, N.Y.: Firebrand Books, 1988.

_____. *Sister Outsider*. Freedom, Calif.: Crossing Press, 1984.

_____. *Undersong*. New York: W. W. Norton, 1992.

_____. *Zami: A New Spelling of My Name*. Freedom, Calif.: Crossing Press, 1982.

McDONALD, Marjorie. *Not By the Color of Their Skin: The Impact of Racial Difference on a Child's Development*. New York: International University Press, 1971.

McNEILL, John J. *The Church and the Homosexual*. Boston: Beacon, 1988.

McFAGUE, Sallie. *Models of God: Theology for an Ecological, Nuclear Age*. Philadelphia: Fortress Press, 1987.

MACK, Burton L. *The Lost Gospel: The Book of Q and Christian Origins*. San Francisco: HarperSanFrancisco, 1993.

MAGID, Barry. *Freud's Case Studies: Self-Psychological Perspectives*. Hillsdale, N.J.: Analytic Press, 1993.

MAHLER, Margaret. *The Psychological Birth of the Human Infant*. New York: Basic Books, 1985.

MALCOLM X. *Malcolm X Speaks*. New York: Pathfinder, 1965.

MARABLE, Manning. *How Capitalism Underdeveloped Black America: Problems in Race, Political Economy, and Society*. Boston: South End Press, 1983.

_____. *Race, Reform, and Rebellion: The Second Reconstruction in Black America*. Jackson, Miss.: University Press of Mississippi, 1991.

MEADE, Michael. *Men and the Water of Life: Initiation and the Tempering of Men*. San Francisco: HarperSanFrancisco, 1994.

MEEKS, M. Douglas. *God the Economist: The Doctrine of God and Political Economy*. Minneapolis: Fortress Press, 1989.

MEEKS, Wayne A., general editor. *The HarperCollins Study Bible*. New York: HarperCollins, 1994.

MEIER, August. *Negro Thought in America: 1880–1915*. Ann Arbor, Mich.: University of Michigan Press, 1966.

MEISSNER, W. W. *Internalization in Psychoanalysis*. New York: International University Press, 1981.

_____. *Treatment of Patients in the Borderline Spectrum*. New York: Jason Aronson, 1988.

MELAND, Bernard. *Essays in Constructive Theology: A Process Perspective*. Perry Lefever, editor. Chicago: Exploration Press, 1988.

_____. *Faith and Culture*. Carbondale, Ill.: Southern Illinois University Press, 1953.

_____. *Fallible Forms and Symbols: Discourses on Method in a Theology of Culture*. Philadelphia: Fortress Press, 1976.

_____. *The Realities of Faith: The Revolution in Cultural Forms*. New York: Oxford University Press, 1962.

MELOY, J. Reid. *The Psychopathic Mind: Origins, Dynamics, and Treatment*. Northvale, N.J.: Jason Aronson, 1992.

_____. *Violent Attachments*. Northvale, N.J.: Jason Aronson, 1992.

MEMMI, Albert. *The Colonizer and the Colonized*. Boston: Beacon, 1965.

MICHAELSON, Robert S., and Wade Clark Roof. *Liberal Protestantism: Realities and Possibilities*. New York: Pilgrim, 1986.

MILES, Margaret R.. *Carnal Knowing: Female Nakedness and Religious Meaning in the Christian West*. New York: Vintage, 1991.

MILLER, Alice. *For Your Own Good: Hidden Cruelty in Child-rearing and the Roots of Violence*. New York: Farrar, Straus, Giroux, 1983.

MILLER-McLEMORE, Bonnie J. *Also a Mother: Work and Family as Theological Dilemma*. Nashville: Abingdon, 1994.

MILLETT, Kate. *The Politics of Cruelty: An Essay on the Literature of Political Imprisonment*. New York: Norton, 1994.

_____. *Sexual Politics*. Garden City, N.Y.: Doubleday, 1970.

MITCHELL, Juliet. *Psychoanalysis and Feminism*. New York: Pantheon, 1974.

_____. *Women: The Longest Revolution*. New York: Pantheon, 1984.

MOLLENKOTT, Virginia Ramey. *Sensuous Spirituality: Out from Fundamentalism*. New York: Crossroad, 1992.

MOORE, Robert, and Douglas Gillette. *King, Warrior, Magician, Lover: Rediscovering the Archetypes of the Mature Masculine.* San Francisco: HarperSanFrancisco, 1990.

MORGANTHAU, Tom. "I.Q.: Is It Destiny?" *Newsweek* (October 24, 1994), 53–55.

MORISON, Samuel Eliot. *The Oxford History of the American People.* New York: Oxford University Press, 1965.

MORRISON, Toni. *Playing in the Dark.* Cambridge, Mass.: Harvard University Press, 1992.

MORRISON, Toni, editor. *Race-ing Justice, En-gendering Power: Essays on Anita Hill, Clarence Thomas, and the Construction of Social Reality.* New York: Pantheon, 1992.

MOSALA, Itumeleng T. *Biblical Hermeneutics and Black Theology in South Africa.* Grand Rapids: Eerdmans, 1989.

MOYNIHAN, Daniel P. *The Negro Family: The Case for National Action.* Washington, D.C.: United States Department of Labor, 1965.

MURRAY, Charles, and Richard Herrenstein. *The Bell Curve: Intelligence and Class Structure in American Life.* New York: Free Press, 1994.

MURRAY, Pauli. *Song in a Weary Throat.* New York: Harper & Row, 1987.

MYERS, Ched. *Binding the Strong Man: A Political Reading of Mark's Story of Jesus.* Maryknoll, N.Y.: Orbis, 1988.

NELSON, James B. *Between Two Gardens: Reflections on Sexuality and Religious Experience.* New York: Pilgrim, 1983.

———. *Body Theology.* Louisville, Ky.: Westminster John Knox, 1992.

———. *Embodiment: An Approach to Sexuality and Christian Theology.* Minneapolis: Augsburg, 1978.

———. *The Intimate Connection: Male Sexuality, Masculine Spirituality.* Philadelphia: Westminster, 1988.

NELSON, James B., and Sandra Longfellow. *Sexuality and the Sacred: Sources for Theological Reflection.* Louisville, Ky.: Westminster John Knox, 1994.

NIEBUHR, Reinhold. *Moral Man and Immoral Society.* New York: Scribner's, 1932.

NODDINGS, Nel. *Caring: A Feminine Approach to Ethics and Moral Education.* Berkeley: University of California Press, 1984.

———. *Women and Evil.* Berkeley, Calif.: University of California Press, 1989.

NORTON, Mary Beth, and Carol Ruth Berkin. *Women of America: A History.* Boston: Houghton Mifflin, 1979.

OMI, Michael, and Howard Winant. *Racial Formation in the United States.* New York: Routledge, 1986.

PASEWARK, Kyle A. *A Theology of Power: Being Beyond Domination.* Minneapolis: Fortress Press, 1993.

PARIS, Peter J. *Black Religious Leaders: Conflict in Unity.* Louisville, Ky.: Westminster John Knox, 1991.

———. *The Social Teaching of the Black Churches.* Philadelphia: Fortress Press, 1985.

_____. *The Spirituality of African People: The Search for a Common Moral Discourse*. Minneapolis: Fortress Press, 1995.

PARK, Andrew Sung. *The Wounded Heart of God: The Asian Concept of Han and the Christian Doctrine of Sin*. Nashville: Abingdon, 1993.

PARKER, Gail, editor. *The Oven Birds: American Women on Womanhood: 1820–1920*. Garden City, N.Y.: Anchor/Doubleday, 1972.

PECK, Scott. *People of the Lie*. New York: Simon & Schuster, 1983.

PETERS, Ted. *Sin: Radical Evil in Soul and Society*. Grand Rapids: Eerdmans, 1994.

PHARR, Suzanne. *Homophobia: A Weapon of Sexism*. Inverness, Calif.: Chardon Press, 1988.

PLASKOW, Judith. "Christian Feminism and Anti-Judaism." *Cross Currents* 27, no. 3 (Fall 1978).

_____. "Christian Feminist Anti-Judaism: Some New Considerations." *New Conversations* (Spring 1987), 20–25.

POLING, James Newton. *The Abuse of Power: A Theological Problem*. Nashville: Abingdon, 1991.

_____. "A Theological Integration of the Personal and Social in Pastoral Care and Counseling: A Process View." Ph.D. diss., School of Theology, Claremont, California, 1980.

_____. "Where I Live Is How I Work." *Pastoral Psychology* 23:3 (January 1995), 177–85.

POLING, James N., and Marie M. Fortune. *Sexual Abuse by Clergy: A Crisis for the Church*. Decatur, Ga.: Journal of Pastoral Care Publications, 1994.

POLING, James N., and Donald E. Miller. *Foundations for a Practical Theology of Ministry*. Nashville: Abingdon, 1985.

POLING, James N., and Lewis Midge, editors. *Formation and Reflection: The Promise of Practical Theology*. Philadelphia: Fortress Press, 1987.

PRONGER, Brian. *The Arena of Masculinity: Sports, Homosexuality, and the Meaning of Sex*. New York: St. Martin's, 1990.

PURVIS, Sally B. *The Power of the Cross: Foundations for a Christian Feminist Ethic of Community*. Nashville: Abingdon, 1993.

RABOTEAU, Albert J. *Slave Religion: The "Invisible Institution" in the Antebellum South*. Oxford: Oxford University Press, 1978.

RAINWATER, Lee, and William L. Yancey. *The Moynihan Report and the Politics of Controversy*. Cambridge: M.I.T. Press, 1967.

RANDALL, William Sterne. *Thomas Jefferson: A Life*. New York: Henry Holt, 1993.

REID, Stephen. *Experience and Tradition: A Primer in Black Biblical Hermeneutics*. Nashville: Abingdon, 1990.

REIST, Benjamin. *Theology in Red, White, and Black*. Philadelphia: Westminster, 1975.

RICH, Adrienne. "Compulsory Heterosexuality and Lesbian Existence." *Signs* (Summer 1980), 631–37. Reprinted in Elizabeth Abel and Emily Abel, editors.

The Signs Reader: Women, Gender, and Scholarship. Chicago: University of Chicago Press, 1983. 139–68.

_____. *Of Woman Born.* Tenth anniversary edition. New York: W. W. Norton, 1986.

ROOF, Wade Clark, and William McKinney, editors. *American Mainline Religion: Its Changing Shape and Future.* New Brunswick, N.J.: Rutgers University Press, 1987.

ROTUNDO, E. Anthony. *American Manhood: Transformations in Masculinity from the Revolution to the Modern Era.* New York: Basic Books, 1993.

RUBENSTEIN, Richard L., and John K. Roth. *Approaches to Auschwitz: The Holocaust and Its Legacy.* Atlanta: John Knox, 1987.

RUETHER, Rosemary Radford. *Gaia and God: An Ecofeminist Theology of Earth Healing.* San Francisco: HarperSanFrancisco, 1993.

RUETHER, Rosemary Radford, and Rosemary Skinner Keller, editors. *Women and Religion in America, Volume 1: The Nineteenth Century.* New York: Harper & Row, 1981.

_____, editors. *Women and Religion in America, Volume 2: The Colonial and Revolutionary Periods.* New York: Harper & Row, 1983.

_____, editors. *Women and Religion in America, Volume 3: 1900–1968.* New York: Harper & Row, 1987.

RUSSELL, Letty M. *Growth in Partnership.* Philadelphia: Westminster, 1981.

RUSSELL, Letty, Kwok Pui-lan, Ada María Isasi-Díaz, and Katie Cannon, editors. *Inheriting our Mothers' Gardens: Feminist Theology in Third World Perspective.* Philadelphia: Westminster, 1988.

RUTTER, Peter. *Sex in the Forbidden Zone: When Men in Power—Therapists, Doctors, Clergy, Teachers, and Others—Betray Women's Trust.* Los Angeles: Jeremy Tarcher, 1989.

RYAN, Mary P. *Womanhood in America: From Colonial Times to the Present.* 3rd edition. New York: Franklin Watts, 1983.

SANFORD, John A. *Evil: The Shadow Side of Reality.* New York: Crossroad, 1986.

SAUSSY, Carroll. *God Images and Self Esteem: Empowering Women in a Patriarchal Society.* Louisville, Ky.: Westminster John Knox, 1991.

SCHWAGER, Raymund. *Must There Be Scapegoats? Violence and Redemption in the Bible.* San Francisco: Harper & Row, 1987.

SEDGWICK, Eve Kosofsky. *Tendencies.* Durham, N.C.: Duke University Press, 1993.

SENNETT, Richard, and Jonathan Cobb. *The Hidden Injuries of Class.* New York: Vintage, 1973.

SERNETT, Milton C., editor. *Afro-American Religious History: A Documentary Witness.* Durham, N.C.: Duke University Press, 1985.

SHIPMAN, Pat. *The Evolution of Racism: Human Differences and the Use and Abuse of Science.* New York: Simon & Schuster, 1994.

SMITH, Christine. *Preaching as Weeping, Confession, and Resistance: Radical Responses to Radical Evil.* Louisville, Ky.: Westminster John Knox, 1992.

SMITH, Hibie Shelton. *In His Image, But . . . : Racism in Southern Religion.* Durham, N.C., Duke University Press, 1972.

SMITH, H. Shelton, Robert T. Hancy, and Lefferts A. Loetscher. *American Christianity: An Historical Interpretation with Representative Documents: 1607–1820.* New York: Scribner's, 1960.

———. *American Christianity: An Historical Interpretation with Representative Documents: 1820–1960.* New York: Scribner's, 1963.

STANTON, William R. *The Leopard's Spots: Scientific Attitudes Toward Race in America, 1815–1859.* Chicago: University of Chicago Press, 1960.

STEVENS, Maryanne, editor. *Reconstructing the Christ Symbol: Essays in Feminist Christology.* New York: Paulist, 1993.

STOLTENBERG, John. *The End of Manhood: A Book for Men of Conscience.* New York: Dutton, 1993.

———. *Refusing to Be a Man: Essays on Sex and Justice.* New York: Penguin, 1989.

STRASSER, Susan. *Never Done: A History of American Housework.* New York: Pantheon, 1982.

STRONG, Augustus Hopkins. *Philosophy and Religion.* New York: A. C. Armstrong, 1888.

STRONG, Josiah. *The New Era or the Coming Kingdom.* New York: Baker and Taylor, 1893.

———. *Our Country: Its Possible Future and Its Present Crisis.* The American Home Missionary Society. New York: Baker and Taylor, 1885, 1891. Reprinted 1963, Belknap Press of Harvard University Press.

SUCHOCKI, Marjorie. *The End of Evil.* Albany, N.Y.: State University of New York Press, 1988.

———. *The Fall to Violence: Original Sin in Relational Theology.* New York: Continuum, 1994.

SUNDQUIST, Eric. *To Wake the Nations: Race in the Making of American Literature.* Cambridge, Mass.: Harvard University Press, 1993.

SWERDLOW, Amy, and Hanna Lessinger, editors. *Class, Race, and Sex: The Dynamics of Control.* Boston: G. K. Hall, 1983.

TAKAKI, Ronald. *A Different Mirror: A History of Multicultural America.* Boston: Little, Brown, 1993.

———. *Iron Cages: Race and Culture in Nineteenth Century America.* New York: Oxford University Press, 1990.

TAVES, Ann, editor. *Religion and Domestic Violence in Early New England: The Memoirs of Abigail Abbot Bailey.* Bloomington: Indiana University Press, 1989.

TAYLOR, Mark Kline. *Remembering Esperanza: A Cultural-Political Theology for North American Praxis.* Maryknoll, N.Y.: Orbis, 1990.

THISTLETHWAITE, Susan Brooks. *Sex, Race, and God: Christian Feminism in Black and White.* New York: Crossroad, 1989.

THISTLETHWAITE, Susan Brooks, and Mary Potter Engel, editors. *Lift Every Voice.* San Francisco: HarperSanFrancisco, 1990.

THISTLETON, Anthony, and Clarence Walhout. *The Responsibility of Hermeneutics.* Grand Rapids: Eerdmans, 1985.

TILLICH, Paul. *Systematic Theology.* 3 vols. Chicago: University of Chicago Press, 1957.

TOWNES, Emilie M. *In a Blaze of Glory: Womanist Spirituality as Social Witness.* Nashville: Abingdon, 1995.

_____. *Womanist Justice, Womanist Hope.* Atlanta: Scholars Press, 1993.

TOWNES, Emilie M., editor. *A Troubling in My Soul: Womanist Perspectives on Evil and Suffering.* Maryknoll, N.Y.: Orbis, 1993.

TRACY, David. *Plurality and Ambiguity: Hermeneutics, Religion, Hope.* San Francisco: Harper & Row, 1987.

VAN HERIK, Judith. *Freud on Femininity and Faith.* Berkeley, Calif.: University of California Press, 1982.

WALKER, Alice. *In Search of Our Mothers' Gardens.* San Diego: Harcourt Brace Jovanovich, 1983.

WASHINGTON, Mary Helen. *Invented Lives: Narratives of Black Women, 1860–1960.* New York: Doubleday, 1987.

WEEMS, Renita J. *I Asked for Intimacy: Stories of Blessings, Betrayals and Birthings.* San Diego: LuraMedia, 1993.

_____. *Just a Sister Away: A Womanist Vision of Women's Relationships in the Bible.* San Diego: LuraMedia, 1988.

WELCH, Sharon D. *Communities of Resistance and Solidarity: A Feminist Theology of Liberation.* Maryknoll, N.Y.: Orbis, 1985.

WELTER, Barbara. *Dimity Convictions: The American Woman in the Nineteenth Century.* Columbus, Oh.: University of Ohio Press, 1976.

WEST, Cornel. *Keeping Faith: Philosophy and Race in America.* New York: Routledge, 1993.

_____. *Prophesy Deliverance! An Afro-American Revolutionary Christianity.* Philadelphia: Westminster, 1982.

_____. *Prophetic Reflections: Notes on Race and Power in America.* Monroe, Mass.: Common Courage Press, 1993.

_____. *Prophetic Thought in Postmodern Times.* Monroe, Mass.: Common Courage Press, 1993.

_____. *Race Matters.* Boston: Beacon, 1993.

WHITE, Deborah Gray. *Ar'n't I a Woman: Female Slaves in the Plantation South.* New York: W. W. Norton, 1985.

WHITE, Evelyn C. *Chain, Chain, Change: For Black Women Dealing with Physical and Emotional Abuse.* Seattle: The Seal Group, 1985.

WHITEHEAD, Alfred North. *Process and Reality.* David Ray Griffin, editor. New York: Macmillan, 1978.

WILLIAMS, Daniel Day. *Essays in Process Theology.* Perry Lefever, editor. Chicago: Exploration Press, 1985.

———. *The Spirit and Forms of Love*. New York: Harper & Row, 1968,

WILLIAMS, Delores S. *Sisters in the Wilderness: The Challenge of Womanist God-Talk*. Maryknoll, N.Y.: Orbis, 1993.

WILMORE, Gayraud S. *Black Religion and Black Radicalism: An Interpretation of the Religious History of Afro-American People*. Maryknoll, N.Y.: Orbis, 1993.

WILMORE, Gayraud S, and James H. Cone, editors. *Black Theology: A Documentary History, Volume 1: 1966–1979*. Maryknoll, N.Y.: Orbis, 1979.

WILSON, William Julius. *The Declining Significance of Race: Blacks and Changing American Institutions*. Chicago: University of Chicago Press, 1980.

———. *Power, Racism, and Privilege*. New York: Macmillan, 1973.

———. *The Truly Disadvantaged*. Chicago: University of Chicago Press, 1987.

WINK, Walter. *Engaging the Powers: Discernment and Resistance in a World of Domination*. Minneapolis: Fortress Press, 1992.

———. *Naming the Powers*. Philadelphia: Fortress Press, 1984.

———. *Unmasking the Powers: The Invisible Forces That Determine Human Existence*. Philadelphia: Fortress Press, 1986.

WONDRA, Ellen, K. *Humanity Has Been a Holy Thing: Toward a Contemporary Feminist Christology*. New York: University Press of America, 1994.

WOOD, Forrest G. *The Arrogance of Faith: Christianity and Race in America from the Colonial Era to the Twentieth Century*. New York: Knopf, 1990.

WUTHNOW, Robert. *The Struggle for America's Soul*. Grand Rapids: Eerdmans, 1989.

INDEX